Sinclair has sifted nearly 30 years experience in one of Christianity's foremost mission agencies working among unreach resource. The result is *A Vision of the Possi* encouragement to all who long to see the c in this generation.

D0537819

missionary ar

This book excites me. I am a pioneer missionary to the core. I long to see churches planted among the most difficult peoples on earth. For years many of us have been groping our way through the miasma of ingrained misconceptions about what it means to plant a church. Here is the best and most practical guide to church planting I have yet seen in print. May it become a stimulus to a new wave of good church starts among unreached peoples across the world!

PATRICK JOHNSTONE
author of *Operation World*

For years prospective church planters among the most resistant peoples, like Muslims, have had to rely largely on a vision that a church was possible. With this book Dan Sinclair has demonstrated through his own and his colleagues' experiences, blended with scripture, how this vision is not only possible but is a reality.

DR. DUDLEY WOODBERRY
Dean Emeritus and Professor of Islamic Studies, Fuller Theological Seminary

Dan Sinclair has the experience of a field church planter coupled with 11 years of being field director, where he tracked progress of nearly 160 field teams, made visits to field teams, and intervened when trouble arose. All of this gives him unique experiences and insight which is wonderfully put in this book of amazing breadth and depth. It is a must read for all those who aspire to plant churches among unreached peoples.

DICK SCOGGINS
co-author of *Church Multiplication Guide* and
mentor for church planting with various other organizations

Pulling upon 20 plus years of experience, *A Vision of the Possible* spells out what is practically needed for today's church planter and fills in the gaps what others books have left out. Dan's message is clear, funny, and easy to read, and he's vulnerable in the process. I highly recommend this book to anyone who thinks they may want to be on a team, or send a team to reveal the glory of God where it is not yet known!

BOB SJOGREN
president of UnveilinGLORY and
author of *Unveiled At Last* and *Cat & Dog Theology*

In the midst of the overconfident generalizations of self-appointed "arm chair" theorists, Dan has "been there; done that" in the Muslim world. *A Vision of the Possible* is an exemplary guide from a veteran who has been a colleague and coach to literally hundreds of "on the ground" practitioners in 40 different countries! He writes reality as one who loves God with His mind as well as his heart!

GREG LIVINGSTONE

founder of Frontiers and author of *Planting Churches In Muslim Cities*

A Vision of the Possible is a future classic; the best book of its type that I have ever read. The style is balanced, entertaining, engaging, and practical. Very well done.

SCOTT BRESLIN

field church planter and co-author of *Understanding Dreams From God*

The beauty of this book is that it is rooted in the Word of God from start to finish. The author has beautifully blended in present-day insights from management, conflict resolution, language learning, and team building, all of which are empowered by a God-given vision to reap a maximum harvest for the Lord. It is so filled with practical wisdom on every phase of church-planting movements by team efforts that it should be a companion volume to the Bible for every Christian working among unreached peoples.

DR. DON MCCURRY

president of Ministries to Muslims, editor of *The Gospel and Islam*, and author of *Healing the Broken Family of Abraham: New Life for Muslims*

A Vision of the Possible not only fills a major hole in the need for information to mobilize more workers among unreached peoples, but also for what to do when they get there! The lessons that Dan has gathered in this book will be critical to our own mission of YWAM, and many other missions and churches, in our common journey on the Emmaus road.

STEVE COCHRANE

International Director of Frontier Missions/Neighbours, Youth With a Mission, India

The first thing I did after reading *A Vision of the Possible* was to give it to a young man preparing for ministry in Pakistan. The clarity, experience, and illustrations of the author help any aspiring "pioneer" understand the practicalities of the challenges ahead as well as the essential nature of serving in a team context. I believe every pioneer church planter—as well as trainers, strategists, or churches desiring to partner with such efforts—should read this book carefully and repeatedly.

PAUL BORTHWICK

speaker and author of *Youth and Missions, Leading the Way, How to Be a World-Class Christian,* and *A Mind for Missions*

a VISION

of the

possible

Pioneer Church Planting in Teams

daniel sinclair

IVP Books

An imprint of InterVarsity Press
Downers Grove, Illinois

InterVarsity Press
P.O. Box 1400, Downers Grove, IL 60515-1426
World Wide Web: www.ivpress.com
E-mail: email@ivpress.com

InterVarsity Press® is the book-publishing division of InterVarsity Christian Fellowship/USA®, a
movement of students and faculty active on campus at hundreds of universities, colleges and schools
of nursing in the United States of America, and a member movement of the International Fellowship
of Evangelical Students. For information about local and regional activities, write Public Relations
Dept., InterVarsity Christian Fellowship/USA, 6400 Schroeder Rd., P.O. Box 7895, Madison, WI
53707-7895, or visit the IVCF website at <www.intervarsity.org>.

All Scripture quotations, unless otherwise indicated, are taken from the New American Standard
Bible®, Copyright ©1960, 1962, 1963, 1968, 1971, 1972, 1973, 1975, 1977, 1995 by The Lockman
Foundation. Used by permission.

Originally published by Biblica.

ISBN 978-0-8308-5779-1

Printed in the United States of America ∞

Cataloging-in-Publication Data is available through the Library of Congress.

P	18	17	16	15	14	13	12	11	10	9	8	7	6	5	4	3	2	1
Y	26	25	24	23	22	21	20	19	18	17	16	15	14	13	12				

Contents

Introduction   vii

1. Apostleship: The Great Neglected Subject   1

2. What Is a Church?—and How to Plant One   15

3. Working in Teams—Foundational Principles   31

4. Working in Teams—Practical Applications   39

5. The Pioneer Church Planting Phases   55

6. Learning the Language   87

7. Role and Residency   109

8. Evangelism   117

9. Discipling Local Believers   139

10. Leadership in the Apostolic Task   159

11. The Role of the Church Planters in Church Planting   181

12. What about Church Planting Movements in Highly   199
    Resistant Cultures?

13. Three Models of Church Planting   211

14. The Crucial First Group of Elders   219

Epilogue   239

Appendices
1. Apostleship in the New Testament   251

2. Becoming Someone to Whom Host People Can Talk   261
   (by Dr. Lyman Campbell)

3. Writing a VSP and MOU   269

4. Orality, Bible Narratives, and Indigenous Reproducing   273
   Churches (by Steve Evans)

5. Top Ten Team Pitfalls   281

Bibliography   283

Endnotes   287

Introduction

"Planting churches among unreached peoples" doesn't strike most people as a gripping topic. Even for Christians, while *missions* has a place in the overall scheme of things, it is just one of many priorities vying for the attention and resources of the church.

But let's stop right here, take a deep breath, step back, and look at the big picture. What are we really talking about? Followers of Christ know that human history is not random, but rather is moving toward the riveting last chapter, which for most will be a *surprise ending*. "This gospel of the kingdom shall be preached in the whole world as a testimony to all the nations, and then the end will come" (Matthew 24:14). All of Scripture points to the reality that bringing the gospel of Christ to all nations is now *the* central drama on the human stage. What develops with Christ's *apostolic envoys* as they work among *all peoples* is the great story—ignored by most—that will affect the destiny of all who live.

What stands between us and the end of history? Only one thing: reaping a harvest among the remaining people groups for whom the gospel has not yet taken root, through establishing healthy, indigenous churches. Therefore, what is the true significance of pioneer church planting? Of taking the gospel to the largest blocs of unreached peoples—Muslims, Hindus, and Buddhists? This is the *main event*, the *holy grail*. Without overstating anything, there is no greater drama unfolding today on Planet Earth! Not only is it the greatest challenge to the church in fulfilling our Lord's Great Commission, it remains the single most determining factor in the course and close of human history.

This book is born out of five core convictions. Firstly, in between His resurrection and His ascension, several times and in different ways Jesus made it clear that bringing His gospel to all peoples must be of paramount importance to all His followers until the task is done. Wherever His followers live or whatever the cost, nothing else is to be of higher priority. "Go and make disciples of all the nations" (Matthew 28:19) is one statement of the Great Commission; being His witnesses "even to the remotest part of the earth" (Acts 1:8) is another. Among approximately one third of the world's population, this assignment remains so very unfinished. Unreached peoples must be the core focus in obeying our Savior's great command.

Secondly, in the wide scope of church history, "church planting" is newly in vogue in the church today, so we might be fooled into thinking it's a new concept. But in fact it is as old and as central as the Great Commission itself. It is exactly what all the apostolic teams of the New Testament did. They preached the gospel and then formed and matured *communities of faith*. How could Paul say, for example, that "from Jerusalem and round about as far as Illyricum [about half the Mediterranean Basin] I have fully preach the gospel of Christ" (Romans 15:19)? Only by dotting the landscape with new churches that would carry on the task of evangelism in their areas.

Thirdly, again following the New Testament example, we must pursue these aims in teams. These needn't be big or elaborate teams. But, as we will see, apostolic works in the Bible were always joint efforts. By the way, those on the home front who are actively engaged as "senders" through prayer, financial, and other vital forms of support, are part of the broader team belonging to those precious field teams. This book is also for you, as you gain a clearer picture of what those with whom you are partnering are grappling with on a daily basis.

Fourthly, the harvest *will* come even in these very difficult fields. We must avoid the temptation to fall into an unbelief, sort of by default, that there will always be major swaths of humanity which the gospel is unable to penetrate, and therefore the people cannot be saved. We simply cannot believe that and the Bible at the same time. Some from "every tribe and tongue and people and nation" (Revelation 5:9) will definitely be a part of heaven's eternal community. Hence this book's title: *A Vision of the Possible*. While reaping a harvest among unreached people is humanly impossible, by our Lord's leading and power it is not only possible but *certain*. This book attempts to unpack what is involved in working in teams to plant churches among the most resistant peoples on earth. Envisioning the steps will fire our faith and lead us to go after the seemingly impossible—for whatever fields might seem to us as *resistant* are in actuality *white unto harvest*.

Lastly, the Word of God is our primary teacher for how to do this. Nearly 2,000 years of experience and missiology is also an incredible aid to today's teams, and some of that is included in these chapters. But throughout I have sought to firstly see what the Lord instructs us in the

Bible. It is amazing how much the Word deals with the questions cross-cultural workers are grappling with today.

Nearly all of today's unreached peoples are Hindu, Muslim, Buddhist (or other Chinese religions), or tribal/animist. By *pioneer* work we mean going, like Paul, to where Christ is not "already named" (Romans 15:20). Indeed, this book emphasizes the work of the gospel among those who are unresponsive, resistant, or even hostile. We speak of apostolic efforts among populations who for centuries have blocked Christ's saving message from gaining any meaningful foothold. This usually means special struggles and persecution for those who do believe, exceptional obstacles to gathering believers, and unique hardship and sacrifices for the workers who go in and labor, laying down their lives—figuratively and sometimes literally—in order that Christ might be formed in the new churches. Examples include the Fulbe of West Africa, the Yadava caste of India, the Khmer of Cambodia, and thousands of peoples in between. However, sometimes it is not so much that they are *resistant*, but that they have been sadly *neglected* by the body of Christ. In any case, the love of Christ compels us to go.

Some Nuts and Bolts

- Some names of people and other particulars have been changed for security reasons.

- The principles in this book apply to all pioneer church planting efforts, despite the fact that most of the examples given arise out of the Muslim context, as that is my main area of experience. It can be equally useful to believers laboring among Hindu, Buddhist, and animist peoples.

- In a number of instances I felt that using an acronym helped the text flow better. These are mostly CP (*church planting*), CPer (*church planter*), MBB (*Muslim-background believer*; likewise HBB for *Hindu-background believer*, and so on), and CPM (*church planting movement*).

- I have intentionally sought to keep the words *missions* or *missionary* to an absolute minimum. Properly understood, these words mean good things. However, in much of the world they are misunderstood and carry quite negative connotations among the people we are seeking to love. We do not wish to reinforce misconceptions of cultural or religious colonialism, coercing or inducing people to change *religions* as if we were in some global religious contest. Jesus calls out to all people to embrace forgiveness of sins in His name, to be changed *in the heart*, and to become His disciples. The outward forms this takes will vary widely across cultures.

I have drawn on the experiences of the last twenty-nine years. In this regard no one has been more important than my wife, as we have been on this wild ride together, being privileged to work among Muslims in the United States, in the Middle East, and from the international office of a large church planting agency, serving as field director. From the beginning, it's been a team effort with my wonderful wife and kids as we have learned together. Thank you for believing it was, and still is, worth it.

Many friends have invested hours of their personal time as the reading/editing team, in giving much-needed advice, in logistics, and just encouraging me to keep pressing on. These include Felicity McLure, Phil Parshall, Darrell Dorr, Dick Scoggins, and Celeste Allen. Others also helped significantly, but have asked not to be mentioned by name for the sake of ongoing ministry in sensitive locations. The Lord knows who they are. I pray that these all receive much blessing and encouragement, knowing how they have helped others. Thank you all!

Finally, words are not adequate for how grateful I feel toward the scores of colleagues on the field around the world, with whom it is my greatest privilege to be your *fellow worker*. Your dedication and giftedness humble me. These insights are your insights. The victories have been your victories. The harvest ahead is your harvest in the Lord. You are the pioneer church planters of this generation.

Dan Sinclair

1

Apostleship:
The Great Neglected Subject

She came up to me immediately after I finished speaking about our life and ministry in the Middle East. "I just want to encourage you, Dan. Your family's willingness to serve the Lord in this way is so special and is a real challenge to us here." Others shared similarly affirming words. When I got home, I realized there was a sub-message in their kind words: "What drinking fountain did you drink from, 'cause I really don't want to catch whatever you've got?!"

Let's face it: Anyone who would leave family and friends; a good job; a home; one's own country, culture, and language; and move to the other side of the world where everything is so different and scary and economically poorer—not to mention hostile to the message—must be a little nuts, right? Numerous other times I've been asked, "So you guys must really like it over there, right?" expecting to hear the affirmative. After all, the reasons for going must be the adventure, the stimulation from other cultures, foreign travel, and the like. Not!

If you're a worker in a foreign country, laboring to bring Christ to an unreached people group, I'm sure you've experienced the same. The reason we seem to be such oddballs is that our calling is different. There's only one reason to do what we're doing: because Christ wants us to. Why? Because He loves all people, not just us. He wants everyone to have the opportunity to know Him—not just those who live in free, comfortable countries. And throughout the centuries He's given the *apostolic call* to certain ones of His children. So they head out, regardless of the cost or whether or not it feels good to them or makes sense to friends back home. It doesn't make us any better than anyone else, but it may make us stranger.

It was a chilly January 1 morning, in the early 1980s, when our family first arrived in our new home in Egypt. The evening before, sitting at the gate at New York's JFK felt like waiting to depart Planet Earth on a mission to Mars. I had recently made an exploratory trip and was fortunate to have already arranged a furnished apartment for us to move right into. We got there, and immediately jetlag hit us like a big brick. But what really got to me was the noise. Turns out our seventh floor flat was on the noisiest avenue in the city and possibly the entire continent of Africa! Egyptian drivers honk their horns all the time. The saying goes that if your horn is broken, park your car—as the horn is more important than the steering wheel. A friend later took a stopwatch and measured the longest duration between horn honks and once got as high as thirty seconds, at two in the morning! In the back of the flat, where our bedroom was, was the tram line. Anytime a tram went by, which was from 6 a.m. to 1 a.m., there came a series of bam-bam-bams . . . at one-second intervals.

My heart sank. There was no way I could live here! But there was also no way I could throw in the towel and return home, though I would've considered this option if it weren't for all the "Let's go out and reach the nations" talks I had just given at our sending church. The point is, pioneer envoys are not inherently tougher. They're just called.

We had been in the city a whole two weeks and were feeling almost settled. Another team family arrived and stayed with us in our apartment, but John and Cindy also wanted to spend a couple nights in a hotel, for the sake of registering their passports. I said, "I know just the place." So we took a taxi to the Venetian. But something wasn't right. Even though it was only 6:30 p.m., the door was locked. Finally, after knocking on the door awhile, a not-very-well-dressed young man answered the door. We had learned a handful of Arabic words prior to coming, so we worked to communicate our wishes for a room. It was all seeming a bit odd, but we just figured that hotels in Egypt must be different from what we were used to. The young man was looking more and more perplexed, but graciously tried to accommodate us. He showed us in, and sure enough there were some rooms with beds and accessories. But things seemed to be missing. And there were no doors. When we struggled to express our concern over the lack of doors and privacy, he appeared very distressed. He didn't know what to do. Then it suddenly hit us: this wasn't a hotel; it was a furniture store! I can't remember feeling so stupid—either before or since. My friend John laughed so hard and so long that even his son pleaded with him to stop, and to get up off the ground.

Are pioneer church planters inherently more cross-culturally aware? Well, I hope that's not a requirement.

For years we have shied away from using the word *apostle* in relation to church planting work overseas. After all, people know that apostles were the "big shots" in the New Testament. To say, "God has called me to be an apostle," sounds somewhere between gross arrogance and a delusional break from reality. This is an unfortunate confusion, because the ministry of apostles is at the very core of the Great Commission as well as the current work to bring the good news to those who have never heard.

Many years ago I took *Perspectives on the World Christian Movement* at the U.S. Center for World Mission. Though it was an outstanding course, I cannot recall a single lesson on apostleship. I later completed a master's degree from seminary. There were no classes offered on apostleship. In fact, I do not recall a single lesson on the subject. Please understand: I do not mean this as a criticism. Given the silence on the subject, this isn't too surprising. But it is ironic in light of how the calling and work of the apostles is at the very core of the expansion of the gospel in the New Testament.[1] If this is true, then the calling, gifting, and nature of apostleship today is more vital to us than even concerns such as cultural anthropology, methodology, and missiology. What was true in the first century is just as true in the twenty-first century: without apostolic ministry the gospel does not break new ground. With regard to pioneer work, apostleship is everything. Indeed, it is why, in the Lord, the impossible is acutally possible.

I would encourage you to read through appendix 1, "Apostleship in the New Testament." To summarize, in the New Testament we find mainly two categories of apostles: the Twelve and pioneer workers in general. The Twelve played a foundational and sacred role in the establishment of the church and had a unique authority from Christ. But the two categories are not fundamentally different. Perhaps the clearest mandate for the apostles is found in Acts 1:8, to be Jesus' witnesses "in Jerusalem, and in all Judea and Samaria, and even to the remotest part of the earth." In fact, the command to the apostles to take this gospel "to the remotest part of the earth" were Jesus' last seven (or however many they were in Aramaic) words before his ascension! This was fulfilled in the book of Acts by both the Twelve and the "non-Twelve" apostles. The non-Twelve apostles included Paul (who seems to have been a sort of bridge between the two apostle types), Barnabas, Silas, Timothy, Apollos, James, and others. The primary way in which *apostle* and *apostleship* are used in the New Testament when not referring to the Twelve is concerning the pioneer work of taking the gospel to unreached peoples, resulting in new communities of the body of Christ. Thus "church planting among unreached people groups" would be a fair description of the New Testament concept of apostolic ministry.

Some Apostle FAQs (Frequently Asked Questions)

1. Are there apostles today?

Yes. Apostles and apostolic ministry are just as needed and mandated today as in the first century. There is no biblical reason to suppose that the way the term was applied to Barnabas, Silas, Timothy, Apollos, James, and others would not continue throughout the church age (and today). The term does not apply simply to all who are *sent out* from their churches (or else many more would have been called apostles in the New Testament), but to those with the special gift of apostleship. Indeed, since the ministries of Ephesians 4:11 exist to bring the church to full maturity, including its growth to all people groups, the role of apostle must still be alive and well!

2. Should pioneer church planters take on the title *apostle* for themselves?

I believe that those engaged with an unreached people group to evangelize and plant churches can unabashedly speak of *apostolic min-*

istry and of being on an *apostolic team*. But out of Christian humility and acknowledgement of the diversity of views concerning apostleship, one should be reluctant to stand up and say, "I am an apostle." Also, while the various teams in the New Testament were no doubt engaged in "apostolic ministry," the actual title *apostle* seems to have been applied somewhat sparingly, perhaps only to those whose calling, gifting, and fruitfulness in pioneer work had become confirmed over time. As 1 Corinthians 9:2 shows, not even Paul's apostleship was universally recognized.

Having said that, I do believe that over time other leaders may come to recognize that a particular person has a clear gift of apostleship, and may legitimately refer to him as an apostle.

In his recent book, *Loving the Church, Blessing the Nations*, George Miley has five very helpful chapters on apostolic leaders. "The word apostle might trigger more concern in some than the word apostolic or even the compound apostolic-type. Notice the difference between saying, 'He is an apostle,' 'He is an apostolic leader,' or, 'He is an apostolic-type leader.' Similarly we can speak of apostolic ministry or even apostolic-type ministry. If we have hesitations about the role of the apostle today, using the adjective might give us more freedom to talk openly about this subject."[2]

3. Can *apostleship* today refer to a positional or leadership role in a denomination?

While I respect those who might use the term in this way, I personally find no evidence of this kind of position in the New Testament. While the twelve apostles were given broad authority in the church by Christ, the focus of their apostleship was not some form of top-level ecclesiastical governing. I do not see support for believing that apostleship today pertains to a kind of positional authority in a local church or hierarchical governing in a church denomination.

4. Is it enough for a pioneer church planting team to possess a general mix of gifts?

In my observations over the past twenty-two years of working with pioneer church planting teams, if a team lacks apostolic gifts (that is, no one on the team seems to have that *breakthrough* type of apostolic gifting), then they are rarely very effective.

5. What about those who are not apostles?

If you do not feel that you have the gift of apostleship, but you are on a pioneer church planting team, is all this apostleship stuff reason for discouragement or for questioning your calling? Certainly not. Many in the New Testament were called to be a part of apostolic teams but were never themselves called *apostles*. Most were called *fellow workers*; and only a handful were called *apostles*. Today, just as then, there are many, many indispensable roles for workers who will not be recognized as apostles themselves.

6. What are apostles like?

I do not believe there is a clear-cut profile—certainly not one you could easily defend simply from the New Testament data. But of those I've observed who seem to truly have the gifting, I can offer some tentative general traits (being very nondogmatic here!):

a. God uses them in a variety of ministries. They are the kind who tend to make things happen. Oftentimes they are good at making something out of nothing, ministry-wise, successfully starting new works from scratch. Generally there is a history of evangelistic and discipleship fruitfulness.

b. People readily catch their vision and feel led to join in.

c. They have gifts of Bible teaching and leadership.

d. They can be quirky and sometimes hard to get along with.

e. They can have thick skins and hard heads. They tend (right or wrong) to not back down very easily—on anything!

f. Areas of the flesh can include self-confidence, overassertiveness, and independence. When this is the case, you can see the Lord taking them through a process to grow in these areas toward greater fruit of the Spirit and total dependence on Christ.

g. They want to have a good handle on everything in the ministry. This can seem like a tendency to *overcontrol*.

h. "They have their own ideas of what they want to do." (Miley:111)

i. "They do not fit the mold. They color 'outside the lines'." (Miley:111)

j. "They have a genuine hunger for a deeper relationship with God." (Miley:111)

k. "They are broad in their horizons and think beyond 'our' church." (Miley:111)

l. "They thrive on doing things that are challenging and risky" (Miley:111)

m. "They tend to become overextended in their commitments." (Miley:111)

n. They can be extroverted or introverted, glittery or non-showy. Apostolic gifting doesn't just come with a particular personality type. Some examples: Apollos was winsome. Paul was driven and task-oriented. Barnabas—whose name means "son of encouragement"—was strongly pastoral.

More could be added to this list. And no doubt some needs to be subtracted from this bit of speculation.

THE NATURE OF APOSTLESHIP TODAY

Apostolically gifted pioneer workers are not supermen or superwomen. They have quirks, character flaws, and soft spots. They can be tall or short, smart or not so clever, impetuous or cautious. But they seem to have this in common: They are always on the lookout for key openings. When the normal ways of getting in seem blocked, they look for other ways to get to the people to show God's love. When those unique opportunities happen, they jump on them.

I think of my friend Bruce, a Presbyterian minister, and his family, who had prayed for years for some way to bring the love of Christ to the Kurds of northern Iraq. In early 1990 they moved to a particular Middle Eastern city to study Arabic, and hoped that somehow an opening might present itself to bring the gospel to this people group that was so inaccessible. When Saddam's tanks rolled into Kuwait City, no one knew that this would mean a way for the gospel to reach the Kurds. A couple weeks after the fighting stopped in April 1991, word went out that the

UN eagerly wanted NGO (nongovernmental organization) help among the Kurds above the thirty-sixth parallel. Within a week, Bruce and his family and their team were on their way to Iraq—not knowing where they would live, whether they would be safe or unsafe, or what would happen the next day. It was a sad day for our kids when their kids left, as they all had become good friends. Other workers soon followed, and they have seen a tremendous harvest for the Lord.

I likewise think of Joe and Cathi, who longed to bring Christ to the people of Albania who were so cut off from the good news because the Communist regime shut off virtually all avenues for the gospel. So Joe and Cathi moved to Kosovo, Yugoslavia, and for a few years learned the language and ministered to ethnic Albanians who lived there. When Communism suddenly and unexpectedly fell in Albania, they immediately went in. Within a week Joe was preaching Christ in the open air in Tirane, standing on a fallen statue of Stalin. A church sprung up at once.

Apostles are not exclusively expatriates. While God is moving people from various nations into the harvest among unreached peoples, He is at the same time raising up nationals, even to go to various cities in their own countries to evangelize and plant churches. I still remember how my heart was moved as I listened for four hours as Jamal, in Central Asia, told me of his conversion and remarkable calling by God. He had a dream in which he was protesting to God not to send him to join other wheat harvesters because he had to care for his family. God directed Jamal's eyes to a high mountain peak; at the pinnacle his infant son was rocking serenely in an cradle. Suddenly God gave a command and the cradle flipped upside down, coming around in a full revolution, finally returning to its former place at the mountain's pinnacle. After Jamal recovered from the horror of witnessing his most prized possession, his first son, meet his certain death by God's command, he looked more closely. There in the cradle was his son, smiling and calm as though nothing had happened. God finally said, "Do you see? I can take care of your family better than you can. You go into my harvest!" This brother has since planted several churches in and around his native city. He and his family have relocated to a new city, having been formally sent out by the MBB church they planted!

In 1984 I sat on a hill overlooking a large swath of Cairo—four- to ten-story buildings as far as the eye could see, all of the same drab light-brown color. The horizon was hazy because of a big cement factory. The population just in this limited viewing area was probably around seven million souls (out of the nearly twenty million of the city). The thought burned through the haze: this is exactly what Paul described in Romans 15:18–21:

> For I will not presume to speak of anything except what Christ has accomplished through me, resulting in the obedience of the Gentiles by word and deed, in the power of signs and wonders, in the power of the Spirit; so that from Jerusalem and round about as far as Illyricum I have fully preached the gospel of Christ. *And thus I aspired to preach the gospel, not where Christ was already named, so that I would not build on another man's foundation; but as it is written, "THEY WHO HAD NO NEWS OF HIM SHALL SEE, AND THEY WHO HAVE NOT HEARD SHALL UNDERSTAND"* (emphasis added).

In this passage Paul shares his heart and his calling, what drove him to do everything he did. It was his life's calling to go to cities where Christ was not yet known, to people groups in which the church had not yet taken root. One of the great privileges of pioneering ministry is that when you share the gospel with a neighbor, friend, or taxi driver, it is the first time they have ever heard—and sadly, may be the last. At that moment, you are truly Jesus' ambassador to them.

Recently my wife and I were visiting the church one of our daughters attends. The pastor was making a reference to *apostleship*, but he stumbled on his words and it came out *impossible-ship*. I thought, "Hold on. That's right. That's really what apostleship is." Apostleship is the work of creating something out of nothing. It is moving to a city and people where virtually no one is following Christ, yet where God uses you to create a body of believers. It normally functions in a hostile environment, which makes things very difficult both for the church planters and for the new church. Humanly speaking, this is an impossible task. It really is a special anointing and gifting.

Why focus in a particular way on Hindus? Or Buddhists? Or Muslims? Though this might seem to some as aggressive or possibly a new form of colonialism, it actually comes from a heart of loving concern. Everyone needs Jesus. For far too long, Christians have failed to give Muslims, for example, an opportunity to understand the peaceable way of Jesus. It is also recognized that the Crusades set a negative historical image. We are grieved that Muslims were mistreated in the name of Christ. Since that time, many Muslim societies have distrusted so-called Christian societies, and vice versa. In addition, Muslims are often taught an incorrect view of what it means to be a follower of Jesus. Therefore gospel workers feel they have a role to play in correcting any misunderstandings about the true nature of Jesus Christ. By becoming proficient in Islamic history and culture and the language of the people, they are better able to maximize their sensitivity and respect for Muslim peoples. In the West we comprehend so little about the typical Muslim's needs and worldview. Only by really caring for these people can we begin to understand. In addition, pioneer church planters have discovered that Muslims have much to teach us. They take the spiritual world quite seriously and generally are open to discuss religious issues. They have a very high respect for God and His power. They place a high value on community and loyalty. Hospitality is very important to them. These are some of the many qualities expatriate workers value in their Muslim friends, and they find that living among Muslims has enriched their lives. Finally, we wish to be for our friends those "People of the Book"[3] spoken of in the Qur'an: "But if you are in doubt regarding what We have sent down to you, then ask those who read the Book before you. Assuredly the truth has come to you from your Lord; so be not among the doubters."[4]

The apostolic heart beats for pioneer church planting—to go where others aren't going or can't go, to engage a populace who have never before heard our message with the great news of forgiveness and eternal life in Christ—without worry of interference from other ministries or of interfering with them. This is the yearning of the apostle. It is why Paul would turn his back on visiting Rome, the center of civilization at the time, with its emerging church and all the excitement, comfort, and prestige that could have meant for him. Instead he stayed on in cities without a vital church, usually in frustration and obscurity, pleading with resistant and hostile people to hear the gospel and building up those who responded.

This pioneering, suffering spirit has always characterized God's special *sent ones*. As C. T. Studd wrote:

> Some wish to live within the sound
> Of Church or Chapel bell;
> I want to run a Rescue Shop
> Within a yard of hell.[5]

A practical application, as alluded to above, is that apostles need "fellow workers" (or teammates) and that these workers, in turn, need apostles. Together they comprise viable apostolic teams. Several times I have observed team leaders who do not yet have a team. Even though they may exhibit signs of apostolic gifting, they can go for long periods without fruit because of not having fellow workers to help them.

I have likewise observed the reverse (and here is where I might get into trouble with some): good-sized church planting teams that do not seem to have anyone on the team with the gift of apostleship—not the team leader nor anyone else. It's perplexing, because these teams have mature and experienced people, but year after year nothing seems to happen. Could it just be that the soil is hard and it's not yet God's timing for a harvest? Of course this is sometimes the case. But I also believe that sometimes the reason is that there is no one on the team with a *breakthrough* gifting, that special anointing that creates something out of nothing for Christ's sake. When this is the case, it may be best for all either to find a new team leader with possible apostolic gifting or let the team break up and the workers join other teams where they can be more effective.

Paul's consciousness of being called as an apostle had a profound impact on his life and ministry. Nothing would ever again be the same. First of all, he knew that his gospel ministry was not his whim, idea, or chosen career path. Rather, it came from God's initiative. And therefore it came with God's authority. How often Paul reminded people in the churches he started of his apostleship—and of his awareness that God was communicating to them *through him*!

Secondly, Paul's awareness of calling eliminated any shrinking back from discharging his ministry with all faithfulness, whatever the cost. "For if I preach the gospel, I have nothing to boast of, for *I am under compulsion; for woe is me if I do not preach the gospel. For if I do this voluntarily, I have a reward; but if against my will, I have a stewardship entrusted to me*" (1 Corinthians 9:16–17; emphasis added). This "stewardship," of course, was his apostolic ministry. As Paul said in his emotional farewell to the elders of the church at Ephesus, "I do not consider my life of any account as dear to myself, so that I may finish my course and *the ministry which I received from the Lord Jesus*" (Acts 20:24; emphasis added). One team leader confided with me, "Paul's sense of apostolic call has had a profound effect on me and my ministry, Dan, forcing me to plead with Christ Jesus constantly to grant me His grace that I might be faithful until the end, not turning to the right or the left in my vocational and ministerial aspirations. I am a bond slave of Christ, called to die to my own will and live for His alone. In addition, when preaching to nonbelievers and exhorting obstinate church members, sometimes, but not often, I have had to plead with them not to sin or reject Christ because God was *at that moment* speaking directly to them through me. Of course, I had better be careful when to invoke my "authority," but such moments have always kept both me and my hearers very serious and careful that our words, spoken with love and humility and extreme self-examination, *at that moment* have eternal weightiness before God."

We're told that today there are still around two billion people who not only do not know the Lord but are also beyond the witness of any church in the midst of their own people and language. They have no news of Him; they have not heard. And they never will until pioneer gospel ambassadors do whatever it takes to bring the gospel to them and plant churches, particularly among Hindus, Muslims, Buddhists, Taoists, and secular Communists, as well as many other kinds of unreached people groups. This is why we do what we do. This is our vision. This is our apostolic calling.

2
What Is a Church?
—and How to Plant One

The BBC recently reported how "the world's first inflatable church went on display to the public for the first time on Tuesday. The blow-up church, which is 47 feet (14.3 meters) high from ground to steeple, 47 feet long and 25 feet (7.6 meters) wide, includes a blow-up organ, altar, pulpit, pews, candles and 'stained glass' windows." Now, if this meaning of *church* became acceptable to the wider gospel worker community, how much easier "church planting among unreached peoples" would be!

Assuming this *isn't* what we mean by church, then what is a church? And how does one plant one? As chapter titles go, this one is pretty audacious. While I cannot offer up a foolproof recipe for planting a church in a resistant context, I do believe there are some generally agreed upon church planting principles that have a lot of power to launch a new team into fruitful ministry. We'll take up the two questions in this chapter in reverse order: first *How do we plant a church?* then *What is a church?*

This chapter presupposes that the workers are committed to church planting among their unreached people group, as opposed to a variety of other field pursuits. I wholeheartedly agree with Trent and Vivian Rowland: "For the least evangelized peoples to be reached, the birth and growth of an indigenous self-propagating church needs to be the central goal and every ministry should be evaluated in light of its contribution toward this goal. People who do not have church planting as their stated goal probably will not do it."[1]

We know that in resistant fields the majority of those who come to faith in Christ eventually leave the faith. But in my experience believers are much more likely to stay in Christ if, from the beginning of their pilgrimage with the Lord, they are woven into fellowship with others from the same background.

How to Plant a Church

Pioneer church planting means starting a church from scratch where no church from that people group yet exists. It is very intentional.

Having a Goal in Mind

A church in an unreached context is like a turtle on a fencepost. It didn't just somehow get there; someone had to make it happen. One has to begin with a goal in mind, a picture, a vision of what must become—something so concrete you can almost touch it, taste it, see it. If God has called you to plant churches among an unreached people group, may He truly give you this special kind of faith and vision. The initial goal will probably be something like this:

a. a group of believers from the particular people group;

b. of some minimum size and social variety (e.g., not just a group of three single guys);

c. committed to Christ, to one another, to being His body together and being taught by His Word;

d. under two or three believers (from that people group) shepherding as elders;

e. with a vision to reproduce.

In most pioneer situations, especially in resistant cultures, the aim should be to start new groups of believers from that background—Hindu-background believers in the Hindu context, Buddhist-background believers in the Buddhist context, and so on—rather than seeking to integrate these new believers into a culturally Christian-background congregation.

As Subbamma writes from Andhra Pradesh, India, "If there is enough flexibility and freedom in our approach to Hindus, house churches will grow naturally among them."[2]

Now some might object that the initial goal I've suggested is too small—that if this is the initial goal then you will be content with it, and you will fail to lay the groundwork for a church planting *movement* (CPM). I would agree and disagree with such an objection. Having a longer-range CPM-type vision is great. To intentionally lay the groundwork for the "DNA of CPM" from the very beginning could be very strategic. And to even cultivate ground in multiple locations simultaneously—especially if you are a larger team—may be exactly what the Lord would have you do. But to have only huge goals (i.e., your *first* goal is a *movement*) and not to have something more concrete, nearer at hand, will paralyze the vast majority of church planters. For a church planting team in a pioneer or resistant city, having a goal that is as simple and specific as the one above will be energizing, as most will realize that it is something that is possible within a reasonable time period, as the Lord works. There is another danger: If you have an impossibly large dream that only Christ can do by a humongous miracle (think on the level of splitting the Red Sea), then you will generally be content with no progress. For pioneer workers, being satisfied with no progress can become a disease.

We had a medium-size team in "Shukranistan."[3] For many, many years the fact that there was absolutely no fruit and little real evangelism did not deter them from claiming hundreds of churches for Christ in their goals. Then the team leader got a new team leader overseer who had a real allergy against such vagueness and directionless-ness. He wouldn't hear about hundreds of churches, but only wanted to know what the team was going to do to get the *first* church. Everyone had to have a plan for their personal evangelism and discipling. Within a year they had two growing fellowships, and the excitement on the team was palpable. This is also a team that prays a lot, and the Lord is answering their prayers, giving them the desires of their hearts.

How to Get Started

It's been my privilege to be a part of starting several new fellow-ships from scratch—three of them with MBBs, and two of those being in the Middle East. These were neither huge nor shining examples of what a church ought to be, but I did learn one thing: Starting a fellowship group is not as complicated as we sometimes make it out to be (though perhaps not as simple as the "inflatable" variety).

In my own experience, in every church plant I've observed, and in all of Paul's church plants, I see that one cannot plant a church until one has believers to work with. This means that we either lead them to faith in Christ ourselves, or else the Lord allows us to find them or them to find us. Many times there is a combination of leading some to faith and discovering an existing believer or two.

Eric and Carla and their two-year-old son moved to a city of three million people in Indonesia, where there were no known believers in the late 1980s. After getting a good start on the language, Eric began to spend most of the day out in various places in the city where men could be found working in markets, socializing near tourist spots, or just relax-ing in their homes. He would meet people, cultivate relationships, share Christ, and return home later in the day. Eric did this faithfully for several years, until one day he shared the gospel with a man named Forest,[4] who was already a follower of Christ. Forest instantly recognized that Eric was a Christ-follower who could disciple him. They became fast friends, and within eighteen months God used these men and their wives to plant a church of twenty believers from Forest's people group.

Another brother, Michael, serving in Central Asia, had worked boldly for quite some time, sharing the gospel and even placing gospel literature in public schools—somehow with official permission. His team also diligently went all over the place showing the *Jesus* film. Fahmi, an engineer who had come to faith in Europe and just returned home, came to one of these showings. God had put a burden on Fahmi's heart for his own people. He immediately recognized in Michael one who was bold and zealous to get the good news out. Within a couple years of working together, the church they started had around 150 members and was plant-ing daughter fellowship groups in neighboring towns.

My own experience was similar. For a year and a half my wife and I labored in evangelism and learning Arabic but saw no fruit. One day Bill, an American friend of mine, told me that an Arab friend of his, a citizen of the country we were living in, was coming back home. Farouk,[5] born and raised as a Muslim, had come to Christ several years back, had grown in his faith, and had been involved in discipleship and ministry outside the country. It wasn't clear if Farouk was coming for a week or possibly longer. "Would I like to meet him?" There was no hesitation. "Absolutely."

Farouk and I met the day he arrived in Bill's apartment and immediately hit it off. We quickly became close friends, drawing on our common commitment to ministry as well as a mutual dry sense of humor. It was later my privilege to be the best man in his wedding, and to this day we are very, very close—a friendship I treasure deeply. A couple of weeks later I headed off to a conference in Germany, where we prayed for a breakthrough in our adopted country. Upon my return Farouk told me that he had met two or three other believers and had pulled them together in fellowship. Was that OK? Did I mind? Did I want to come and meet these brothers? The group was off and running. (Never mind that one of these brothers had been a fighter in the Lebanese civil war and later tried to kill Farouk. One must learn to overlook minor ups and downs in this work!)

Some advocate an approach to evangelism and church planting that seeks to work with a whole group of people who are not yet believers, regularly getting together around the teachings of Christ and building deeper relationships together in the context of learning more about Him from the Gospels or the whole New Testament. An excellent example of this among tribal peoples would be the intentional approach of forming "listening groups" of nonbelievers in the largely oral Kui people of Orissa, India.[6] I really applaud these efforts to form groups of nonbelievers, and wherever we can see it being fruitful is truly exciting. The hope in this methodology is that at some point most or all will come to saving faith in Christ. Of course, even with this approach, at some point there have to be believers who become the community of faith.

Oftentimes this approach of casting wider nets means investing a lot in a particular family or clan. Don and Carol and their team worked among the "Buran"[7] in a major city in South Asia. For several years they had seen only a little progress, including the ongoing discipling of Bruce,[8] a Buran believer. Though Bruce's family lived in a village around four hours away, and though Bruce's brother Hank[9] was a zealot who had trained with the Taliban, Don and Bruce would visit them periodically and seek to share Christ. There is not space here to share the exciting details, but once Don, Bruce, and another brother drove very early out to visit the family, arriving around eight in the morning. Just a few hours prior to their arrival Hank had a dream in which Christ told him these men were about to arrive and that he and the whole family should receive their message from God. This they did, and the whole family was baptized the next day! Now not only has a church been planted among this extended family, but many other embryonic fellowships among the Buran have sprung up as well. And through this the gospel has even spread into another four or five related people groups in different areas, including one in a neighboring country. We can never know what we will set in motion by the simple obedience of sharing the good news!

How to Gather

Now let's assume that your team is in regular contact with two or more believers, but that these believers are not yet seeing each other regularly. There is not yet a fellowship group. The best thing at this stage would be for someone on the team to be regularly discipling each believer. In other words, they see each other often, study the Word and pray together, and are involved in each other's lives in an ever-growing relationship.

Gathering these new believers into a functional fellowship—even a small one—will probably take more time and care than would be required back in your home country. Each believer is already aware that following Christ is risky business. The threat of persecution from family, neighbors, employers, and the government is very real indeed. Also, Hindu, Muslim, and Buddhist societies are typically Eastern in culture and therefore more family and clan oriented. Getting to know people from outside one's clan is not easy in general, and particularly daunting in sensitive matters of faith. All of these factors can create an absence of trust—a force which can keep believers apart, or pull them apart soon after initial introductions.

Some have proposed that the answer to this large difficulty is to "fish in ponds"; that is, only seek to lead people to Christ in a particular clan or social network, so that when some do come to faith they already know each other. I admire this approach, and wherever the Lord's workers believe this is how they should proceed I say "Go for it." But be aware that this may really limit your sphere of contacts, as we really do not know where the Lord is going to stir people's hearts. Likewise, I've seen in a situation or two that some believers prefer relating to others outside their family or social circle. Relationships inside families are always complex and have their own set of challenges.

So which approach do I personally favor: casting our nets widely and then later having to bring strangers together—or only working inside one family or circle, hoping to create a fellowship group from those who already have a natural relationship with each other? My answer is that it really depends on the context and one's sense of the Lord's strategic leading. Overall, I would say that the jury is still out on which works best across the board. Failed attempts at gathering do not exist only in the former approach to church planting.

Regardless of your approach on this matter, there are forces that keep believers apart. But there are also forces that can serve to pull them together. One of these positive factors is *you*. If your relationship with them is one of good friendship and is spiritually beneficial, then they will not mind meeting other friends of yours—i.e., other believers. You can be the glue. Another key factor is how they will see, as they become more acquainted with the New Testament, that believers are supposed to be in community. And finally, following Christ will result in overwhelming psychological pressure if a believer is isolated: he or she will feel odd and vulnerable in society, and under a great burden of dealing with such challenges alone. People naturally want others supporting them when they are dealing with really hard things.

There are basically four things you need to nurture when beginning to bring multiple believers together who may or may not know each other:

1. *Learning biblical principles about community.*

Even working one-on-one you can begin to unfold the Lord's teaching about relationships between believers: why this is nonnegotiable, an indispensable aspect of fellowship that they will come to experience as precious. Of course at first this will only be conceptual. Nonetheless, we start this process with the Word of God.

2. *Comfort.*

Think of creative ways for them to meet each other in nonthreatening contexts. It will likely take time for them to begin to feel comfortable with each other. Again, you are probably the initial glue.

3. *Trust.*

—in the long run, so very, very vital.

4. *Healthy interaction.*

Eventually they can begin to be there for each other: to encourage, strengthen, and minister to each other. They can begin to carry out all the various "one another" functions and exhortations found in Scripture.

Most of the time you will need a stage of pre-gathering. You will probably want to let new believers know of the existence of other believers early on. And you will begin teaching about the community life of believers, and how staying in isolation in the long run is unbiblical and a recipe for disaster. Going over passages such as Acts 2:41–47 and Ephesians 4:11–16 is a good start.

A nonthreatening way to introduce people to each other is through parties. With birthdays and holidays (both Christian and local), there are unlimited occasions to have a dinner or party. We have found that meals and parties in our home are seen by all as warm and inviting. Believers and seekers who might steer clear of a meeting will gladly come out for a meal. Indeed, to not come is to offend the host, which people are eager to avoid.

The fellowship meetings we'd been having weren't well attended. But it was someone's birthday, so we decided to invite many believers and some seekers to a party and dinner. We made it clear to all that this was a birthday party but that we were also going to worship, pray, and have some time in the Word. I couldn't believe that nearly twenty-five people showed up. We barely fit in Fred's apartment and had to take special measures to make the food stretch. Surprisingly, a young believer named Tawfiq, who hadn't shown much commitment to the Lord up till then, not only came to the party but brought an unbelieving friend—knowing that we'd be sharing about the Lord Jesus.

These parties can be merely social. Or, if you feel the situation will allow it, the event can also have a spiritual dimension, even if your invited friends include those who are not believers yet. It can be perfectly natural—for example, at Easter—to read and share from God's Word and have a time where some people pray out loud.

The final step of pre-gathering can be get-togethers consisting only of believers, expressly for the purpose of fellowship, Bible study, and prayer. These gatherings might take place on an evening, or perhaps even as an overnight retreat somewhere. Hopefully these times are meeting needs in people's souls, and an appetite for more is growing.

In my setting, the believers often enjoyed picnics together on Friday afternoons. These gatherings were usually one to two hours away by car, up in the hills in the midst of pine trees and fresh air. I remember one time when many of us piled into cars. We had chairs, blankets, Bibles, lots of food, charcoal, matches, and—whoops!—no grill. Mahmood, a particularly enterprising young man, searched the hillside high and low and found the front section, or grill, of a 1957 pickup truck, which served as a perfect barbeque grill! I still have a photo of it. I also remember how, even as the sun went down, no one wanted to go home.

At some point, then, you will want to propose—if the believers haven't proposed it already—that the group get together regularly. This may very well require all your resources of personal influence, relationship, and bringing forward persuasive truths from the New Testament. You may have to tear down fear barriers. And prayer will need to bathe

the whole process, as ultimately only God can overcome this hurdle. And He will. He is committed to you, to them, and to the life of the body.

Some would contend that these regular fellowship times should not be in the expatriate's home; other locations would be better. But most would agree that it's better to have a fellowship in a less-than-ideal place than none at all.

Then What?

According to the "Pioneer Church Planting Phases" (see chapter 5 and www.churchplantingphases.com), once you have three or more believers getting together regularly, the group is in Phase V. There is nothing magical about the number three, of course, though it does seem to be a sort of minimum for a group to be a group. In a pioneer context this is a huge achievement, and it represents exhilarating potential for now growing the body of Christ.

One of the most gratifying bits of affirmation concerning ministry we ever received came from an unusual source. Sometime after the events mentioned before, Farouk was questioned frequently by a senior officer of the secret police. He was basically the head of the department concerning Christian activities, specifically responsible to make sure that Christian evangelism didn't rock the boat. With unusual candor, he finally told Farouk that he'd been working in these affairs for twenty years and that our group of Christ-followers, because of its potential, was the first thing to really get his department scared. And so it is, when God's children begin to form together into a body. Of course, as people begin to follow Christ in reality they bring all kinds of beneficial influence to society, but the security services may not realize that.

Once at this stage, the focus of the church planters becomes the fourfold task of 1) teaching the Word; 2) shepherding the believers; 3) developing community and New Testament body life; and 4) beginning to develop potential leaders. This is the subject of chapter 14. However, let me be quick to point out that this does *not* mean that the evangelistic activity of the church planters ceases. This continues on, as well as possibly seeking to start new groups in other places, as the team is able.

There are some very important things we haven't mentioned concerning this process of planting a church from scratch in a pioneering or hostile environment. We haven't said much about prayer, which of course is absolutely crucial—both for the CP team and for mobilizing prayer all over the world. We haven't talked about praying for the sick, or about several other things some might feel are central.

WHAT IS A CHURCH?

I have heard fellow workers proudly proclaim their aim to plant a *contextualized* church—one that is maximally indigenous and fitting to the culture—as if they have just discovered the Rosetta stone of pioneer work. Personally, I have never met a church planting worker who intended to simply transplant or import "church" just as it was back home to the new culture. Everyone gladly embraces to one degree or another the principle that forms and flavors of church life are not biblically absolute and therefore ought to come from and fit in well with the host culture. Specific areas include clothing, interaction of men and women, sitting in pews or chairs or on the floor, modes of worship, the role of and type of music, religious terminology, greetings, meeting components, food, finances, prayer positions, and the list goes on and on. And besides all these externals lie the meanings behind the forms and the strategy for thinking through contextualization, so that the church is truly at home in its context and the only objection or stumbling block to this new faith is that of the cross of Christ. As Subbamma describes in the Hindu context, "It is consequently entirely in line with the historical practice of the Church that we should fit the churches to the needs of the populations becoming Christian."[10]

Issues of contextualization don't apply only to the propogation of the gospel. Indeed, it was Buddhism's closeness to Taoism that enabled it to be accepted so widely into Chinese society in the second century A.D.[11]

Until Jesus returns, church planters will differ on the very important issues of contextualization and approaches to culture. This is natural. But all will agree with the need to give birth to an indigenous church. Whatever our approach, we should not allow cultural concerns to paralyze us or the progress in church planting. We must learn the language and culture well (see chapter 6) and strive to minister in culturally appropriate ways. But mistakes will be made; no one is going to get it perfectly "right." As the church planters play a smaller and smaller role—eventually leaving all together—the church will naturally drop off any unintended and unhelpful foreign baggage.

Therefore, what ought to engage us more than the *cultural* concerns regarding how to plant a church are the *biblical* concerns. What is a church? What does it look like? How is it birthed? How is it to function? How is it led? And because the apostolic church planter is not going to be around forever, not going to implement or teach everything from A to Z, the question becomes, What are the minimums or core essentials of the New Testament with regard to "church" for this people group God has called me to? Coming to grips with these matters is the central steward-ship for the apostolic church planter. Then, with these biblical principles in view, he can begin to visualize how it might look in the new culture.

Some Basics

The predominant Greek word in the New Testament for "church," as you may know, is *ekklesia*. It is used 114 times and, except for 5 times, always refers to the church. By this time, *ekklesia* had both a Jewish and a Gentile meaning. To the Jews it denoted a religious gathering or body, the congregation of faith. To the Romans and Greeks it meant a func-tioning social entity, such as a city's assembly. It seems that the New Testament writers drew upon both understandings in their use of the word. There are two other Greek words—*plethos* and *sunagogay*—that are used a few times for church. Interestingly, *koinonia* ("fellowship") is never used to denote a local church (e.g., "the Antioch Fellowship").

In the New Testament, *ekklesia* often refers to the church at large, the *universal* church. Many times, however, it refers to specific local churches. As someone has said, "While there are many churches, there is but one Church." As such, unity is inherent because of our organic relationship together in Christ; yet at the same time, on a practical level, there is an ongoing necessity of working hard to preserve it.

There were no purposely built church buildings until Constantine. Churches often met in homes. There could be several house churches in one city, while maintaining a larger sense of "church" under a common leadership, such as was apparently the case in Corinth.

The key mark of the church is faith. Jesus' inaugural use of *ekklesia* was upon Peter's full confession of faith in Jesus as Messiah (Matthew 16:18). "Primarily the church is a society not of thinkers or workers or even of worshippers, but of believers. Hence, we find that 'believers' or 'they that believed' is constantly used as a synonym for the members of the Christian society (e.g. Acts 2:44; 4:32; 5:14; 1 Timothy 4:12)."[12] Drawing upon old covenant terminology, all members in Christ are now "a chosen race, a royal priesthood, a holy nation, a people for God's own possession" (1 Peter 2:9).

The Operation of the Church

In numerous references, baptism is the confirming entrance point upon which an individual or group embraces Christ and is brought into the church. While it might not be possible to say the New Testament asserts that one cannot be a member of the church without baptism, its normative treatment of the practice would suggest that an unbaptized believer is certainly lacking a vital step in following Christ and being in union with His body.

By the spring of 1990 our fellowship group was growing and doing pretty well. Farouk and I were partnering to give leadership to his exciting new group. Three of them hadn't been baptized yet and were eager to do so. So for weeks we taught on baptism, as well as counseling these three individuals to make sure they understood its meaning and ramifications. Finally the Friday came when about eight of us headed off for the baptism. We had all agreed that, for security reasons, none of us would talk about this event to anyone. We walked together through a beautiful canyon, after a while coming to a pool and small waterfall area. Total privacy and an incredibly beautiful spot on earth! The baptisms were wonderful, and the fellowship was so very rich. One of the men had a false tooth that fell out during the baptism, which we still laugh about to this day. By 3:30 that afternoon the phones were buzzing with people who had heard about the baptisms from the men. So much for security!

As there is a clear point of joining the church through faith and baptism, there is likewise to be a clear demarcation to know who has left. There are three ways for this to occur: 1) being removed for failure to turn from sin (Matthew 18:15–20; 1 Corinthians 5); 2) abandoning the faith (1 Timothy 1:19); or 3) simply ceasing active involvement in the church (1 John 2:19). By God's grace, restoration is possible in all three cases. One result of this clarity in entry and exit is that it ought to be possible at any time to know fairly well who are the visible disciples of Christ and members of His body. While this doesn't necessarily rule out the possibility of "closet believers," that would clearly be an inferior spiritual state—with impaired obedience to Christ and some question about the reality of one's faith and salvation.

Local churches *assemble*, or *come together* or *meet* (cf. Acts 2:42; 5:12; 1 Corinthians 5:4; 14:23, 26; Hebrews 10:25; James 2:2). They are not merely an amorphous network of believers who have occasional ties. The context of the local church in the New Testament is always on *active* community life, rather than some theoretical sense of membership. Never are people viewed as being *in* the church if they are not *active* in the church. This is a crucial point in hostile contexts: despite the pressures and risks believers must find a way to spend time together, whether in small groupings or larger ones.

A local church in the New Testament is under a common leadership of *elders*. Thirteen times in the New Testament we find the term *elders* in the plural with *local church* being in the singular. Indeed, usually the first application of the term *church* with regard to a new group of believers is in the context of the leadership or eldership over them (e.g., Antioch [Acts 11:26]; the churches of Paul's first missionary journey [Acts 14:23]; Ephesus [Acts 20:17]; the churches of Crete [Titus 1:5]). This is probably an indicator that an absolutely essential structural component to a local body of Christ is being under the vital leadership, teaching, and shepherding of elders.

Neither Jesus nor the writers of the New Testament give us a detailed order for local church organization; no church constitution or bylaws are found on Scripture's pages. The one thing that is normative for local church leadership across all New Testament churches is the role of *elders* (or *overseers* or *pastors*)—with plural *elders* shepherding the singular *church*. It seems highly likely, therefore, that within this one norm, there is nearly complete latitude for different churches of varying cultures and times to organize themselves as best fits the situation.

Our Lord directed us to "make disciples of all the nations . . . teaching them to observe all that [He] commanded." Throughout His time on earth He consistently taught that all His followers are to be together in community, in unity, and in service to one another as we grow in Him. This community He called *church*. So as church planting is implicit in the Great Commission, the goal of pioneering work must be to leave behind believers in community. And while there will be many philosophical and strategic issues for us to grapple with along the way, we move forward by keeping the all-crucial biblical teachings concerning church and church planting before us.

3
Working in Teams
—Foundational Principles

Different things go in and out of style in pioneer gospel endeavor. One emphasis very much in vogue today is working in teams. Common wisdom says that workers thirty years ago believed in cooperation on the field, but were pretty individualistic in their actual ministries. Then came the Baby Boomers, who were more relational, touchy-feely, and wanted to do things together. And now the Gen-Xers are *really* into doing things as a group; relationships are a top priority. Today's candidate sees being in close community as absolutely essential. This stereotype may not be always true, but there is no doubt that the younger wave of workers are much more into "team" and "community" than their predecessors. Mission agencies know this, as even a cursory look at current recruiting advertisements will bear out.

As one who has had the privilege (and sometimes the overwhelming *challenge*) of overseeing more than 160 teams—most of them still carrying on, thankfully—I know that *team* is a matter of great contrasts. As workers begin their pre-field preparation, *team* connotes only the warmest of images and future hopes: close fellowship, need-meeting friendship, sharing Christ arm in arm in the bazaar, mutual encouragement when things are tough, a sense of belonging, and cherishing the direction of the team leader as he[1] wisely steers the ministry ship in the Lord's way. One can almost smell those pies in the oven during future team meetings on the field!

Though sometimes those expectations are actually fulfilled, reality tells another side of the story: probably the biggest source of pain on the field for workers is from fellow teammates. Interpersonal conflicts, clashing expectations and opinions, unresolved offenses, and irreconcilable differences with leaders often bring healthy team life grinding to a halt. I'm sad to report that many times I've seen teams stuck for a year or longer, frozen and unable to have good team life or any effective ministry at all. How the devil must laugh when workers pay the enormous price of leaving home and enduring many hardships, believers back home are giving and praying, and the team knows the language and culture—but then the ministry becomes stymied or even destroyed because of the team's internal conflict and dysfunction. As a field overseer I could get really frustrated by that, except I've been in the thick of those things myself as a co-sinner with my teammates.

The first church planting team I led was in Egypt. The first six months as a team were quite rocky, with a lot of dissatisfaction, focused largely on some decisions I made or the way I made them. I sort of expected the problems to just go away, but they didn't. Tension on the team grew worse, and contentiousness became a serious problem. Two or three on the team were making it impossible for me to lead, and it was becoming really unbearable. I still remember the day I told my wife, with tears in my eyes, that I couldn't go on, that I was quitting as team leader. Three years of preparation at a dead end. I never felt so low. All our hopes and dreams had failed, or so it seemed. By God's grace, we eventually worked things out as a team—and I didn't quit. I grew from the mistakes I had made, some difficult team members changed their attitudes, and soon the Lord pulled us together into a deeply satisfying unity. Before long, we as a team were discipling several believers and a fellowship meeting began. But I would never forget those lows and highs of team life—and I've got the gray hairs to prove it!

So do we give up on working in teams? Certainly not. As I'll share below, working in teams is an essential part of the apostolic task. God doesn't call *lone rangers* to build communities of faith. But what are the lessons we can learn?

Most workers feel that they finally get a handle on team life and ministry only after a term or two on the field. This chapter is an attempt to give the reader a head start. There are several models of team out there. Are some better than others? What works? What does it mean to be a team? Does *team* necessarily mean *big team*? (Hint: No.)

Why Plant Churches in Teams?

1. *It's the only New Testament model.*

A very interesting study is to trace all the occurrences in the New Testament of "the work" (Greek *ton ergon*). Most of the time this is a very special phrase referring specifically to the expansion work of the gospel, taking the good news to cities and regions that are as yet unevangelized. The end result, as the Lord works, is consistently the founding of new communities of faith in Christ—churches. The people involved are apostles, evangelists, and those intriguingly referred to many times as "fellow workers" (Greek *sunergous*). Likewise, the New Testament mentions thirty to forty individuals by name who had left their homes and were actively engaged in pioneer apostolic work. They seem to be full-time in ministry, or nearly so, and most probably received some form of financial assistance to enable them to do so. The point is this: every single one of those mentioned worked in joint effort with other workers.[2] Teams are not just the latest fad; they are the New Testament model and mandate.

2. *One person can't do it.*

Throughout history lone rangers usually see little or no lasting fruit and are often unable to persevere in the task long enough to have enduring impact, to leave behind lasting fruit. There are rare exceptions to this, of course. But I believe the Bruchkos[3] are the exceptions that prove the rule.

In Acts 13:2 the Holy Spirit did not say, "Set apart for Me Barnabas for the work to which I have called him in Cyprus; and then also set apart Paul for Me to go to Asia Minor by himself. This way we'll get more done in less time." No. He called them to go out together, knowing well that either one of them by himself would be lonely, vulnerable, and ineffective. Jesus sent out the Twelve two by two (Mark 6:7), as well as seventy others (Luke 10:1). The Lord then continued on with this model in the early church.

While Barnabas and Paul had some overlapping gifts—for example, in preaching and teaching—they also had differing gifts and personalities. It was God's intent to use these differences and this apostolic gift-mix to plant and strengthen each of the churches on this first journey. They also experienced many disappointments, problems, and fierce opposition (like Paul being stoned and left for dead). Truly, when one of them was down, the other could pull him up.

Isn't it interesting that at the end of Acts 15 when Paul and Barnabas had their falling out, neither of them threw in the towel on the team concept? Neither one said, "OK, that's it. I'm done trying to work with others. It's too hard." Rather, both quickly went out and formed new teams!

Steve Richardson of Pioneers writes about dramatic change in apostolic work in Indonesia in the mid-1980s, where a new pattern emerged in which attrition went way down and fruitfulness increased. "The common distinguishing factor in West Java was that new arrivals after 1985 almost without exception were persons affiliated with organizations that prioritized, or were seriously endeavoring to develop, a *team* approach to ministry. Each of these organizations was characterized, in varying degrees, by a pervasive and integrated emphasis on nurturing biblical community among their personnel on the mission field."[4]

3. *You need to stay vibrant in body life relationships yourself.*

Pioneer workers are there not only to share the gospel, but also to disciple newer believers and older believers, gather them, teach the Word, lead, counsel, and solve problems. Overall, they are there to build up and develop a new body of believers. Therefore, we've got to be able to model biblical relationships between believers. As Paul said, essentially, in 1 Corinthians 4:16: "Imitate me!" We've got to be experiencing and practicing the love of Christ ourselves to be able to teach it. This includes all the aspects of the "one another" commands in the New Testament, preserving unity, confronting sin, helping others in spiritual transformation, and generally ministering to one another. It's certainly important to do this with our teammates, even if there are only a couple of them. The apostolic team itself, as a microcosm of community, should be a great place for us to grow in biblical relationships and to be an example to local believers.

4. *You need to stay "on task" and spiritually thriving.*

This has become something of a mantra for many of us: the focus of our coaching a team and each member of it is that he or she be on task and thriving spiritually. They need to have a clear sense of the particular aspect of ministry they need to be zeroing in on at each stage, and then helped to work at that daily, and effectively. Most of the time there aren't ten things I need to be focused on, but just one or two (for example, learning the language or majoring on evangelism). So it's vital that I spend my time and energies on those things and not get distracted by other things. Likewise, there is nothing more important for workers than being in close fellowship with the Lord and drawing on His life. Only by the power of the Holy Spirit can we see progress in anything of a spiritual nature.

That's another reason we need a team around us. Our lives on the field are hard. We're away from home and from our normal church life. So often we feel like strangers, culturally out of sync and out of touch. We're attempting a humanly impossible task in a sometimes hostile environment. This task will likely take several years rather than just a few months. Add to this being "afflicted, perplexed, persecuted, and struck down," which Paul says is par for the course for apostles (2 Corinthians 4:8–9). Not even the most rock-like among us is unaffected. We need our fellow workers to keep pointing us to the Lord, to His adequacy, to His life. Isn't it instructive that in that great 2 Corinthians 4 passage about suffering and overcoming on the field, Paul always used the first-person plural: "we" and "us"?

When we moved into our present house a few years ago some of the upstairs floorboards were squeaking. So I grabbed some screws and my drill, pulled back the carpet, and began setting in new screws to better lock those boards down. After a few minutes I drilled a hole and heard a new sound: Hhhisssss. "Hmmm," I thought, "I didn't know wood made sounds like that." When I pulled back the board, I got squirted in the eye with water. I had hit a water pipe. Panic ensued as the hallway was beginning to resemble a water feature. Fortunately Liz kept her head and phoned a friend of ours, who is a doctor. He quickly performed emergency surgery on the pipe and we were saved! Isn't it great having friends around in a time of need?

Not long ago Hans and Karen, a team leader couple in Africa, went through a really tough patch. They and their team live in one of the poorest cities on earth and are engaged in a vibrant humanitarian project that has blessed tens of thousands of people, and they have also planted a some-what large multicell church. They were thrilled to learn that Karen was pregnant with their second child. But soon she began having difficulties and eventually had to fly home for the remainder of her pregnancy, as too much activity would've resulted in the loss of the child. Hans stayed back, and they would periodically talk on the phone. Then a wave of attacks broke out against workers and local believers. One expatriate family survived a vicious murder attempt. Another worker was shot at. The bullet hit his daughter, but thankfully both were OK. A local leader was knifed, but miraculously survived. Then, finally, Hans received a series of death threats from someone connected with terrorists.

What should Hans do? Stay? Go home? Go to the authorities? He and Karen had some really difficult and intense conversations over the intercontinental phone lines. Such times are not fun. But their team was able to rally around them both, providing strength, counsel, and encouragement. As a result, Hans and Karen were able to weather the storm; and they remain today in incredibly fruitful work. The point is this: because of working in a team, they were able to stay and become instrumental in leading dozens into eternal life in Christ, and a lampstand for Him is now well established. If there hadn't been a team, the work would've likely come to an end prematurely.

FORMING, STORMING, NORMING, AND PERFORMING

Let's take a look at Rick Love's description of the "Four Stages of Team Development" as applied to apostolic teams:

1. Forming.

The beginning of team life. Expectations are unclear. Members test the water. Interactions are superficial. This is the honeymoon stage.

2. Storming.

Conflict and resistance to the group's task and structure. The team is struggling through its differences.

There are healthy and unhealthy types of storming. We must work through the healthy types and minimize the unhealthy types (which, since we live in a fallen world, are unavoidable). As a team leader and coach, I have found that conflict usually occurs in five major areas: character problems, gifting fit, authority issues, vision and values dissonance, and personality and cultural differences. However, if dealt with biblically, these five stumbling blocks of storming can be turned into five stepping stones of performing.

3. Norming.

A sense of group cohesion develops. Members accept the team and develop norms for resolving conflicts, making decisions, and completing assignments.

Norming takes place in three ways. First, as storming is overcome, the team becomes more relaxed and steady. Conflicts are no longer as frequent and no longer throw the team off course. Second, norming occurs when the team develops a routine. Scheduled team meetings give a sense of predictability and orientation. Third, norming is cultivated through team-building events and activities, such as celebrations, public and private affirmation, retreats, and fun get-togethers.

The team's goal, however, is performing, not just norming. Yet, norming is a necessary transition stage. A team can't perform if it doesn't norm.

4. Performing.

This is the payoff stage. The group has developed its relationships, structure, and purpose. It's beginning to tackle the task. The stumbling blocks of storming have been turned into stepping stones of performing.[5]

Now, in the next chapter, let's turn our attention to the skills of successful team life. Successfully ministering as a team is what will powerfully impact our church planting, as the Lord gives fruit.

4
Working in Teams
—Practical Applications

In the last chapter we took an in-depth look at what working in teams means, both biblically and in today's environments among unreached people groups. Along with the biblical imperative of apostolic ministry functioning in teams, we've seen the reality of common frustrations that team life often brings. In this chapter we move even more from theory to practical applications. What will it take for *my* team to be successful? What might cause failure or even team disintegration? What skills do we need as a team, not only to have a good team experience but to operate together fruitfully in church planting?

KEYS TO SUCCESSFUL TEAM LIFE

Here are eight practical tips for helping teams to work together well and to be effective. Let me also recommend that these eight points would make for good group discussion about how *your* team is doing.

1. Team leadership.

The best team leaders are those who are strong, secure, and gracious in their exercise of leadership. Organizations should appoint leaders who have a measure of maturity and who have a track record in leadership roles, at least in their home country—though this second criteria should not necessarily rule out younger leaders. Insecurity causes leaders to overreact to situations and often leads to insecurity in the team. Teams can then drift. It is very important for both the team leader and the team members that the team leader's role is defined and well-understood by the team. Accountability for each person on the team is also a critical factor for success (see the section on accountability in chapter 10). It is vital that team leaders learn how to stay graciously firm in regard to team standards.

2. Oversight and coaching from outside the team.

All team leaders need someone to whom they report and to whom they are accountable: an outside pair of eyes, an encourager and problem solver. In our organization this is the role of the team leader overseer (TLO). Other organizations use different titles. Whatever the role is called, it is essential. This person can help the team leader become a better leader, as well as assist him when intra-team problems arise.

3. Careful recruiting.

Some teams seem to have only two qualifications for new workers: 1) they can raise their support; and 2) they have a pulse! There are no perfect teams and no perfect team members, but I personally do not recommend a "whosoever will may come" approach to team building. It can be a team's downfall.

This is not to say that a team should set super-high qualifications for joining. As Steve Richardson writes, "We had members from almost every imaginable background. Some had been involved in drugs and gangs, others in rock bands, some had been suicidal, or had been abused as children. One had seen four different stepfathers come through the home, while another had been employed as a bartender and simultaneously operated a large illegal gambling racket in the United States. 'And such were some of you,' the Scriptures say."[1]

Every team or team leader must consider two questions in regard to recruitment: 1) What level of maturity is minimum, especially in areas such as marriage, getting along with others, working under authority, and their spiritual walk with God? 2) How much of a prior track record of ministry in the candidates' home country is required? If they are expected to share the gospel, disciple young believers, or teach the Bible on the field, surely they should've done it already back home in their own culture.

The best teams are indeed a place where each member can continue to grow in Christlikeness and gain victory in an ongoing way over areas of sin. But teams that are absorbed in character issues can become little more than a MASH unit, or spiritual hospital, for themselves, and little church planting takes place. One of the most common regrets I hear from team leaders is how they have recruited a wrong individual onto the team.

While we're on the topic of recruiting, let me say again that every team should have at least one member with apostolic gifting—whether it be the team leader or someone else.

4. Godly relationships and unity in the team.

The good news is that most pioneer teams eventually attain this, and God refines us in the process. This usually involves a very practical thing: learning to be realistic with each other. The Bible calls this *grace*. It calls it *accepting one another* (Romans 15:7) and *showing tolerance for one another in love* (Ephesians 4:2). None of us, starting with me, has "arrived" yet. We all have sins, habits, and ways of communicating or doing things that are irritating or offensive to our fellow workers. Get used to it!

The other key issue in this area pertains to offenses or sins: knowing when and how to confront or discipline one of our brothers or sisters. All teams are urged to invest a series of team meetings in working through Rick Love's *Peacemaking* manual.[2] This takes time, but pays huge dividends over the long run.

5. Being willing to change the makeup of the team.

Sometimes it is perfectly fine for a team member to leave the team and go somewhere else. Maybe there's a team leader in another part of the country whose style or philosophy of ministry is a better match for that person. Luke doesn't criticize Paul or Barnabas for their parting of the ways, and both carried on in effective work for Christ afterward.

Likewise, team leaders must sometimes be willing to confront team members about serious problems and even be willing, at some point, to ask them to leave. *This should not happen without cause, and without giv-*

ing the team member plenty of opportunity to change. But sometimes it is necessary for the good of the team, and for the team member as well.

Jerry and the team he led prepared for a couple of years to live in a certain country in the Middle East. After building up the team to seven members, they moved to the field. It was soon apparent that Jerry and Frank were not on the same page. Jerry would try to lead the team to *zig*, and Frank would insist they *zag*. Conflicts between them would occur around almost every issue: Jerry's leadership, the team's objectives and strategy, tentmaking decisions for Frank, or even what day to hold team meetings. Jerry—patient to a fault—would take hours to talk with Frank, to try to persuade him or come to agreement; but most of the time that didn't work. Meanwhile, the rest of the team looked on with frustration. The situation began to eat at everyone. Frank was never willing to say, "God has called me to work under Jerry's leadership, so I'm going to co-operate and support him, even when I don't agree." And Jerry was never willing to bring their relationship to a crisis point, where the problem would get fixed or else Frank would have to leave. After about six years on the field—most of it characterized by lots of personal turmoil and little fruit—the team busted up completely. I do not recommend such passivity.

6. Keep the focus on the ministry God has called you to.

We've talked about the problem of team strife. There exists an opposite and equal problem: *too much* coziness. Some teams seem to believe that their primary purpose is to be the perfect team. Usually these are large teams, with lots of team meetings and socials and perhaps an over-emphasis on "community." They aim at growing super close together and at becoming the ideal environment for personal development. Sadly, I've seen some model teams, in terms of team life, that are accomplishing nearly zero in regard to reaching their target people and are largely just raising their children in a foreign country. When the team becomes everything—the focal point and the measure by which we gauge our success—then church planting will necessarily get lost.

Interestingly, we don't help the matter by calling the team leader "team leader." That title implies that the person's main job is to *lead the team*, as if that were an end in itself. The team leader's main aim should be to plant the church(es), and leading a team is a means to that end. People often get confused about this. One of these days I'm going to propose a change in title. Pioneer church planting teams have the singular objective of planting churches, e.g., among Buddhists, Hindus, or Muslims. We can succeed at that or we can fail at that. You can measure our progress by that one thing. Therefore it is vital that teams avoid falling into the trap of becoming a cozy club or a monastic order. We're there for one reason: to plant churches. (OK, I'll stop preaching!)

7. Oneness of ministry objectives.

A team is not merely a confederation of adults, all of them doing their own thing. A true team will have a clear vision of what they are attempting to accomplish for Christ together; every member's activities will somehow fit into making that happen and will be subordinate to that goal.

I remember getting to know a new team in Cairo: five couples who had arrived around the same time. Soon they were mostly spread out far and wide, in a city where it can take an hour to get from point A to point B. Within a year, one couple was focused on a humanitarian project outside the city; another was mainly working with Christian-background Egyptians, teaching Sunday school in a Christian church; another was working on media full-time; while the other two couples were trying to really learn Arabic and share Christ with the majority people, frustrated because they had assumed the whole team would be doing that. This "team" was actually no longer a team. A real team has a cohesive vision and a plan to work together toward making it a reality. NOTE

8. Strategic use of your time together.

Let me suggest three essentials:

Firstly, my dear friend and valued mentor, David Roper, once told me that the way to develop "teamness" and unity in a group is to study the Word together. This is true for elder boards as well as ministry teams. When you study the Bible together you see how each one responds to the Lord, and there are unique opportunities to speak into each other's lives. You are mutually in submission to the Lord and His word. Listening and obedience are the order of the day. You grow together in your grip on Scripture, as well as developing a common philosophy of ministry. And the Lord loves to speak from His word on specific situations the group may be facing.

Secondly, pray together. Let me share a confession: I've been terrible at this as a leader. And my ministry has suffered as a result. Teams must have extended times together in corporate prayer and worship. There's so much to pray about, both in terms of each other's lives and for the ministry. Again, you're all together, in God's presence, and in submission to His leadership of the team. In my ten years of serving as field director, I noticed a strong correlation between teams that pray a lot and teams that see a lot of fruit. Hmmmm.

Thirdly, take time as a team to communicate together about all aspects of the work, and to plan. At one of our annual leaders' conferences, we were privileged to have Haik Hospesian, Armenian bishop of Iran, as a special guest. Six months later Haik was martyred. Something led me back then to ask him about goal-setting, and his words still ring in my ears: He shared how in their ministry, in which they had seen thousands come into the kingdom, "planning" was regarded as a great act of faith. So may it be with us. Normally the best team decisions about direction and strategy are made together—in consensus, if possible. Never underestimate people's need to share their viewpoints (whether or not their position prevails), to be heard, and then to own the direction. You may be tempted to think, "But that will take too much time." Remember the adage: If you don't have enough time today to do it right, what makes you think you'll have more time tomorrow to do it over again? Likewise, to under-process key team decisions and directions will cost you down the road. Been there, done that.

None of these three elements can be left out of healthy team life. But don't make the mistake I've often made: trying to accomplish all three in one weekly meeting. They won't fit. Team prayer especially needs its own separate get-together, free from diversions. Haven't we all been in "prayer meetings" where deciding who brings the potato salad to the team retreat somehow took up most of the time? Protect your team prayer times.

VSP &MOy

VSP AND MOU

As future team leaders begin to put together their plans for the field, they rather quickly face two key challenges: How can I share this vision with others? What information do prospective team members need before they can make a decision to join us? And what is vital for folks to understand so that we are all *on the same page*?

First of all, there are a host of reasons why a prospective team leader needs to write what we call a Vision and Strategy Paper (VSP), which is normally about three to five pages:

- It forces him to articulate, in writing, the team's vision. This is a good thing. What may have been fuzzy becomes clearer. Who exactly are we seeking to plant the church among? Where? If the Lord accomplishes what we believe He has put on our hearts, what will it look like? In broad strokes, how are we going to pursue this? In short, a VSP addresses the what, who, where, and how.

- The leadership of the workers' agency may require this document to help them evaluate whether or not to approve this leader and this new team.

- Recruiting and sending entities really need this paper in order to help the team come together.

- Supporting churches need it.

- And last but not least, this paper can be the most powerful vehicle for prospective team members to clearly grasp the vision and have it resonate in their hearts by the Holy Spirit.

Secondly, as candidates begin to seriously consider committing to this team, it is vitally important that they understand as much as possible the particulars of how this leader intends to lead, what life will be like on the field, and how the team will function. This comes together in a more detailed document we call the team's Memo of Understanding (MOU). The aim here is to minimize surprises and conflicting expectations later down the road. Mismatched expectations is perhaps the number one cause of conflict on the field. For more on how to write a VSP and MOU, see appendix 3.

Team Formation: Size and Gifting

One of the first practical questions a new team leader will have to grapple with is this: How large should my team be? How many people will we need?

A couple of years ago some of us were interacting with an authority on the subject of church planting movements. I asked him, "From what you've seen on the field, what kind of team size seems to be best?" He replied, "We've found that team size is inversely proportional to church planting fruit." Jaws dropped, drinks were spilled, and silence took over the room. Bear in mind that we place a high value on *team*, and for many in our ranks, it is "the more the merrier." We quickly realized the speaker was joking or exaggerating to make a point—probably both. But his point was clear: larger teams of necessity end up making a huge investment in the intra-team relationships themselves, and too often have little energy left to really focus on the local people, language, and culture. In the experience of this leader and his organization, it was the small teams that were generally most fruitful.

From what I have seen over the years, I would have to say that my observations are similar. Several times I've been concerned for a team because I thought they were too small. When are they going to add team members, so that they can *then* become effective? I would persist in my concerns only to discover one day that they were planting churches and appointing elders!

In one case a team leader and his wife tried for many years to build a team. Several couples joined them, only to leave—for various reasons: health, children, hardships, etc.—a year or two or three down the line. Finally we encouraged this couple to stop trying to build a team and just get on with the work. Within a couple of years they planted three churches in this resistant environment! Why? Because they focused more on local people, and as they teamed up with some of them, they saw fruit together. Would I recommend this approach for everyone? No. (Reread the four points under "Why Plant Churches in Teams?" in the previous chapter.) But for many, trying to build a large expatriate team will *slow down* the actual planting of churches.

My first team in Egypt consisted of fifteen adults and I can't even remember how many children. I entered the field with high hopes of learning the language well, sharing Christ, and teaching the Scriptures to those wanting to follow Him. What I actually found myself doing was managing and administrating a large team. I discovered that with every "pair of boots" on the ground, the burden of things like relationship building, communications, oversight, and coordination goes up. And it goes up exponentially, not linearly.

Try a little exercise: If you have X points, there are Y lines or links between them. If you have three points—a triangle—there are just three links. If you have four points, there aren't just four links—there are six. Five points have ten links; and so on. You get the picture.

Over the years I've worked closely with one of our teams in Central Asia that is a bit remote or isolated. It was first led by the Wilsons and then by the Hortons. There has never been more than two families on-site, and most of the time there has only been one family there. As a result, both families have struggled with a lack of fellowship, along with health and education issues, and have often been on the verge of throwing in the towel. Now there is no question that this was not ideal, and that it would've been better over the years to have more fellow workers. But God has used first the Wilsons and then the Hortons—and the three other adults who were with them in the early days—to plant the church, which consists of five house churches and is still growing. They were forced, in a way, to go deep into the culture and into relationships with the local people. Over the years, despite really wanting teammates, the right teammates, Bob Horton insisted on being selective, even though most of us urged him not to be so picky. In time God brought along another couple who had solid maturity and field experience and even knew the language. As a result this new couple was able to move quickly into ministry, including discipling elders and teaching them how to plant daughter churches.

I personally do not buy the model that you must have a large team in order to have *all* the necessary gifts to plant a church. Some would say that in addition to gifts of apostleship, evangelism, and Bible teaching, you also need gifts of worship leading, administration, children's ministries, women's ministries, Bible translation, pastoral care (especially since you now have a large team with lots of pastoral needs), financial giving, computer expertise, ethnomusicology, mercy, media, language learning, visa renewal, car repair, and web page design. Don't get me wrong. Those things are important, and you may indeed want individuals on your team who are strong in them. But this is a model that feeds on itself: the more team members you have, the more other team members you need to help take care of them, and so on. And it all has the net effect of pulling team members inward into the team and away from creating and deepening relationships with locals. Gravity is gravity.

How were the few examples of teams in the New Testament able to be effective? Since they generally were made up of only two or three individuals, it is unlikely that they had all the gifts. Rather, it seems that they did have a few essential gifts: namely teaching, leading (especially the ability to pull believers together into good body life), and probably the gift of faith. Perhaps these three gifts are the *irreducible core* of apostolic gifting. They also had spiritual authority, of course, because of their maturity and calling and the Spirit working effectively within them. I don't even think that they necessarily always had a "gift of evangelism," though they were obviously committed to evangelism and must have had at least a "C+" ability in communicating the good news with boldness.

So is there a case to be made for larger teams? Believe it or not, I think the answer is yes. While I and others may tend toward smaller teams, others are working effectively in larger teams, and for good reasons. Here are some reasons that you—if you are a team leader—might conclude that a larger team is right for you:

1. If you are the type of leader who needs lots of team members, and you are very good at making it all work together well and especially at leading people to be effective in their ministries. I think of a friend who I believe would shrivel up and blow away if he didn't have a large team with lots of activity going on. And he's made it work. I can also think of another friend who used to operate this way, but eventually gave up on the three-ring-circus model because it was killing him and his wife. He eventually stepped out of leading expatriate workers altogether (and is being very fruitful).

2. If it is part of your calling to invest in green, inexperienced workers, so that five years down the road they will be effective. Though Paul usually worked in small teams, he always mentored at least one up-and-comer, most notably Timothy. A delightful model related to this is to grow a team and then hive off part of the team to become a new team, and to keep doing this in ongoing "team reproduction." A key is make sure you have a leader in the making who can take over the new team.

3. If your aim is to have a larger team that will operate in multiple small church planting "squads." I think of one of our teams in Turkey that is large and the team leader has done an excellent job of pulling people together and providing a good, nurturing environment; but for ministry they are broken up into three or four sub-teams that each seeks to plant a church in a different part of the city.

4. If you must operate a humanitarian project that absolutely requires a large number of expatriates to run it.

Other than for these four reasons, I would suggest being selective and keeping your team small.

Three Pauline Models

We all know of Paul's three "apostolic journeys" in the book of Acts:

1. Acts 13:4–14:28 (Cyprus and southern Turkey)
2. Acts 15:39–18:22 (central Turkey, Greece, western Turkey)
3. Acts 18:23–21:17 (expanding the gospel in previously visited regions, with a long stay in Ephesus)

It occurred to me recently that these three ventures each had a different model of "team," and that these somewhat reflect what we find today among pioneering teams around the world:

1. Quickly go out with a good friend or partner (Barnabas).
2. More deliberately build a team, over time (Silas, then Timothy, then Luke [i.e., starting with the "we" passages that begin in Acts 16:10], then incorporating Aquila and Priscilla).

3. After becoming a respected veteran, base in one place (Ephesus) and network with a wide variety of workers to reach a whole region. Paul probably functioned in a broad leadership role, directing multiple individuals and small teams to plant churches all around western Turkey, "so that all who lived in Asia heard the word of the Lord, both Jews and Greeks" (Acts 19:10). It was probably during this time that Paul began to network with the couple dozen "fellow workers" he wrote about in various passages.

On his fourth journey—to Crete, Spain, and perhaps elsewhere—Paul may have gone back to the first or second model. During this time he was also able to effectively direct ministries from a distance, most notably Titus in Crete. But we speculate . . .

TEAM DECISION-MAKING

One last practical matter: How should teams make decisions? What we're talking about here are especially decisions that affect the team as a whole (as opposed, for example, to whether someone should take a particular tentmaking job or a family should rent a particular apartment).

Of course, not all decisions are created equally. There are trivial issues, there are medium-weight issues, and there are foundational issues of goal-setting, strategy, and doctrine.

One thing I've learned the hard way is the value of consensus. People need to feel heard. People need to process and know that they have at least some influence in the process. All this is good, because at the end of it all they will feel more ownership of the decisions. Normally, team leaders are held accountable for the team's overall well-being and direction, and for the progress in church planting. Therefore the team leader has authority commensurate with this high level of responsibility. Team leaders are encouraged to exert strong leadership when appropriate, which will not always be popular.

However, even though team leaders could be highly directive and make all decisions unilaterally, I don't encourage that. The team will feel that the leader is being authoritarian and heavy-handed. While that level of taking authority may be necessary once in awhile, most of the time consensus-building works better. Here's a quote from one office's Memo of Understanding (MOU) regarding how they operate:

> We value participative leadership.
>
> We reject leadership styles that are autocratic. On the other hand, we also reject a purely democratic approach to decision-making. Participative leadership means that everyone gets a say. It does not mean, however, that everyone gets a vote.
>
> The goal of any leader is to discern the will of God. To do so s/he must listen to God and to the people s/he leads. Thus, in the spirit of James 3:17, the leader guides the decision-making process, facilitating honest and open discussion, receiving the team's counsel and input. In this atmosphere of "speaking the truth in love" (Ephesians 4:15), the leaders generally seek to lead the team to consensus.
>
> Failure to attain consensus on important matters is regarded as a call to prayer for further guidance. While we value participation and seek consensus, the International Director and other directors at International Office always maintain the right to make unilateral decisions within the purview of their responsibility and authority.

As you read that you probably noted a couple of things. First of all, not everyone's input will be weighed equally. Some may have more experience or insight on a particular issue. Secondly, consensus does not necessarily mean unanimity (i.e., that all vote yes). And finally, consensus leadership does not work well in emergency situations, turmoil, or in extreme conflict. It's better to have strong, directive leadership at those times.

In summary, there are three ways in which team decisions are usually made:

1. A final decision is made only with team consensus. Soon after all the turmoil was resolved in our team in Egypt, we were

encouraged by a leader from another organization to spend time as a whole team doing major goal-setting, since we were closing in on the two-year mark. He gave us a set of steps that their organization used. It was fantastic! The team pulled together like never before, and by God's grace everyone felt really blessed to be on this team. We were able to hear each other out, to articulate our team ministry objective, and to identify milestones we expected to aim at in the coming twenty-four months. It was fully a team process with no one person—including me, as team leader—being dominant. The more significant and lasting a decision will be, the more valuable it will be to gain consensus.

We find a delightful example of this in Acts 16:6–10 when the Spirit was leading the team to take the gospel into Europe for the first time in history. Paul initiated with what he felt to be the Lord's leading. But the final decision was made as a group: note that "concluding that God had called us to preach the gospel to them" (v. 10) is in the plural.

2. Nonetheless, there are times when the team leader will need to make a final decision himself. There may be touchy situations, sensitive personnel issues, or occasions when a consensus is unattainable. Even here, however, the team leader should allow for good discussion and consultation. This consultation doesn't always have to involve everyone at the same level; for example, if a decision is especially pertinent to only a few on the team who have the most stake in something or bear the most responsibility.

3. Some decisions should be delegated. For example, if the team is planning a retreat you may delegate certain things to an individual (e.g., choosing the location) and empower that person to make the decision.

Group Discussion Questions for Your Team

I would recommend that you allocate forty-five minutes in your next two or three team meetings to openly and honestly discuss the following questions. Alternatively, work on these questions in multiple sessions during a team retreat, assigning different team members to moderate different sessions.

1. Would you say that your expectations for team life and ministry are overly optimistic (or "blue sky"), too pessimistic (or jaded), or pretty realistic? (Go around the room and let each person respond.)

2. Does the New Testament *really* only give examples of pioneer work in teams? Support your answer.

3. What is *our* model of team?

4. What are the gifts present in our team?

5. Is our team a good environment for biblical body life? Are we modeling this well for local believers (or will we able to in the future)?

6. Does this team help you or hinder you in being *on task* and *thriving spiritually*?

7. Where are we on the "Forming, Storming, Norming, and Performing" sequence?

8. What's the right size for our team?

9. Does this team help me to have a healthy outward focus on ministry and majoring on the local people, or is there a danger of too much inwardness on our team?

10. Review the eight "Keys to Successful Team Life" in this chapter. How do we stand?   *P 39-44*

11. How do we make team decisions? Does that process need any adjustment?

5

The Pioneer Church
Planting Phases

The Pioneer Church Planting Phases (often referred to as the CP
Phases, for short) have been broadly welcomed since their launch in 1994.
One leader of an older, major agency remarked that their organization had
started out solidly focused on church planting about a hundred years ago,
then drifted from that, and more recently has come back to their church
planting moorings. He shared how the Church Planting Phases had been
a significant help to them in that process and that their teams now use the
phases quite a bit. The current version is a major upgrade from earlier
versions, with a fresh emphasis on reproduction, nonlinearity, groups,
and preparing for a movement. This new version can be found at the
end of this chapter, as well as at http://www.churchplantingphases.com,
along with accompanying papers.

WHAT ARE THE CHURCH PLANTING PHASES?

The CP Phases, as developed by Scoggins and Rockford, are a broad
description of the process of planting churches in a pioneer (unreached
people group) context. They can be a guide in planting one such church,
though the emphasis is on planting multiple churches and reproducing
churches. They outline the general stages church planting teams go
through to win people to Christ, gather them together as His body in that
locale, and develop them into a functioning, biblical *ekklesia* (church)—
leaving them with indigenous leaders and a vision for spreading the
gospel and reproducing daughter churches. The CP Phases identify key
milestones along the way.

While this resource might apply anywhere—even in the West—the intent is that it be a tool for places where Christ is not "already named" (Romans 15:20). This generally means there is an ignorance of the gospel, misconceptions about Christ, special difficulties for church planters, hostility toward the message, and persecution for believers who determine to follow Christ. As a result, in particularly resistant environments it can often take quite some time before the church planting team will reach the final phase. The tool takes a team all the way from pre-field work and the initial "landing"—when they don't yet know the language or culture—to the planting of reproducing churches. The CP Phases are a unique sketch of how something that is humanly impossible actually *is* possible, in the Lord. Here's an overview:

Phase I: *Forming, Preparing, and Launching the Team*

All the stuff before you get on the plane: recruiting, planning, support-raising, pre-field training, working on the team's relational kinks, etc.

Phase II: *Learning the Language and Culture*

Starts when the team first "lands." Pioneer workers typically spend the first two to three years in full-time language learning. Of course, during this time they are building relationships and sharing Christ as opportunities arise. Workers must not wait for perfect language proficiency before bearing witness to Christ.

Phase III: *Preaching the Gospel to Groups and Individuals*

To be fully in this phase means the team has reached a functional level of proficiency in the language (see chapter 6), so most of their time is now spent in evangelism rather than in language work. Normally there are no believers to disciple yet, though some teams skip over this phase if a number of local people come to faith while the church planting team is still learning the language. But, of course, no team really "skips over" evangelism, which should remain a priority throughout the church planting process. Other teams may spend ten years or longer in Phase III, if people are especially unreceptive to the gospel message.

Phase IV: *Discipling Believers and Working toward Gathering*

One or more believers from the people group are being discipled prior to gathering taking place. Like Phase III, sometimes this phase is skipped over when gathering occurs early. Having a distinct phase here does *not* mean that keeping believers isolated for a period of time is advocated. Quite the opposite, as church planters are encouraged to bring believers together as soon as feasible. But it's not uncommon for church planting workers to be in this discipling-but-not-gathering phase for quite a while.

Phase V: *Developing the Body of Believers*

The ministry of gathering believers together and leading that fellowship toward maturity begins once three or more believers start meeting together regularly for fellowship in Christ.

Phase VI: *Empowering and Installing Leaders, and the Beginnings of Reproduction*

Preparing the fellowship for being on their own as a church, particularly by developing leaders—specifically a plurality of leaders who can soon assume eldership. This is similar to Phase V, but now the group is further along. The focus is on leadership development and reproduction.

Phase VII: *Reproduction and Movement*

Begins once elders are appointed. Focus is now fully on helping the church(es) become reproductive in planting daughter churches and working toward becoming a church planting movement.

The CP Phases are based on examples in the New Testament and on the personal experience of field teams, mixed with common sense. For example, you can't have a group of believers until there are individual believers. Even if a team's strategy is to bring together a group of seekers who regularly study about Jesus together, and even pray and worship together, they are not yet a local body of Christ until some of them are born again. Likewise, if the church planters are going to become fluent in the language—a high priority among most pioneer workers—it makes sense that they would make this a priority from the beginning on the field. Pre-field preparation for a team comes even before that. At the other end, it makes sense that the church planters will invest heavily in developing potential elders *after* a fellowship has begun to meet. And one can find these same kinds of steps—except for language learning—in the New Testament (see examples below). See David Hesselgrave's "The Pauline Cycle"[1] for similar factors.

It really helps to break up the overwhelming task into smaller chunks. As Nido Qubein said, "One of the greatest reasons people cannot mobilize themselves is that they try to do great things. Most worthwhile achievements are a result of many little things done in a single direction."[2]

Apostolic teams oftentimes envision planting large churches, an expanding network of smaller house churches, or even a full-blown church planting movement. As mentioned, planting churches that reproduce is crucial. Some teams operate in regions where the gospel hasn't yet made any inroads at all; and therefore, perhaps appropriately, they have smaller visions. But there is always a certain minimum objective for all teams, even in the most resistant and unresponsive environment. This is to establish a group of believers, of a minimum "critical mass" of size and diversity, committed together to being the body of Christ, under the eldership of at least two or three local elders, where those elders are installed and operating, giving indigenous shepherding to the church. The point is, whether a team has huge goals or more modest goals, the primary goal is always church planting. That is a narrow aim. And that narrowness is intentional in the CP Phases.

The Church Planting Phases are a combination of two tools in one:
1. A *measure* or *yardstick*: Seven distinct phases, with definitions that endeavor to make as clear as possible what phase a team is in and precisely when they will pass into the next phase.
2. A *guidebook*: This refers mainly to the specific, numbered activities under each phase. While this is certainly not meant to be a "cookbook" consisting of recipes guaranteed for success, nor a list of mandatory steps that all teams must do, it does seek to comprehensively identify most of the activities you should be focused on in each phase and it forces you to look ahead to the next phase. Regardless of what phase you are in as a team,

the priorities for you at that time ought to be clear, and the CP Phases try to make that possible. Having a large number of possible activities under each phase is especially helpful for teams in resistant soils who tend to try a few activities over and over again, often losing hope and creativity.

Here is the basic structure. Each phase has these components:

- *Title*

- *Definition*: a short description of what is to be accomplished in this phase.

- *Crestpoint*. A term such as "endpoint" is not used because oftentimes the primary activity of that phase does not in fact end (e.g., language learning, evangelism, or discipling). The *crestpoint*, however, is meant to mark the target point of that phase and when a team essentially moves from that phase into the next phase. For example, a team in Phase IV is discipling one or more believers. Once three or more believers begin meeting together in fellowship as a body of believers, the team is regarded as being in Phase V. But that certainly does not mean individual discipling or mentoring stops. The crestpoint is a clear, intermediate goal that should be out in front of the team in a given phase.

- Various *activities* that the team should consider undertaking for that phase.

In addition to being a measuring tool for team progress, the Church Planting Phases are also useful for describing the growth and progress of new churches. Note the specific criteria for a fellowship's development in the crestpoint of Phase V and Phase VI. When a fellowship meets the specific criteria for group commitment, size, breadth, leadership, and strength at the end of Phase V, it is said to be a Phase VI church. When such a church has installed a plurality of elders per the crestpoint of Phase VI, it is said to be a Phase VII church.

Again, the titles, definitions, and crestpoints comprise the measuring tool of the CP Phases. The aim is to be as unambiguous as possible with regard to what phase a team is in at any given time, just like the lines on a ruler are not fuzzy but sharp. One of those transition points may be more subjective than exact: the "shifting of gears" between Phase II (language learning) and Phase III (evangelism). I suggest to team leaders that this transition occurs when the team switches from spending 80 percent of their energies in language learning and 20 percent in evangelism to vice versa.

As mentioned, even though a team will be in one particular phase it is very common for ministry activities from various phases to be going on at the same time. For instance, language learning will certainly carry through all the remaining phases, as vocabulary will need to be developed and refined as the team goes deeper into the ministry required by the later phases. And though a team may be in Phase V (a new fellowship having gathered), newer team members may be in Phases 2 and 3 and there may be pre-field team members in Phase I. But in the church planting arena, the team is seen as operating at Phase V when they are giving leadership to a group of believers who regularly gather. In addition, there may be a few Phase VI activities (leadership development) going on even before the work is fully at Phase VI. Again, the phase the team is in is the highest one that is completely attained according to the definition and crestpoint criteria.

It is very common for a work to go backwards in the CP Phases. For example, imagine a team which has brought believers together in fellowship, hence going into Phase V. That group might eventually attain the maturity criteria at the end of Phase V, hence going into Phase VI. Then suddenly persecution hits, or serious division and strife occur, and the whole thing falls apart. The work would then be back to Phase IV or possibly earlier. Unfortunately, this is not unusual and should not surprise us.

The ministry activities within each phase form the "guidebook" tool for church planting. These suggested activities are meant to be *descriptive* rather than *prescriptive*. That is, they are suggestions. No team is going to do all of them, nor should they. The team should look at them together and decide which ones are applicable, which ones are not, and how to proceed. The suggested activities are especially helpful when the team is stuck at a phase and not making any forward progress.

Of course, the reality on the field is that nothing is predictable. At a recent consultation a friend shared how their team in Indonesia regularly prays for the healing of the sick. One of his teammates prayed earnestly for a sick Muslim friend who subsequently died. As a result, twenty family members came to faith in Christ. When the gospel worker asked them how his friend's death (after being prayed for in the name of Jesus) influenced them toward faith, they replied that Jesus obviously had the power to take a person away from this life in peace!

The question often arises: What should the apostolic workers do once local elders are installed? Many have discovered that after having planted one or more churches, including the appointing of local elders, they still felt that the Lord wanted them to stay on and minister in church planting and reproduction. At first this seemed to go against the grain a bit. Once you appoint elders, the last thing you want to do is hang around in a way that undermines their leadership. Also, pioneer church planting is by nature *itinerant*. In the New Testament the apostles planted a church and then generally moved on. But clearly in some cases it really does make sense to stay, especially to be a catalyst for reproducing daughter churches, particularly in surrounding cities and towns. After all, Paul did stay in Ephesus more than two years after the Ephesian church was planted, and during this time he seems to have had a broader church planting ministry in the region, while based in Ephesus.

This Phase VII ministry generally falls into two spheres:

A. Working with the newly planted church or churches to help them reproduce and work toward a CP movement; and/or

B. Mobilizing, training, facilitating, and possibly overseeing local CPers. This option may eventually mean creating a national sending structure.

How the Church Planting Phases Can Help You and Your Team

The alternative to having and using a tool like this is to have no tool at all: no measuring rod to mark progress, no guidebook to suggest key activities. One of the most debilitating situations in this business is when you can't see any progress. If a team has only a vague sense of where they are, where they are going, and of movement—relying just on anecdotes or feelings—that is pretty disheartening.

As the saying goes, "You cannot manage what you cannot measure." Vision-casting, goal-setting, planning, and accountability have no place if a team doesn't have a clear sense of where they are going and how they are going to get there. Of course, if you don't have a goal, then there is no possibility of failure. But that is not something we should take comfort in, in view of the two billion souls within unreached people groups who are in desperate need of Christ. We embrace Jesus' exhortation in the parable of the ten minas (Luke 19:11–27) where He urges risk-taking and *going for it*, for His sake. It is likewise true that "you cannot motivate what you cannot manage." In the absence of a tool like the CP Phases, it is very hard for leaders to encourage and motivate church planters in the task. When you can see a step or two ahead, you gain confidence. Faith is enhanced. As C. T. Studd said about faith endeavors in the kingdom of God, "Things first look impossible. Then difficult. Then done."

I have heard of some teams who repeat together—almost mantra-like—at the beginning of every team meeting: "Where are we? Where are we heading?" After a while team members roll their eyes and it sounds a bit like a broken record. But a very positive message is driven home each week: We're here for a purpose. We're going in this direction for a reason. God is going to use us to accomplish something concrete and amazing for Christ's glory. The CP Phases become the vehicle for bringing this hope out into the open.

This chapter isn't long enough to enumerate all the activities on the field that workers can get into *other than* evangelism, discipling, and church planting. These are often interesting things, satisfying things; they are sometimes good things, and occasionally even necessary things. But much of the time they have the effect of causing the team to go in circles, to run in place; they create a kind of centrifugal inertia to just keep doing what they're doing. An apostolic team doesn't want to become like a spinning top: lots of motion, but no forward progress. A friend of mine wrote, "There are millions of dollars being spent on good projects in our country, but one wonders how many of them are really distractions from the real task which we use to make ourselves feel useful because the real task is so hard and sometimes goes so slowly."

While on the field I spent thousands of hours in tentmaking pursuits. Some of that was necessary and very positive in helping my role in society make sense to my friends; some of it was not. It is said that there are three ways to waste our years: Do nothing. Do the wrong thing. Or do so many things that none of them have sustained impact. We are all in desperate need of focus, to be on task with regard to whatever is the most important thing at that stage in our ministry. The CP Phases can be like the person who comes alongside those in the valley, points up to the crest of the mountain, and says, "Remember, that's where we're headed. And here's the way forward!"

A friend of mine talks about "the curse of the *so-thats*": We're going to do this, *so that* this happens, *so that* that comes about, *so that* it helps cause this, all of which will ultimately help people come to faith, *so that* the church gets established. Isn't it interesting that in the New Testament the apostles didn't have so many *so-thats*?

Anyway, a team can frequently review together its aim and progress using the CP Phases. When it's clear to the whole team where the work is and where it needs to go, then it's also easier for people to see how they personally fit in and what their particular contribution is according to their gifts. Conflicts are reduced. Expectations are equalized. Individual team members aren't left behind, wondering if they fit in. And there is at least a starting point for healthy discussion and debate about the way forward.

Communication between people working together is so important! Take, for example, this transcript of a 1995 radio transmission off the coast of Newfoundland between a US Navy vessel and some Canadians:

> **Canadians:** Please divert your course 15 degrees to the south to avoid collision.
>
> **US Ship:** Recommend you divert your course 15 degrees to the north to avoid collision.
>
> **Canadians:** Negative. You will have to divert your course 15 degrees to the south to avoid a collision.

US Ship: This is the captain of a US Navy ship. I say again, divert *your* course.

Canadians: Negative. I say again, you will have to divert your course.

US Ship: This is the aircraft carrier, USS Lincoln, the second-largest vessel in the United States Atlantic Fleet. We are accompanied by three destroyers, three cruisers, and numerous support vessels. I demand that you change your course 15 degrees north, I say again, 15 degrees north, or countermeasures will be undertaken to ensure the safety of this ship and its escort vessels.

Canadians: We're a lighthouse. Your call.[3]

Finally, the CP Phases provide a common language to communicate easily with others within the frontier church planting framework about the work. For example, your team might say, "We were at Phase V, but that fell apart; so we're back to Phase IV, following up the believers." People know exactly what you mean.

SOME MISUNDERSTANDINGS

As the CP Phases have been around for several years now, a variety of misunderstandings have cropped up. Let me try to clear the air on some of these.

1. "They claim it to be a cookbook, a guaranteed recipe for success. A magic bullet."
   Answer: Of course, it is not. CP is more like an art than a science.

2. "Those using the CP Phases feel less of a need to depend on God."
   Answer: The team's need for creativity and ingenuity from the Spirit to find the keys that will unlock the doors in their particular context are not diminished in the slightest.

3. "The CP Phases promote a kind of homogenous, or cookie-cutter, approach to pioneer church planting."

Answer: Diversity and experimentation are still very much alive and well among teams using the CP Phases! The phases are simply broad categories. They are *descriptive* of where you are heading rather than *prescriptive* of an exact method to get there.

4. "The CP Phases are rigidly sequential, and therefore prevent the laying of a groundwork for a movement."
   Answer: On the contrary, a thoughtful and flexible usage of the phases can help facilitate church planting movements. It should be noted that while experienced church planters can more easily work in a multiphase, nonsequential approach, younger teams are likely to really benefit from the simplicity of the CP Phases. This is perhaps analogous to a master chef doing many things all at once in the kitchen in preparing a fancy meal, whereas a less experienced cook will carefully follow a recipe's steps.

5. "The CP Phases emphasize working with individuals, and this can slow down getting to groups and movements."
   Answer: This used to be true. But the new version, having been informed by more years of field data, now emphasizes going after groups early on, as well as helping an individual believer to bring the message of Christ to his or her family and friends.

6. "The tool is specifically bound to the house church approach to church planting."
   Answer: New fellowships in unreached people group contexts are almost always *underground* fellowships, at least at first. This influences toward a house church approach. However, the CP Phases are intended to be model-neutral—that is, not tied to any particular model. They are currently used by teams employing the cell model as well as those developing larger, central churches.

NEW TESTAMENT AND CONTEMPORARY EXAMPLES

- Titus 1:5: "For this reason I [Paul] left you [Titus] in Crete, that you would set in order what remains and appoint elders in every city as I directed you." This is a good example of a team having multiple Phase V and VI church plants, with all of them hopefully moving toward Phase VII.

- 2 Corinthians 2:12–13: "Now when I [Paul] came to Troas for the gospel of Christ and when a door was opened for me in the Lord, I had no rest for my spirit, not finding Titus my brother; but taking my leave of them, I went on to Macedonia." A promising Phase III that got aborted.

- Acts 16 and Philippians 1:1: Luke's exciting narrative of how the church in Philippi got started, and then Paul's later letter "to all the saints in Christ Jesus who are in Philippi, including the overseers and deacons." This is a delightful portrayal of Phases I–VII (minus Phase II, language learning), including pre-field preparations, evangelism, discipling, gathering, developing leaders, and the eventual appointment of elders.

- Acts 13–14: Other examples of Phases I–VII, except for language learning, are found here in Paul's first journey.

- Acts 19:1–20: The Lord had previously prevented Paul and Silas from going toward Ephesus (see Acts 16:6). But now, in Paul's third journey, God's timing was right. Paul had learned valuable lessons about working with urbanized Greeks, especially during his year and a half in Corinth. God had now linked Paul up with Priscilla and Aquila, and this husband-wife team had done valuable groundwork in Ephesus (Acts 18:19). Now the church becomes well-planted through Phase VII (as we learn from Acts 20:13–38). We also learn from Acts 19 and other passages how Paul was based in Ephesus for more than two years, and trained a variety of other church planters so that all the Jews and Greeks who lived in the province of Asia "heard the word of the Lord" (Acts 19:10)—i.e., an extended Phase VII. One example of mobilizing "nationals" was probably Epaphras' successful church planting venture to Colossae, a hundred miles down the valley (see Colossians 1:1–8).

- Previously I described our first team on the field, in Egypt. Phase I for us was in Pasadena, California, where most of the team planned together, prayed, and did the Myers-Briggs personality test as a way of getting to know each other. We all landed on the field more or less at the same time, found places to live, and jumped into concerted Arabic learning. That's Phase II, though none of us reached fluency before we had to leave the country. During this time all of us were able to share Christ with Egyptian friends, and over time three or four came to faith. Individuals on the team began discipling these new believers, which is Phase IV, though, of course, hard work in learning Arabic continued. After around a year and a half a small gathering of believers was formed, which is Phase V. The Lord brought about this fruit, and surely knowing where we were going helped accelerate the pace.

- One of our teams in Central Asia consisted of a married couple and Ted, a single man. Ted and Aref, a Muslim father of three and an engineer at a factory, became friends. Ted gave Aref a New Testament, but Aref literally threw it aside, saying he wasn't interested in reading that book. This took place during Phase II, as all three team members were working hard on the language. One day the Lord pricked Aref's heart or his curiosity, and he wound up reading a large part of the New Testament. He got down on his knees and surrendered his life to this new Lord, Jesus. Immediately the team was thus into Phase IV, as they helped Aref along in his newfound faith, especially in the midst of severe harassment at work, in the neighborhood, and from his wife and children. Fast forwarding a year or so, Aref's family came to faith, as well as a handful of neighbors, and they began to meet regularly under Aref's spiritual leadership. Phase V. Then the group grew quite a bit, including a number of heads of households. They were meeting in the church building of the local Russian Baptists. Clearly the threshold to Phase VI had been crossed (see Phase V crestpoint criteria). When a summer of persecution fell against the church, they broke up into underground house groups—which led to even more growth, including the further development of leaders. Finally the team leader took six elder candidates through three months of study, culminating in the appointing of four elders who assumed overall leadership of this network of house churches. That is the crossing over from Phase VI to Phase VII. Today the expatriate workers there are few, and they are only in an advisory or catalytic role vis-à-vis the churches. Aref and his family have been sent by the planted church to another city as apostolic workers.

FAQs

1 *Is it possible to skip phases?*
Yes, as described above.

2. *If you've jumped quickly ahead, does that mean you can now just skip certain previous things, like language learning?*
No. While the phases are broadly sequential for the overall work, the specific activities for individuals are not necessarily so. Those whose church planting jumps ahead still need to learn the language and culture well, as well as develop good patterns of evangelism.

3. *Is evangelism just one phase: you do it for a while, then leave it?*
I wouldn't recommend that. The new church needs to see how boldly spreading the good news is a vital part of following Christ, whatever "phase" one is in. New churches that don't have this in their "DNA" become stale and stagnant. We need to be evangelizing until we exit, serving as examples to the flock, even if it is a minor part of what we might be doing at Phase V, VI, and VII. Also, certain members of the team may be exceptional evangelists and highly effective in training national evangelists. We don't want to shackle them to Phase V and VI activities that may not be their strength. Others on the team will have gifts in the areas that can cause groups to blossom and deepen.

4. *How can the Church Planting Phases be compatible with going after a church planting movement?*
As mentioned, the CP Phases can be misunderstood to be at odds with CPMs, but it doesn't have to be that way. There is a strong emphasis on working with the end in view, and the groundwork for leadership development and reproduction can be laid as early as possible, even in Phase III. David Garrison describes an intriguing example of this from a Buddhist field:

In Church Planting Movements prospective converts often begin serving Christ even before they become his follower. A Southeast Asia missionary began meeting regularly with a group of Vietnamese physicians. Though the physicians were not yet Christian, they met weekly for prayer, Bible study, and sharing a vision of what they perceived to be God's desire for them and their people. After a few months, one of the doctors said, "I am not yet a Christian. But when I do become a Christian, I think I want to be the kind of Christian who brings a Church Planting Movement to my people both in this country and across the border."[4]

George Patterson says, "Begin with the end in view."[5] The phase list keeps the overall process, and thus the end, in view.

5. *Does the phase mark where the team is or where the fellowship or church is at?*
   Both. It is the farthest point at which the team's work is, and is also very useful in describing groups. Let's say a team has three church plants: one at Phase V, one at Phase VI, and one at Phase VII. You would say the team is at Phase VII.

6. *Are the CP Phases just a tool for expatriate CPers?*
   No. Some national church planters are also using them.

7. *Does this tool foster a fleshly sense of competition between teams?*
   The leaders of our agency's 140 teams get together every other year, and it's very common for them to use the CP Phases to describe to each other where the ministries are at. In general, it simply helps to build mutual understanding. The result is a supportive fraternity of church planters rather than a competition.

Dick Scoggins summarizes well: "Anytime a tracking device such as the Seven Phases is developed it can be misused. We do not want to see it used as a slavish, sequential, discreet formula that guarantees the planting of a church. Only Jesus can truly plant a church (Matthew 16:18) through His Holy Spirit and by His grace. We church planters are but midwives. But it is helpful to understand the patterns that God uses so that we can be cooperative as midwives."[6]

Suggestions for Using the CP Phases as a Team

1. The team leader and whoever oversees him should know this tool well, and review it often as a basis for looking ahead.

2. All team members could read this chapter and the CP Phases, in order to be prepared as a team for group discussions.

3. All on the team should know what phase the work is at and what activities are most strategic at the present time.

4. The team can discuss their particular philosophy of ministry and approach to church planting and how that fits into the phases. For example, are you mostly pursuing groups or individuals? How does that affect evangelism, or even language learning? Do you foresee a house church model, a cell model, or a larger, central church? How does that affect your discipling of individuals?

Pioneer Church Planting Phases

by Dick Scoggins & James Rockford

Version 3.0,[7] copyright June 2005

SEE WWW.CHURCHPLANTINGPHASES.COM FOR THE LATEST
VERSION AND RELATED PAPERS.

☑ means see related paper(s) on the website.

I. Forming, Preparing and Launching the Team

This phase begins when someone is confirmed to form and lead a new church planting (CP) team. This new leader may already be on the field as a member of an existing team. This phase is comprised of all of the vital pre-launch activities aimed at forming the team and preparing for its effectiveness.

CRESTPOINT: Phase I ends and Phase II begins when the first team members (TMs) join the team leader (TL) on the field (though others may follow later).

SUGGESTED ACTIVITIES:

1. The TL prepares a Vision & Strategy Paper (VSP). ☑

2. The TL and TMs obtain approval from their sending church(es).

3. TL is appointed from sending organization.

4. Research best information available on language, history and culture of country and people group. Learn to see the people as God sees them. Research issues women in the country particularly face.

5. Research work roles and residency. Lay the groundwork for residency and identity (one's visa, as well as being able to answer, "Why are you here?").

6. Research practical life issues (e.g. housing, schooling, banking).

7. Prepare for communications, including secure e-mail.

8. Research existing church planting efforts currently underway, if any, and begin communications with workers.

9. Plan for security issues.

10. Prepare family and prospective TMs for the transition to the field.

11. Resolve conflicts within the family that may arise from your calling and moving overseas.

12. Recruit the right team. Plan the kind of TMs and team you want. Whether you are starting on the field or from your home country, begin working with sending offices to identify candidates and initiate contact.

13. Develop a Memorandum of Understanding (MOU). ☑ Anticipate issues of life and ministry together; pro-actively communicate about them. TL and TMs discuss mutual expectations. Ensure each TM has a copy of and understands the policy on "recourse."

14. Clarify the role of the TL wife.

15. Each member/family budgets for one-time outgoing needs and monthly needs. Raise sufficient financial support.

16. Develop a strong home prayer team.

17. Identify pre-field training needs, and see that this is carried out (e.g. in the people group's religion, evangelism, culture, contextualization).

18. In particular, plan and get training for creating an excellent team language-learning program.

19. Get the team to own the vision and strategy for CP, adjusting it as appropriate. Build your team unity and identity together.

20. Line up a ministry coach, as well as a business/NGO coach where appropriate.

II. Learning the Language and Culture

The CP team is now on-site and laboring to reach a level of proficiency in the language sufficient to effectively plant churches, which also involves an ever-deepening understanding of the culture. While the level of fluency aimed at may vary from person to person, depending on envisioned ministry roles, most will need to be in a mode of concerted language learning (LL) for 2–3 years. The workers develop a growing identity as *belongers* among their host people.

CRESTPOINT: Phase II ends and Phase III begins when most of the CP team have reached their appropriate level of fluency, and now are ready to spend most of their ministry time in disciple-making rather than language learning. Whereas evangelism probably took place before this point, it now begins in earnest.

SUGGESTED ACTIVITIES:

1. Members "land" and secure suitable housing. Learn how to function and enjoy life in your new environment. Adapt and renew your devotional life. Enable family to do the same. Make a plan for regular rest and a day off; develop a sustainable pace.

2. Continue to develop your role in society (i.e. job, business, humanitarian project, etc.). However, because being fulltime in language learning (or nearly so) is so important during this phase, job expectations should be kept as minimal as possible.

3. Address conflicts arising in the home.

4. Work through the *Peacemaking* manual[8] together as a team. Address conflicts arising in the team.

5. Develop your team life, in relationships, communications, accountability, and mutual support. Develop a spiritual team life that sustains members. Team meetings should include prayer, time in the Word, and strategic planning.

6. Appoint a Team Language Coordinator, who receives intensive training and creates a strong team LL program, including training and accountability. Link up with a language learning coach and other essential resources.

7. All work hard at learning the language. Husbands and wives work out respective strategies for appropriate goals.

8. Begin developing spiritual components of your language, such as learning special vocabulary and memorizing Scripture.

9. Clarify roles for team women and men. Work through differing expectations (e.g. regarding mothers of young children, business facilitators, etc.).

10. Develop relationships of varying depths with many local people, especially those who do *not* speak *your* language. Enable family members to do the same.

11. Bring redemptive elements into your relationships. Look for those who already know the Lord or are spiritually sensitive.

12. Learn local forms of hospitality and become hospitable in that culture.

13. Seek opportunities to demonstrate God's love for the people practically and culturally, standing alongside those in need in appropriate ways.

14. Grow in character through the stresses of adapting to your new life, not only personally, but also as a family and as a team. Develop the mindset when stressed by new things: "It's not right. It's not wrong. It's just different."

15. Collect evangelistic tools available in your new language.

16. Form links with any others in your area who are engaged in ministry to your intended people group.

17. Before too long, bring in a coach—preferably a couple—to help in all of the above.

18. If not done already, seek to enter a relationship with a Team Leader Overseer (and wife) who can eagerly support your vision and give appropriate help.

III. Preaching the Gospel to Groups and Individuals

As most of the team has now reached a good level of fluency, they spend most of their ministry time seeking to share the gospel and persuade people to become followers of Christ. Some may share mostly with individuals, while others may seek to evangelize whole groups of naturally connected people. All team members will be engaged in "friendship evangelism." Most teams will also begin experimenting with different kinds of "apostolic evangelism."[9] It is also common that teams *discover* one or more who already know the Lord, with whom close relationships are formed for the sake of fellowship, discipling and moving forward in CP. The team develops a tentative approach for how new believers can identify themselves in their faith to their broader community.

CRESTPOINT: The team is recognized as having moved to Phase IV when a member of the team is discipling a believer from the intended people group, who has a potential group of friends or relatives. However, members of the team do not stop sharing the gospel, for the sake of reaching more and more, breaking into new social networks, and being examples to the believers.

SUGGESTED ACTIVITIES:

1. If one's ministry time in Phase II was perhaps 80 percent language-learning and 20 percent evangelism, it shifts to 80/20 the other way in Phase III. Develop a revised LL plan for the reduced but ongoing pace.

2. Develop an extensive network of prayer-partners in your home countries who can regularly intercede for your work. Every day tell God you are available and ask Him to direct you to those in whose hearts He is working.

3. Cultivate faith to believe God will lead friends to Himself.

4. Model Christ's life before your friends and in your relationships, especially when difficulties arise.

5. If necessary, strengthen and adjust your role in society in terms of work, residency, and viability.

6. Grow in your understanding on what are people's felt needs, as well as their spiritual obstacles and opportunities.

7. Train together in effective ways to communicate the good news and in vital apologetics.

8. Learn to share key Biblical truths and promises in the language. Memorize key Scripture verses, and possibly some verses from their holy book as well.

9. Share Jesus with many, and see an openness to the gospel develop in friendships.

10. Evaluate team members' abilities and gifting in light of CP. Regardless of team members' gifts, all can use their gifts *evangelistically* and contribute to the team's overall outreach. Where helpful, two or three team members can work together, combining complementary skills (e.g. relationship-building with hospitality). Discern who from the team should be involved in which social networks.

11. Develop a strategy for reaching receptive people's social and work-related networks.

12. Develop outreach tools and materials, bearing in mind different audiences (socially, men/women, children).

13. Start a Bible Study with a friend and see it grow into his or her social network.

14. Regularly pray in Jesus' name for those who are sick or have urgent needs.

15. Lead someone into following Jesus, preferably with others in their social network.

16. Learn what are the marks of a "man or woman of peace" (M/WOP), or "respected person" in the culture.

17. Prayerfully evaluate your friend as a respected person in society (i.e. M/WOP) or as an avenue to such.

18. Identify one or more potential respected persons.

19. Begin to discern what is the good news for this social network and the respected persons in it.

20. Somehow introduce Jesus into the conversation within 30 minutes of every new person you meet.

21. Follow up any leads regarding existing believers.

22. Plan and begin to implement some kinds of "Apostolic Evangelism." ☑

23. Every team member should develop multiple ways of meeting new people (e.g. clubs, sports, etc.).

24. Implement a systematic way within the team to stay focused and motivated in the invaluable job of sowing many seeds. ☑

25. As you lead people to Christ, or you form relationships with existing believers, invite faithful ones to a deeper discipling relationship.

26. CPer baptizes the believer(s).

IV. Discipling Believers and Working Toward Gathering

Discipling one or more believers, especially working with them to win their social network to the Lord. From the earliest days with new believers, CPers teach that truly following Christ is *in community*, and that Christ wants to form a new group of His followers, committed to one another and, indeed, committed to growing and reproducing. As people come to faith and grow in Christ, the CPers seek to form individuals and existing groups together as the Body of Christ. Progress toward *gathering* will likely involve a variety of *pre-gathering* activities (e.g one-time get-togethers, building bridges between believers, etc.).

CRESTPOINT: Discipling never stops. But the team moves to Phase V once there is a fellowship group of 3 or more believers of the people group regularly meeting together.

SUGGESTED ACTIVITIES:

1. Use a plan of Bible study for the believer's personal growth and development.

2. The believer(s) learn Bible stories that will impact life practices.

3. Come to understand the place of suffering in the Christian life (such as we see in 1 Peter).

4. Respond to sin by repentance and developing new patterns of life.

5. Live out Christ's life in the extended family (e.g. Matthew 5–7).

6. Develop godly patterns in husband-wife relations including: godly submission and loving leadership, resolving conflict, forgiveness, and reconciliation.

7. Develop godly patterns of child raising.

8. Develop a regular habit of turning to Scripture and prayer.

9. The believer(s) shares the good news with family and friends and God's plan for Kingdom communities.

10. CPer(s) helps new believers break any occult involvement.

11. Believers who are already baptized baptize new believers.

12. Where appropriate introduce local believers to each other with the aim of fostering trust and fellowship. Host one-time events (e.g. birthday parties) as a "safe" venue for trust relationships to form over time.

13. The CPers decide which believers should be gathered together in fellowship, and which should be developed as starting points for separate fellowships.

14. Continually teach believers the New Testament concepts of fellowship and community, so that they will own the conviction of being linked with other believers in *ekklesia*.[10] Help them obey Christ's teaching about relationships with other believers, conceptually and in practice. ☑ See a fellowship group formed.

15. Begin to identify believers' gifts and calling in the Kingdom.

16. Implement godly patterns of conflict resolution with you, the church-planter, and with others.

17. Become familiar with God's plan for the extension of the Kingdom from the book of Acts.

18. Men disciple men and women disciple women.

19. Help the believer(s) develop how to present their identity in Jesus to family and friends.

V.   Developing the Body of Believers

Working with the new community of faith—and especially with emerging leaders—in order for them to grow numerically, in personal and corporate *koinonia* maturity. This crucial phase includes them developing a group identity and mutual commitment to one another as the Body of Christ, and also grasping a vision for leading others to Christ and forming new fellowships, locally or in neighboring places. Generally speaking, the team is either working with a single fellowship at this point that they hope will grow to medium or large size, or else they are aiming at a network of small house fellowships. In the case of house fellowships, the numbers below are evaluated collectively, in total.

CRESTPOINT: Phase V ends and Phase VI begins when the fellowship reaches these criteria of size and depth ("critical mass"):

GROUP COMMITMENT: The local believers have committed to one another and see their assembling together as an expression of being a local *church* (using whatever word is most suitable for *ekklesia* reality).

SIZE: Around 10 or more believers of the people group regularly involved, including older believing children. This does not necessarily mean that meetings average 10 or more, just that there is regular involvement of the 10+.

BREADTH: 3 or more married men (heads of households), and 2 or more mature women, of local believers regularly involved (whether or not their spouses are believers, though that is clearly stronger).

LEADERSHIP: At least 2 key believers who seem to be "elders in the making," who are assuming more and more shepherding and overseeing, and whom the others recognize as leaders.[11]

STRENGTH: Not all hidden believers with hidden faith. Some believers are baptized and have already faced serious threats and persevered, maintaining their faith and their "confession of Christ before men" (Mt.10:32). Believers regularly share their faith; prayer and planning have begun for starting a *sister* fellowship.

SUGGESTED ACTIVITIES:

1. The community is meeting together regularly for worship, fellowship, instruction, and prayer. Passages such as Acts 2:42–47 are studied as an example to follow.

2. It is not uncommon for CPers to do substantial teaching and leading in the group early on, depending on the maturity of the believers and the group.

3. Local believers develop their identity together as a community of faith (e.g. through *covenanting*). ☑

4. The group develops their sense of spiritual identity to those outside as well.

5. Older believers determine appropriate way for membership in the community.

6. Older believers understand and model Biblical "one anothers" which define community.

7. Believers learn to break previous or active occult involvement of new members. (See Acts 19:11–20)

8. The community celebrates the Lord's Supper, with older believers presiding.

9. The believers are doing the work of evangelism with their family and friends.

10. Older believers have baptized new believers.

11. Older believers disciple new believers.

12. Older women believers disciple newer women in Titus 2 skills and other needs.

13. Believers learn to support each other through persecution, interrogation and hard times.

14. Believers develop an attitude of sacrificial generosity towards the poor and needy, particularly to other believers in need. They begin to seek opportunities to demonstrate in practical ways Christ's love for those in need.

15. Community meetings are organized by believers. Older believers trained to lead community meetings (various components). Certain mature or gifted believers given opportunities to teach the Word.

16. Appropriate male/female roles in public meetings determined and practiced.

17. Mature believers are emerging and begin functioning as shepherds.

18. Growth in godliness in the home of emerging leaders sets the pace for the community.

19. Multitude of gifts encouraged and developed for edification of the community.

20. *Peacemaking* skills exercised by the community. Believers forgive and forbear as normal hurts occur.

21. Past family hurts explored and forgiven.

22. Believers adequately contribute to the support of their extended family.

23. Confronting, exhorting, reproving of erring members.

24. Shunning and disfellowshipping those persisting in sin.

VI. Empowering and Installing Leaders, and the Beginnings of Reproduction

A continuation in the growth of *body life* and Kingdom commitment in the new *ekklesia*, with the CPers now focusing primarily on developing multiple leaders, especially potential elders. The CPers intentionally take a lower profile in the fellowship. They are also looking to recognize those believers with possible evangelistic gifts who are keen to share the gospel and initiate CP ministry in other locations.

CRESTPOINT: The appointment of 2 or more elders from the people group over the church (or network of house churches).[12] And the church has embraced a Great Commission vision.

SUGGESTED ACTIVITIES:

1. Some or most CPers withdraw from believers meetings and focus on starting new fellowships. One or more CPer(s) remain involved, but adopt lower profile. Leaders-in-training spend time with the CPers in all sorts of contexts—not just teaching or worship settings—so that CPers' behavior can be modeled in every setting.

2. If not already in place, the church commits to times of corporate prayer, acknowledging their full dependency on Christ as His Body.

3. Older believers exercise deliverance ministries in the community.

4. Gifts encouraged and developed for edification.

5. Married believers are specifically helped in their marriage relationship and character issues by older believers or CPers.

6. Church life and leadership concepts are taught and implemented. Believers determine ways to develop healthy biblical community life.

7. If there are other churches around, begin to network emerging leaders with leaders of other groups as appropriate.

8. Intense teaching on reproducing communities. Community embraces goal of reproducing and networking.

9. Local believers and expatriate CPers look for new men and women of influence around whom to start new fellowships.

10. Older, more mature believers trained to take leadership of community gatherings. Believers take responsibility for Biblical instruction. Several given chance to "try out" leading meetings, teaching the Word, and leading the body in worship.

11. Respective avenues for men's and women's leadership identified and promoted.

12. Mature believers preside at the Lord's table.

13. If there is one strong leader, he or she is taught and implored with the biblical necessity of plural leadership in the church and enlisted to make that a reality. Their broader ministry should be encouraged in multiple fellowships.

14. Erring members are confronted, exhorted, reproved, and helped. Those persisting in sin receive church discipline according to the NT.

15. Discerning the will of the Lord by leaders and community taught and practiced.

16. The body continues to discuss and refine their identity vis. society around them. They decide whether to be an underground church or an open, perhaps registered church.

17. There are special activities, parties, or retreats outside regular meetings for outreach and fellowship.

18. Leaders' place in conflict and peacemaking in the community taught and practiced.

19. Ephesians 4:11–12 giftings recognized and appropriate forums established for developing these gifts. CPers encourage believers with possible evangelistic gifts to share the gospel boldly and start ministries in other locations, with substantial prayer backing from the body.

20. CPers select elder candidates in consultation with the believers. Those who agree to undertake this process are introduced to the church as "elder candidates," and the body is urged to help.

21. Elder candidates begin special process of character growth, examination of motives, and intensive learning about *ekklesia* and shepherding.

22. Meetings of leaders begin with CPer present. Team spirit develops amongst leadership. [Men and women leaders may meet separately or together, as appropriate.]

23. Conflicts about leadership appointment dealt with. Those not selected may need special encouragement.

24. Leaders look for new ones to develop as leaders and begin to mentor them (e.g. prospective deacons).

25. CPer often absent from fellowship meetings. New leaders lead.

26. CPer sometimes absent from leadership meetings.

27. CPers appoint some or all of the elder candidates (if there are two or more; preferably three or more). Elders formally ordained.

VII. Reproduction & Movement

The church or churches are now somewhat mature and are under the leadership of local elders from the people group. The CPers now labor for a wider spread of the gospel, with emphasis on church reproduction and a CP movement. There are two primary avenues for the CPers to make this happen:

A. Working with the newly planted church or churches to help them reproduce and work toward a CP movement. AND/OR

B. Mobilizing, training, facilitating, and possibly overseeing local CPers. This option may eventually mean creating a national sending structure.

CRESTPOINT: In a sense, this phase never ends, as the ministry has hopefully ignited a spreading of the gospel and multiplication of churches that becomes a movement. CPers may exit after the completion of Phase VI (appointing elders). Some, however, may stay on for varying lengths of time in order to strategically catalyze church planting reproduction and/or mobilization of local CPers.

SUGGESTED ACTIVITIES:

1. The local elders fully assume shepherding and feeding responsibilities in the church, including protecting the faith and doctrine of the community (Titus 1:9).

2. Deacons are appointed, as needed, to help the elders.

3. Vision developed for planting new churches in the local area.

4. Role of expatriate CPers determined (see 'A' and 'B' *primary avenues* and *Crestpoint* above). Responsibilities between CPers and local elders defined for the new community.

5. CPer(s) redefines relationship to leaders as *coach*, attending leadership meetings only when invited.

6. Great Commission vision includes recognizing, training, and sending local evangelists and church planters to other cities, and even to other countries.

7. Vision given by leaders to congregation.

8. Evangelists guided to go out to other cities, towns, or villages.

9. Indigenous CP teams sent out by themselves or with expatriate team.

10. New gatherings started.

11. Ephesians 4:11–13 gifted believers regularly visit other churches and emerging fellowships.

12. Elders and Ephesians 4 ministers take responsibility to develop new leaders and new Ephesians 4 ministers.

13. Leaders begin to network with emerging leaders of new gatherings including taking some responsibility for their training.

14. Communities concerned for each other and resources shared (especially Ephesians 4 equippers).

15. Peacemaking skills are practiced among leaders.

16. Leaders formally recognize newer emerging leaders (e.g. new elders or deacons).

17. Expatriate CPer(s) commends old community to God and leaves community meetings, but may visit on occasion.

18. Elders (with church planter(s)) lay hands on new elders in the newer community.

19. Relationship between different communities and leaders worked out and formalized.

20. Peacemaking skills between communities and leaders communities exercised.

21. Especially with model 'B' above, some means developed to mobilize gifted and proven national CPers (e.g. bivocational roles, administration, etc.).

6
Learning the Language

The wonderful world of "language learning" in my life has taken the form of seeking proficiency in Arabic: the Egyptian dialect, a second dialect, and Modern Standard Arabic—necessary for reading, writing, and understanding formal speech. This was an incredible challenge for me and, to be honest, always a frustration—I never did get as proficient as I thought I should have. My qualifications to write on the subject of field language learning include having made most of the mistakes possible and having experienced the failures and discouragements which are all too common. I think the Lord also sovereignly directed my steps to experience over the span of two decades the wide spectrum of language learning approaches. Before going to Egypt, I took a night class in Arabic at a university. I was also attending seminary, so I took Arabic in a class full of graduate students in Semitic languages, who seemed to have already mastered Hebrew, Aramaic, and Ugaritic, and so were moving on to Arabic as a lark. I was also privileged to take the two-week intensive class, "Language Acquisition Made Practical" (LAMP), under Tom and Betty Sue Brewster.

When we hit the field I jumped into my LAMP methodology, having loaded up with tape recorders and "loop tapes." Soon I had developed a route of around thirty shops where the men were happy to have me practice my weekly texts on them.[1] I had hired a young man who would serve as my "language helper" or tutor—an arrangement which worked well only some of the time. Soon my drive for self-directed learning was flagging, and I found myself in a local night course. After nearly two years in Egypt, my language was nowhere near what I had hoped for, though the blame for that rests on me and on my team-leading responsibilities, rather than on LAMP.

When we moved to another Arab country, I immediately jumped into a full-time Arabic program for a year and a half. After that I did a semester at the local university. For years after that I kept pressing ahead, especially on vocabulary, accumulating a couple thousand index cards of new words and phrases.

So where did all that leave me? It was a mixed picture. There was certainly a measure of fluency and functionality. I was able to conduct my tentmaking business in Arabic, as well as teach many Bible studies. I even taught a serious course on the Gospel of Mark in Arabic. One day the tax man was coming to my office to audit me, and he didn't speak English! "No problem," I thought, "my accountant is fluent in English and Arabic." But because he was involved in a traffic accident, he never arrived. What an experience it was to interact about accounting and taxes in Arabic, since there were many technical terms I didn't know. But I knew them by the end of the day! While all this might sound good, it's also true that I would often lose the thread in conversations. I never really attained the fluency I wanted.

From my personal experience with language learning, as well as from overseeing teams as a field director, I would like to offer some perspectives and suggestions. This isn't going to be a chapter on methodology, as I don't claim to have the expertise for that. Team leaders and language coordinators will have to get training in language learning principles and methods beyond this brief, simple chapter on perspectives. Please see the excellent appendix by Dr. Lyman Campbell on methodology and training.

A small minority of English-speaking workers will feel called to work only with English-speakers or entirely through a translator. Generally I would really recommend against this approach. For the rest of us, learning the language and learning it well is absolutely vital in the course of pioneer church planting. Besides the tactical reasons for this, we are also taught in Scripture how Jesus left heaven and "became flesh (or *incarnate*)" among us. He fully became man in order to reach man. We cannot become "incarnate" among the people God has called us to love without becoming able to readily communicate with them in their language and in their cultural framework.

Likewise, in chapter 11 we will examine the multifaceted ministry of the apostolic church planter, particularly noting what the various Pauline teams did in diverse places. One cannot practically teach, disciple, model, and build up leaders operating completely in English or other nonindigenous languages. We are called to follow Paul's example, who said, "I have become all things to all men, so that I may by all means save some. I do all things for the sake of the gospel, so that I may become a fellow partaker of it" (1 Corinthians 9:22–23). This "becoming all things" requires an investment of time and effort. Jesus spent thirty years becoming a man who could minister and teach as a "belonger" in a particular culture and language community. Though it wasn't in language learning per se, God took about eleven years to craft Paul into the apostolic worker He wanted before Paul's first apostolic journey.[2] We mustn't shy away from the time it takes to prepare us. Months and years in learning the language is an apostolic investment. These years of investment will actually prove to be God's ministry in and through us as well, laying a foundation (of humility and flexibility, among other things) for the other church planting roles that will come later.

I find that the vast majority of workers are conceptually committed to learning the language before they depart to the field. At the same time, most are also carrying nagging doubts in the back of their minds about whether or not they will succeed. In this chapter I would like to draw a lot upon the work and teaching of Greg Thomson, a leading expert in the field of second language acquisition. Greg writes, "Any normal person can learn any language, given enough contact with speakers of that language. But it does help to be realistic. A simplistic view of a language learning challenge can lead to disappointment and discouragement. An unrealistically pessimistic view can lead to giving up before getting started."[3]

Though most workers believe in the importance of language learning, it's amazing how much things can vary in practice. Language learning is an absolute commitment for some teams, with a carefully thought-out program, with resources and oversight; and nothing is allowed to deter workers from attaining fluency. For other teams, language learning is almost an afterthought. Sadly, our "default" mode can be pretty bad. Workers might take a month-long class or make a few attempts to work with a tutor, but pretty soon they get swamped with many responsibilities and diversions and become discouraged.

I remember a trip I made to Central Asia where I saw both extremes in the same week. I spent some time with a couple who had been there five years but were only at maybe an FSI[4] Level 1 Plus (sort of a basic "buy vegetables" level). I went on to visit a team in another city which had developed a fantastic "language center" for the whole team. Even before new team members stepped off the plane, everyone knew they would be in full-time language work for at least two years. They used the latest methods and there was much variety, fun, and even "rewards" in the language learning activities. In less than two years most of the team members were fluent and fully able to minister in the language. I was so impressed!

This chapter is for all workers, but primarily aimed at the team leader. I hope to persuade you to do whatever it takes to create an excellent language learning environment and to point you to some tools to help you in this task.

WHAT ARE YOU AIMING AT?

As the saying goes, "If you aim at nothing, you'll hit it every time!" What is fluency? What is a good level to attain before shifting to other kinds of ministry? Does a bell ring or a light go off when you've hit it?

A few points should be apparent to all:

- We will never become completely, perfectly fluent. We won't reach an FSI Level 5 (total fluency, like a native), and probably not even a Level 4. *That's OK.* The aim is to reach a high level of fluency in the language *and* the culture, which will enable us to function well in relationships and communication, opening the door to fruitful ministry.

- We don't remain in full-time, concerted language learning forever. We've all got to shift into majoring on other things at some point.

- For the tougher languages especially, even after our initial learning period we will want to continue to regularly invest some time in language improvement.

Greg Thomson offers a good introduction to this question of fluency:

A learner who has studied a language, no matter how extensively, but who has not done much extemporaneous speaking, will find that using the language in extended, unrehearsed communication will require great effort at first, becoming easier over time. When it becomes apparently effortless (note the word *apparently*), we say that the person is "fluent," having either "high-quality" fluency or "low-quality" fluency. The first type depends on massive exposure, since it requires a language familiarity that can come only through taking in large amounts of comprehensible input. Low-quality fluency, on the other hand, can occur when the learner becomes highly adept at the creative use of a limited range of language. This second type may be adequate for certain purposes. But often, I believe, low-quality fluency is all that is achieved when high-quality fluency is possible.[5]

As very much a nonexpert, I would suggest a few simple points regarding the definition of fluency. We want to gain fluency in six key facets of language:

1. *Listening comprehension.* This is numero uno. Just like a child, we first must be able to understand what is being said around us and to us. This will be the foundation for our own speaking.

2. *Speaking.* While some may define fluency only in terms of speaking, it is in reality only an obvious part of a bigger whole.

3. *Reading.* For some, this won't be essential. But for those who are called to minister the Word, reading will be a integral part of

what "fluency" will mean for you. I am not including writing, as rarely is that essential in one's ministry.

4. *Pronunciation.* Think of the last time you heard your native language spoken by a foreigner who seemed to know all the words to say, but whose accent was so bad that it was painful to listen. Like fingernails on a chalkboard. We don't want to be like that. Whatever methods you use, they must include helping you say things the way local people say them. Sometimes the differences seem subtle and minor to us, but make a big difference to the ears of our friends.

5. *Vocabulary.* Eventually you will want to acquire thousands of words. For me this usually occurred in two stages: first, trying to learn a word—making a card, drawing a picture, whatever; then, as I began recognizing that word in speech and naturally using it myself, it became mine. As one of our workers recently remarked, "Once one's vocabulary increases it's amazing how often one hears those words!"

6. *Grammar.* How much explicit teaching on grammar principles is needed will vary from person to person. But even for the most intuitive and social of learners some grasp of the structure and rules of a language will help them avoid perennial mistakes and accelerate their speaking ability.

The latter three points are sort of "below the water line," or less visible. Of course, we mainly want to get really good at understanding what we are hearing and to be able to speak comfortably. I urge workers to work hard, full-time, until they are around an FSI Level 3 Plus. This generally means you can interact well in a small group Bible study context, as well as teach the study. Depending on the language and the learning situation, this requires two to three years for most of us.

How to Create a Quality Language Acquisition Environment

The rest of this chapter concentrates on five things, *five critical aspects* to crafting an environment and program that really brings about effective language and culture learning. I can almost guarantee that if you have a team that facilitates these five critical aspects well, then you will have a team full of fluent language speakers. These are:

1 Motivation, perspectives, and perseverance (otherwise known as the "affective filters")

2. People connections

3. Methodology

4. Time stewardship

5. Oversight

Obviously, there is a lot of overlap between these and they are really an integral whole. When these five elements are functioning well, they propel the language and culture learner to success.

Fact number one: Self-starters are able, over time, to work out a decent language learning approach and weekly structure for themselves and to keep on track over many months, monitoring their progress and making adjustments. Fact number two: At least 80 percent of us are *not* self-starters. That is why it is truly the responsibility of the team leader and/or team language coordinator to ensure that these five aspects are in place. Anything less is a disservice to your fellow teammates. But with these, you can give them one of the greatest gifts possible: the achievement of becoming incarnate in the local culture, in order to make their God-ordained contribution to the planting of the church in your unreached people group, for Christ's eternal glory.

1. Motivation, Perspectives, and Perseverance

Anyone can be excited about learning the language for the first month or so. We jump in with enthusiasm, waking each morning confident that today new secrets of this precious new language will be unlocked to us. Each week we sense a slightly greater ability to understand and be understood. But what about in the twelfth or eighteenth or twenty-fourth month, after we have been through a few discouraging plateaus? As human beings we are wired to need affirmation. We require the encouragement and reinforcement of seeing the product of our labors. But language learning isn't like building a cabinet, repairing a car, or preaching a good sermon. Usually it's hard to see our accomplishments. This is one reason why I advocate having progress assessments about every six months, as this can be a powerful motivator. In any case, most of us will want to set out on around two years of full-time language learning, and we need to plead for the Lord to sustain our drive and "hope levels" during this time.

"Commit to the LORD whatever you do, and your plans will succeed" (Proverbs 16:3; NIV). This exhortation applies so wonderfully to our sacred task of learning well the language and culture of the people God has brought us to in order to lift up Christ and plant His church! This is His work, and we need to commit our language learning and entrust ourselves to Him on a daily basis—not only as individuals but our whole team as well. Every team meeting should include prayer for those in language learning, for the Lord to give them success.

Outlook is everything. It's sort of like the classified ad in the newspaper that read, "Lost dog. Brown splotches. Ear bit off. Broken leg. Eye gouged out. Answers to the name 'Lucky.'" Our mindset will have an enormous effect on how well and how quickly we learn, as well as how much we can enjoy the process. Some call our conscious and subconscious perspectives "affective filters," and these will impact our learning as much or more than our methods. For example, if you think you're *not* going to learn the language, you probably won't (or at least it will be harder). If you believe you *are* going to learn it, this perspective will propel you forward. The experts declare that you *can* learn any language, given sufficient time and exposure and effort. *You will learn the language.* You will arrive at a good level of proficiency that will enable you to have effective relationships and ministry, while always continuing to grow further. Fear not!

Thomson writes:

> You can take heart. Large numbers of people who felt they were "not good at languages" have learned languages perfectly well. The real danger in connection with aptitude is that your ideas about your own aptitude will lead to self-fulfilling prophecies regarding your ability to learn a

language. There is evidence that good self-esteem with regard to language learning goes hand in hand with good language learning. As a matter of fact, it helps if you feel generally positive about yourself at the outset, but it helps even more if you feel OK about yourself *as a language learner*. If you don't, it may help for you to get at the root of your low language learning self-esteem. That root may lie in your negative past experiences with foreign language courses. Be assured that for most people, most foreign language courses are doomed from the outset. You may have felt other students were doing better than you, but the fact is that almost none of them really became fluent speakers of the language through that course. If you now face the prospect of learning a language that you will actually be using extensively in communication situations, then consider yourself to be starting with a clean slate. Those past negative experiences are largely irrelevant.[6]

Another wrong message you don't want to let the devil play in your head is that it's too much work and it's not worth it. As the Brewsters so often said, "Language learning *is* ministry." Not only are you portraying the love of Christ for the people in your learning as they see your respect for them and their culture, but every day's efforts are serving Christ and are a sacrifice pleasing in His sight. Your daily language learning activities are a real way to love Christ and love the people, even as you are investing in future fruitfulness for the gospel among them. Some will be so "itching to get going" in more direct ministry that they will be tempted to look for shortcuts in learning the language. For them, these two years or so in full-time language learning will be a test of patience, of being stretched as they learn not to "despise the day of small things" (Zechariah 4:10).

2. People Connections

Let's state the obvious: We learn the language primarily from our interactions with *people*—our friends, neighbors, and others around us. This is not primarily an endeavor in books, classrooms, vocabulary cards, and deskwork, though all of these have their place.

If we believe this, there are some practical implications:

a. Building and cultivating many relationships should be a priority from the beginning.

b. These relationships should predominantly be with local people who do *not* speak English (or your native language). It is natural to gravitate toward English-speakers. But if we end up spending much time with them instead of with others, this will inevitably have a detrimental effect on our learning. It may be helpful for your language helper to be an English-speaker. But your friends for language practice should not be English-speakers, if possible.

c. A key responsibility of a team's language learning coordinator is to help learners assess and consider ways to develop the relationships they have with local people.

d. Your children—even babies and toddlers—can be a great asset in relationship-building. Over the years we were on the field, probably half of our relationships somehow came about through our kids, especially for my wife. On our very first day in Egypt we went on a walk in a park, with our two-year-old daughter in a stroller. Within ten minutes we met a delightful Egyptian couple with a similar-age son, and later went out for dinner together! I want to be clear about this, because it's easy for parents to view their children as a hindrance to language learning. To be sure, husbands and wives will need to juggle schedules so that each can have study and preparation time. But what wonderful bridge-builders our kids can be! And with mothers especially, it is such a natural thing for mothers to visit each other in their homes for hours with their little ones running around their ankles.

3. Methodology

It shouldn't surprise us that *how* we go about language acquisition will make a huge difference over the course of two years and beyond. One of the saddest things I've seen on our fields is some workers who are receiving no help and oversight. With no team structure actively guiding them in language learning, each day they wake up and face a situation where they are more or less "making it up" as they go along. This becomes a sort of slow "Chinese water torture" that erodes confidence and hope, leading to overall discouragement about language learning. The good news is that it doesn't need to be this way at all.

Thomson writes, "Even in a relatively easy situation, you will get further faster with an effective strategy, but it probably won't mean the difference between success and failure. In the most difficult situations, success or failure will almost certainly depend on the effectiveness of your strategy."[7] "I generally find that people facing challenging language learning situations are initially confident that they will succeed. But gradually their confidence can turn into a conviction that success is impossible. It saddens me to see enthusiasm and dedication go unrewarded, or under-rewarded. I believe that I have seen cases where a better strategy would have made all the difference in the world."[8]

The Bare Minimum

Whatever methods we end up using, we ignore certain essentials at our peril. Thomson writes of "A Bare Minimum for Successful Language-learning":

> When all is said and done, anyone who fulfills the following three requirements will become a reasonably proficient speaker of a language, and anyone who does not fulfill them will develop limited proficiency, at best.
>
> 1. *Lots of exposure to comprehensible input.* Only through massive meaningful exposure to the language—that is, through receiving large amounts of comprehensible input—will the learner become familiar with the language and develop a confident feel for how it is spoken.
>
> 2. *Lots of extemporaneous speaking practice.* In extemporaneous speaking practice, the learner expresses a continual flow of new ideas with no pauses or hesitations for overt language processing. S/he produces countless sentences that s/he has not heard before, and does this flexibly in the flow of conversation or other speaking activities such as story telling.
>
> 3. *Steady acquisition of in-depth knowledge of the people who speak the language, knowledge of their shared experience and*

beliefs. The third requirement may be less obvious. And it is easy to pay lip service to it without appreciating its full and profound significance. It is not possible to understand people if one does not have a clue about what they are talking about, even if one knows all of the words and sentence patterns they are using. Learning to understand what lies behind all that people commonly discuss, including learning the ins and outs of common local activities and experiences, is a large part of what is meant by culture learning. A person who truly learns the culture in conjunction with learning the language will learn the vocabulary of the language in the process.[9]

What's Out There?

Approaches to language acquisition more or less fall into three camps:

Traditional. Think classrooms, grammar, drills, tests, exercises, and memorization. Usually there's not a lot of emphasis on actually *using* the language in normal situations. While I would not advocate this approach being the main one, I do think that some of its activities can be very helpful supplements to the other two approaches (i.e., we don't want to throw the baby out with the bath water).

Speech-led. A good example of speech-led learning is the LAMP methodology made popular by the Brewsters that I referenced above.[10] I actually contracted with Tom Brewster to receive seminary credit for doing fifteen complete cycles in Egypt. Essentially you develop a brief text in the language with the aid of a language helper, record it on tape, memorize it, and then practice it many, many times out on your "route" with real people.

Communicative. Thomson explains that the aim in this approach is "to force the learners to understand what is said to them in the target language, and to express their ideas using whatever ability they have at that point . . . Communicative activities directly develop the ability to use the language in communication."[11] More and more new language learners are going with this emphasis, which has been developed by Thomson and his associates. Please read appendix 2 where "comprehension-led learning" is explained. The key to this approach is to receive lots of comprehensible input, whether via normal human interaction, from audio tapes, recorded radio and TV programs, or reading appropriate to our level. We learn our second language the way we learned our first one: by hearing hundreds of hours of speaking, with visual and contextual clues helping us catch the meaning, which we begin to grasp more and more over time. For example, there were some popular radio call-in shows which, in hindsight, I really wish I had recorded and then listened to over and over until I fully grasped it all. Other good sources to tape include excerpts of our sessions with language helpers, soap operas, simple movies, children's cartoons, and taped sermons from the mosque, temple, or church. Of course, a fully developed methodology for this whole approach exists and training is available.

Providing Supportive Structures for Language Learners

Some language learners are simply on their own. They can nonetheless benefit from the special training increasingly offered on comprehension-led learning, and by language learning workshops being offered in their area. Others, likewise, are learning as individuals but are on a larger church planting team and reap the benefits of encouragement and oversight from others on the team who are already fluent. One of the best situations for effective language learning is to be in a group of learners at a similar level. Some of our teams have developed "language acquisition centers" for their team and others in the country. Evidence is mounting that real learning is accelerated by the support of such centers, so that multiple teams are pulling together within a country to create their own language acquisition center based on comprehension-led learning. Sometimes this means that the new worker will not go straight to his or her intended city, but rather spend a year or so at another city in the country. That's not always a bad thing.

Learning Styles

Next, a brief word about learning styles. We have different personalities and varying strengths and weaknesses in the various aspects of language learning. Think of "Polly the people person." She immediately hits it off with new people she meets. She loves spending time with people, and people are comfortable around her and love to talk to her. Polly picks up meanings very intuitively in conversations, subconsciously being an expert at emotions, situational clues, and body language. In contrast we find "Alan the academic learner." He'll get the A+s in the language class. He'll breeze through the grammar because, after all, it makes perfectly good sense. At the eighteen-month mark Polly will easily be grasping most things in conversations, while Alan will get lost in those same conversations, with a squinting look on his face. Meanwhile Alan will be reading and writing, and perhaps translating difficult texts, while Polly wouldn't recognize a participle if it hit her in the nose.

These are, of course, stereotypes, but they often hold true to form. Research has shown that a lot of our learning differences are due to the two different sides of the brain, the "left brain" being more dominant for some individuals and the "right brain" for others. While the left brain is more logical, sequential, rational, analytical, and objective, the right brain tends to be more random, intuitive, holistic, synthesizing, and subjective. The left brain focuses on parts, whereas the right brain looks at the whole.[12] Polly would be right-brained and Alan would be left-brained.

Should we let our differing learning styles or "brains" or personalities impact our language learning? The answer is an obvious yes; actually, we don't have much choice. For starters, you will want to reap the benefits of what you are strong at. Ride that horse. Let your strengths and preferences propel you forward. Likewise, customizing your language learning around *you* will help learning be more enjoyable rather than feeling like you're chewing on oatmeal every day. We also adapt our learning activities to fit our language level. What we do in month eleven won't be exactly the same as what we did in month two.

However, if we only go with what feels good, with what fits nicely with our personality, we will become warped learners and speakers. The people person has got to exercise discipline and self-control to make sure he or she gets time on their own, reflecting upon and internalizing what they are learning, moving forward on language structure and broadening their vocabulary beyond their daily conversations. Likewise, the more analytical learner will really need to push past internal barriers to get out with people—a lot. They can retreat to their desks and VCRs to some extent, but their language program and routine must include getting out with real people, engaging in real communication. Language acquisition is probably more of a right brain process, so having a good method and program structure will be doubly important for those of us who are left-brained. Having said that, I truly believe that all personality types can learn a second language and learn it well!

Pre-Field Preparation

Finally, what about pre-field preparation? Most agree these days that it does *not* make sense to try to learn the language before going to the field. If you're not immersed in relationships with the host people and language, it's too easy to learn things incorrectly, develop wrong pronunciation, and even acquire improper social habits. Who wants to have to spend time *unlearning* things after they arrive on the field? On the other hand, experts say that it is hugely important to learn *language acquisition skills* before going to the field. If a team already has a strong language program on the field with a very capable language coordinator, then it might not be so necessary for new workers to go to a language acquisition class beforehand. But for all other situations, I believe going to such a class is essential. These are generally two-week intensive courses offered around the United States and Europe throughout the year by a variety of organizations. In my observations, these classes will give the learner at least a 20 percent advantage in their future learning. Over two years that translates to a five-month head start, for just a two-week investment! Do the math. Whatever it costs, it's worth it.

4. Time Stewardship

What a precious resource time is! God tells us to "[make] the most of your time, because the days are evil" (Ephesians 5:16). We live in a fallen world, and there is so much the Lord wants to do through us for His redemptive purposes; we are compelled to become very good at using time wisely and well. "Do you not know . . . that you are not your own? For you have been bought with a price . . ." (1 Corinthians 6:19–20). Therefore we know that we are stewards of our time rather than masters of it. If this applies anywhere to Christian life and ministry, it really applies to language learning. After two years, the level of our attainment will be impacted more by how we actually used our hours and days and weeks than by our original good intentions. And, as I mentioned earlier, since most of us are not naturally strong self-starters and self-managers, we really need leaders in our lives to help us stay focused and on task.

Some of the languages teams need to learn are particularly challenging: for example, Kashmiri, Arabic, and Mandarin. Others, I am told, come more readily, such as Turkish or Indonesian. Nevertheless, in general I advocate that pioneer church planting teams establish a policy that new workers will focus full-time on language learning for two to three years. A good rule of thumb is thirty or more hours per week engaged in language activities for two years. Of course, there is no magic number of months. But a reasonable level of fluency should be reached before moving out of full-time language mode (such as attaining an FSI Level 3 Plus, as described above). This might actually take less than twenty-four months, or it might take a bit longer. *Key point*: It is absolutely vital that this requirement be spelled out clearly in a team's memo of understanding, and that new members are well aware of it *before* leaving for the field. This way they arrive mentally and emotionally prepared to jump into this challenge. It also provides a light at the end of the tunnel. If this isn't spelled out ahead of time and is a matter of debate after they have arrived, then in a sense you have already lost the battle.

There are a couple of possible exceptions to this. One is mothers of small children. Some couples feel that due to heavy household responsibilities, the wife should not have a time-demanding requirement placed upon her, such as spending a minimum of thirty hours per week in language learning. They would contend that the wife should try to move forward, though in her own time and not under rigorous accountability. Some couples on my team in Egypt felt strongly this way. Others on the team felt exactly the opposite: that if I did *not* hold the wife firmly accountable, then I was saying her part was unimportant. This calls for wisdom and flexibility on the part of the team leader! Regardless, language learning should be a high priority for all, even for a mother of young children who isn't able to invest as much time in it per week as others. If she doesn't eventually attain a certain level of fluency, she risks never becoming at ease and functional in the new country and never being able to make a strong contribution to the team's church planting. She risks not having local friends and becoming very unhappy, perhaps wanting to return home. This reality should motivate husbands to be flexible and helpful for the sake of their wives' language growth.

The second possible exception is those who must work in their tentmaking early on, whether that be in their job, business, humanitarian project, or whatever. Sometimes this is necessary to obtain a residence permit, if an ongoing tourist permit isn't obtainable. If this is the case, I would urge the worker and team leader to take a good, hard look at the situation. Is it really necessary, or is it just that the worker might feel more comfortable having a normal job and firmer visa? Is it possible to stay on a tourist visa for a while? Can the worker get by for a while with a lesser residency status in order to be full-time in language for two years? Many countries have universities that offer the country's language for credit, and students can enroll and get a student residence permit.

But if the conclusion remains that it's essential to have a work visa, then I would suggest three ways yet to maximize language learning during this time:

1. Plan to move into the job or NGO, but delay it as much as possible. For example, for those coming in to work in an NGO, sometimes the host country will insist on them being engaged in the work early. But the NGO leader can emphasize to the government the importance of the workers speaking the language, and obtain an agreement that they will be full-time in language for nine months first and then do their NGO work.

2. Be involved in your job, but negotiate with your supervisor to reduce your hours as much as absolutely possible in order to give more time to language. This, of course, will ultimately make you more effective on the job.

3. Work out ways to do your work on the job in the language.

If your working will mean that your language time goes down to fifteen to twenty hours per week, then obviously it will take longer to reach an acceptable level of fluency.

Finally, if the environment simply does not allow for concerted language work for an extended period, then workers should seriously consider going somewhere else first to learn the language full-time, perhaps for two years, before landing in their intended city.

That's sort of the *macro* picture. What about how our time stewardship works out on a weekly basis? That's really where the rubber meets the road. Let's assume that we will be engaged in thirty hours or more each week. This would include all sorts of language activities, including such things as buying vegetables, riding in a taxi and conversing with the driver, watching TV in the language, as well as more direct planned language learning activities. By the way, the reason it is only thirty hours is that the workers will no doubt have other things required of them in their ministry, such as team gatherings and a certain amount of administration and communications.

As explained above, every team member will need a program or plan—hopefully one worked out with someone trained and further ahead in the language. A good plan should employ lots of variety, such as vocabulary work, time with a tutor, Total Physical Response drills,[13] studying, speaking cycles, plenty of active listening, and lots of time interacting with local people. Again, the methodologies and principles available to undergird learners these days are much better than what we used to have. The learner and language coordinator have a large menu of strategic activities from which to choose in building a person's personal program. All of us need variety, and it's not hard now to build that into a good weekly plan.

Secondly, as human beings we need structure. Without it most of us would get really stressed out, and that opens the door to discouragement. Therefore I strongly encourage that the plan include a weekly schedule of activities. Of course, it needs to be flexible since time with local people is a key component and that can't always be "scheduled." But it's better to start with a schedule and then bend it than to have no schedule at all. Team leaders commonly require a form to be filled out weekly, reporting time spent in various aspects of language learning, and this can be very helpful.

Finally, watch out for time potholes. Think of all the things that can trip you up and cause you to fail to achieve your thirty hours per week on a consistent basis. For example, a major seduction that pulls people away from staying on task—in this case, learning the language—is e-mail. We know we should be pressing on in some language pursuit, but the computer sits in the corner of the room singing out its siren song, pulling us away to spend hours at its keyboard, *supposedly* for some important matters. Of course, easy and secure e-mail is a wonderful thing today. It enables us to communicate around the world so quickly. And some of this is truly vital. But it can also grow to become a millstone around our neck, compromising what we're really there for—which isn't computer stuff. I'm not being judgmental. I confess that I blew it in this area. I spent too much time in front of the computer. Of course, it didn't help that my tentmaking job involved computers. Could it be that the reason the apostle Paul was so effective is that he didn't own a computer?!

5. Oversight

After the previous section on time stewardship, it's probably fairly apparent why we need oversight. As someone has said about athletics, "The job of the coach is to force you to do what you don't want to do so that you will achieve what you want to achieve." We need godly leadership to lay out the big picture, to work out a program with us, to assist us in consistently using our time well, to help us periodically evaluate how we are doing, and to hold us accountable. We need encouragement. And we need practical help in working out the particular activities. It doesn't matter to me if you call this role that of a language coordinator, language encourager, language supervisor, or something else. This person may or may not be the team leader. In fact, for larger teams it's usually better if the language coordinator is *not* the team leader. Since the team leader is necessarily involved in many things, it's preferable to have a language coordinator who can specialize and focus on language. But if it must be the team leader, so be it. This oversight shouldn't be heavy-handed, but it must be real. The Bible speaks a lot about oversight and accountability, ingredients that are so very vital during this initial period of language learning.

The team leader must not shrink back from providing this language oversight, either directly or through a language coordinator, for without it learning on the team is sure to flounder. And since language learning can be very challenging and it can be difficult to keep our outlook positive month after month, the main tone of this oversight should be positive and encouraging. We need to lift up those branches that have fallen to the ground. There is sometimes a certain unhelpful irony: most team leaders feel a bit insecure at first, and so they are tempted to be woefully under-assertive in their leadership. They assume this will help the contentment level on the team, whereas in fact the opposite is true. Insecurity in the team leader translates into insecurity in the team.

As I've already mentioned, I believe language learners need to evaluate their progress about every six months. Staying motivated during the first two years is often the largest hurdle. Some might react that a language test or evaluation will be intimidating and discouraging. That is possible if it is done wrong. But done well it can be the most powerful motivator in keeping us pressing on. It also has the practical benefit of helping us see where we are strong and where we need improvement, so we can make course corrections.

How can we conduct semiannual assessments on our team? The answer to that is unfortunately beyond the scope of this chapter, and I would mostly commend you to the experts in learning how to do it for your team. Greg Thomson says, "It is common to distinguish between *achievement tests*, which are tied closely to content that learners have made an effort to learn, and *proficiency tests*, which aim to reflect the learner's general ability. Another distinction is made between *discrete-point testing*, where, for example, the learner is tested on the past perfect form of the verb, and *integrative testing*, where the learner is tested by being required to use the language in more genuine ways. Traditionally, integrative proficiency tests are considered more meaningful than discrete-point achievement tests, as the latter may say little about actual language ability."[14]

I believe the best evaluations:

a. Are simple to conduct;

b. Utilize at least one native speaker;

c. Primarily measure listening comprehension and speaking ability, with perhaps some check on pronunciation and reading; and

d. Are in some way quantitative, in order for the learner and leader to track progress and to gauge when the learner is approaching a sufficient level of fluency.

One method of evaluation being advocated on fields now is that of testing as a means of planning the next set of language learning activities—a type of "placement" or "course adjustment" testing. For example, a learner records the evaluation session with his language helper, during which they interact about a section of a picture story book. Then the learner reviews this tape with his helper (or another host language speaker), taking note of errors he has made in language use and pronunciation. He then uses this to plan the focus for his next set of language sessions. The tape and evaluation form are kept in his "portfolio" as a steadily accumulating history of his progress in language learning. Such evaluations can be profitably used even monthly.

Another objection to evaluations that is sometimes raised is that if one's language achievement is known by others on the team, then this creates an atmosphere of unhealthy competition. I agree, and believe the answer lies in keeping results confidential between the learner and the language coordinator (and team leader).

There's an expression that some Arabs use when they wish to complement someone learning their language. When they see you are somehow clever, and that you are working hard to become proficient in the Arabic language, they say, "You are going to be dangerous!" They mean it positively, with affection and a twinkle in their eye. They mean that you are about to merge two things into a powerful combination: your abilities from your home country with the newfound ability to operate these in your adopted country.

Many workers come from their home country with strong spiritual gifts, valuable training, and proven fruitfulness in ministry back home. For a while they cannot function in those roles that they felt so confident in before, and this is certainly a frustrating period of time. But over time, as they acquire more and more facility in the language, they realize that those old abilities in ministry are returning—but now in the host language! They have become tools in the hands of the Master, able to help plant churches in the target language for His glory. That's what it's all about.

7
Role and Residency

The primary purpose of an apostolic team is to win the people of an unreached people group to Christ, planting churches that lead to movements. However, few countries where we are laboring grant visas for that purpose. In pioneer ministry today, full-time church planting is a rarity. Usually, workers need some other job, business, or role in order to remain in the country and be understood by society. Often these roles are referred to as *tentmaking*[1] or *residency platforms*.

Is this duality somehow deceptive? Is there an ethical problem in having a particular vocation you fulfill in your day-to-day life which is not exactly the same as your primary purpose for coming to the country, namely church planting? No. Definitely not.

Consider these four truths:

1. It is simply normal life for a Christian to have a vocational identity in addition to an overarching life purpose. Consider, for example, a Christian database programmer in Frankfurt. His life purpose is to know Christ and make Him known. But when people ask, "What do you do?" he does not answer "I endeavor to know Christ and make Him known." Rather, he says he's a database programmer. As opportunities arise, he is happy to unfold the deeper things that shape his life. No deception. No schizophrenia. It's no different with today's cross-cultural workers among unreached peoples. This is simply referred to as being bivocational.

2. In 1 Samuel 16:1–13 we find a fascinating precedent. The Lord instructed Samuel to go to Bethlehem and anoint one of Jesse's sons to succeed Saul as king. Samuel objected that if he set out for that purpose Saul would hear about it and kill him. The Lord's

solution was this: "Take a heifer with you and say, 'I have come to sacrifice to the LORD.'" Was this a lie, a ruse? No. Samuel really was to perform the sacrifice with Bethlehem's leaders. But God gave this to him as an additional purpose. The aim was not to deceive, but only to work around the practical reality of avoiding serious trouble with Saul's henchmen.

3. When church planters are tentmakers—whether in a humanitarian project, a job, or a business—invariably they are providing valuable services for the people, which oftentimes provide jobs and a tangible benefit to the local economy. They are serving people out of Christ's love.

4. These vocations are *real*, not fake—not a mere cover. I cannot think of a single tentmaking gospel worker who says he or she is doing such-and-such (e.g., teaching English) but is not in reality doing it.

We have got to get this sorted out in our heads. This is a big issue. It is the lens through which local people will first view you. Your bivocationality should actually enhance rather than hinder your CP goals. All who have been on the field awhile have experienced the tension of not getting it right. The taxi driver asks what we do. We hesitate, freeze up, and mutter some vague answer. If we don't get comfortable with our *raison d'etre*, insecurity grows.

This is especially true if you have entered the country temporarily on a tourist visa, which often is necessary for a time in order to be free for full-time language work. Very few people on apostolic teams will have solid jobs right from the beginning. In most situations it's best to major on language learning for about two years, which can be a challenge in regard to residency. Most will move into more tangible roles only after being in the country awhile, and that is OK.

Having a reasonable purpose for being in-country is driven by two very practical needs: 1) To have a viable answer for the question that comes to you several times a week: "Why are you here?" 2) To obtain a visa or residence permit. It is possible to have one without the other. (i.e. viability without a residence permit or vice versa). A good discussion question for your next team meeting might be: "Which is more important: viability or residence permit?"

TYPES OF RESIDENCY PLATFORMS

These seem to be the primary categories of residency:

1. Job. Not the book before Psalms, but being an employee of a local company. Examples include teaching English, computer work, medical work, management, sales, teaching in a school or university.

2. Owning and running a business, self-employed or with a partner.

3. Working in a nongovernmental organization (NGO), usually providing valuable humanitarian or economic services to people.

4. Working officially in a church capacity. This is sometimes an option in countries where a Christian minority exists, especially if there is a supportive local sponsor.

5. Student (e.g., postgraduate, research, or in-depth language study).

6. Not having any official role or residency other than a tourist visa, but having a reasonable purpose for being in the country (e.g., researching business opportunities).

7. Other (e.g., retirement).

One can perhaps think of other categories, but the ones above probably cover 95 percent of tentmaking workers.

DISCOVERING THE RIGHT ROLE FOR YOU

The myriad of choices for what vocational role you might adopt can really become overwhelming. What is your professional background? What do you like to do? What are real options in the country you are going to versus what probably wouldn't work? These are practical considerations that we must grapple with. But as important as all these are, there is another vital question that may trump all these others: What do you wish to accomplish through your residency platform for the sake of your intended church planting ministry? Are you looking for a very minimal job that will allow you to be as free as possible for direct ministry? Or are you open to a more time-consuming vocation if you can accomplish more *through* that job for the kingdom of God?

Here are ten benefits that your tentmaking role might provide:

1. Excellent viability in society—an identity that is real and makes good sense. For example, a five-hour per week English teaching job probably won't provide you much viability, whereas a foreigner working full-time as general manager of a company is likely to make perfect sense. Likewise, the more solid your role is, the less likely that the government will seek to expel you if ministry becomes sensitive later on (though there are no guarantees).

2. A residence permit.

3. Contacts—helping you meet a wide variety of people and establish bonds of friendship and trust.

4. Opportunities for witness, to demonstrate the good news by word and deed.

5. An example of an exemplary work ethic to local believers.

6. "Normalcy"—that is, being in a normal kind of job, with normal hours, in a normal way. While many apostolic workers realize they have to live and minister in a different sort of work life, others may crave having a job no different than what they would do "back home."

7. An arena for using the language a lot; an opportunity to grow, while on the job, in language proficiency and cultural understanding.

8. A demonstration of the love of Christ through meeting people's urgent needs, usually through a humanitarian project.

9. Income. For example, it usually takes a full-time job to get residency in Arab Gulf countries, but those jobs also pay well.

10. Permission to travel to certain areas. This is sometimes a factor if the people you want to reach with the gospel live in an area in which the government restricts travel.

I recently received a touching example of the eighth point above:

The Miracle Center. That is what our handicap center has been labeled in the community. Praise the Lord! One girl first came to the center in a wheelchair and is now walking to the center. A boy had no use of his arms when he first came, but now is able to ride a specialized tricycle using his arms to move the wheels. Now we have a third success story. Last October a mother from the countryside brought to the center her "lame" daughter. This little girl could not move her arms or legs and had a hard time even keeping her head up. She would just lay in her mother's arms like a vegetable. One of our local therapists taught the mother some basic physical therapy techniques and sent her on her way. Because she lived in the countryside nobody saw her for several months. Earlier this month the mother returned to the center with her daughter. This time the little girl couldn't stop jumping up and down and running all around the center. Her mother says it's a miracle. Her words have spread throughout the city. Now this mother is planning on selling some of the family livestock in order to rent an apartment near the center to be able to bring her daughter in more regularly.

No job or role is going to provide all ten benefits outlined above. Obviously there are tradeoffs between one kind of role and another. Again, the biggest tradeoff of all is probably time. Many bivocational workers will want to spend only a very minimal amount of time each week in their tentmaking job in order to have as much time as absolutely possible for language learning, evangelism, discipling believers, teaching the Bible, etc. Sometimes workers will have a good position in a company; and because of having an employer who is sympathetic to their CP goals, they have lots of flexibility in their hours. Others will be more drawn to having a full-time job or NGO project, or even sometimes to more than full-time hours. They hope to make their biggest contribution to the CP goals through the job itself. Perhaps the majority of pioneer workers will be somewhere in the middle: less than full-time in their tentmaking, and less than full-time in their CP ministry. (One caution: In my observations, those with full-time or greater than full-time jobs often do not make a huge direct contribution to church planting. May each team member have a clear sense from the Lord what role is the best fit for him or her!)

The profession we adopt on the field may not be the same as our profession back home. The apostle Paul was trained at the highest level of religious law, yet that sort of career only worked in long-term, stable situations. So he adopted a vocation that better fit his itinerant calling: making tents. It was a job well below his education and deserved status. And yet it was ideal for ministry. I have seen many church planters leave very lucrative and prestigious careers in law, medicine, or business, only to take on much "lower" jobs on the field—but jobs that better fit the team's ministry goals. That's OK!

Sooner or later workers come to realize that "What is your work?" and "Why are you here?" are not identical questions. I personally ran a small business in the Middle East. We had some of the top businesses in the country as clients, and we were able to employ a handful of locals. But I always found it very liberating to share with friends that my deeper interest in coming to the country was to serve the kingdom of God in the lives of people.

Inevitably, when cross-cultural workers are in a country for five years, ten years, or more, they end up changing jobs. They're able to shift their role or circumstances to better fit their life and ministry. This is good. New workers mustn't feel that they have to get it perfect from the very beginning. Personally, I've been on a tourist visa for a long time (with a plausible reason for being in the country), I've been a full-time student, I've been an employee of a computer company, and I've run a business. Over time, new doors open up.

For most men, the sooner they can work outside the home the better. Too many make the mistake of basing whatever they do from home. In most of the countries and cultures we work in, this doesn't make sense to local people. A man may wonder, "Why is Bob home all day? I'm not comfortable with him being around my wife all day long in the apartment building." Even if one's full-time role is language learning, having the primary base for this being a rented office can be a tremendous boost. I've heard over and over from men—and it has been my own experience—that two things really help you feel normal in your host city: 1) having an office, and 2) having business cards. It seems simple, but can make a huge psychological difference. Besides, if one's aim is to build relationships with local men, it's more effective to do so in the workplace rather than family to family from home.

We are called to live and work among these precious peoples for Christ's sake, as His emissaries of love and truth. I don't advocate a form of tentmaking that is deceptive, but rather that we adopt vocations that are real and legitimate. Whether in humanitarian service, for-profit business, or work in the academic sphere, our aim is to demonstrate the love of Christ through caring—by meeting needs and doing excellent work. This will make sense to people and only enhance our message. As Paul said, "Whatever you do, do your work heartily, as for the Lord rather than for men, knowing that from the Lord you will receive the reward of the inheritance. It is the Lord Christ whom you serve" (Colossians 3:23–24).

8

Evangelism

How lovely on the mountains
Are the feet of him who brings good news,
Who announces peace
And brings good news of happiness,
Who announces salvation,
And says to Zion, "Your God reigns!" (Isaiah 52:7)

Imagine being that runner who brought home the wonderful news that the Babylonian exile was finally over! He paid such a high price: he had run for days, was exhausted, and had blistery and bleeding feet that might take months to recover. But he also had the historic joy of bearing the *gospel* that a couple of generations had longed to hear: the people of God would be reborn in their own land, as God had promised through Isaiah. Gospel envoys working among unreached people groups are usually well aware of the punishment their feet have born—that is, what they have left behind and the ongoing dangers and hardships they and their families endure for Christ's sake. Speaking personally, there was also the continual exciting reality that in the case of every person I shared the good news with on the field, it was almost always the first time that he or she had the chance to hear God's offer of salvation accurately (and, sadly, he or she might not ever hear it again). What an unspeakable privilege!

Apostolic ministry among unreached people groups can be multifaceted. Church planting is the main theme of this book; but proclaiming Jesus is so utterly central to why we have gone out. Sharing Christ is at the core of the apostolic calling. "How then will they call on Him in whom they have not believed? How will they believe in Him whom they have not heard? And how will they hear without a preacher? How will they preach unless they are sent?" (Romans 10:14–15; Paul then goes on to quote Isaiah about the *beautiful feet* of the *sent ones*). Jesus' heart is full of compassion for those around us, and as we walk in that, we long to lead our friends and neighbors to faith in Christ, that they might be with us in eternity. Practically speaking, apostolic workers sharing Christ *a lot* is normally essential for getting a fellowship, not to mention a church planting movement, started in a pioneer setting.

Will the spread of the gospel in a highly resistant culture occur primarily at the hands of foreigners? The answer, of course, is certainly not. Sooner or later the local believers themselves will be the more prolific and more effective witnesses, by far. This sort of story—from a team leader report—is typical: "A coworker led a young country woman named Ari to Christ in India. Ari in turn successfully shared the gospel with the man who later would become her husband. She also led to Christ, and baptized, eight other women, including a woman over eighty years of age. Recently Ari was confronted publicly in the market by a furious fundamentalist uncle, who has pledged to have her arrested." Thus, we will want to continually model for the local believers a passion and practice in evangelism, that they too will catch this and take it further.

How you read this chapter will depend a lot on where you are and what your people group is like. Are you involved in a ministry in which there are already many believers and you are engaged in discipling and teaching the Word? If so, evangelism is important for you, but you must balance it with other types of pressing ministry. Or are you, like many of God's ambassadors, in a situation where there aren't yet believers—and so evangelism is *the* primary ministry focus? Likewise, are you in a strictly policed country where overt public evangelism would probably get you booted?[1] Or are you in a country where workers can publicly show the *Jesus* film, advertise free New Testaments in the newspaper, or even invite the public to a large hotel to hear a speaker? Whether we're in Agra or Bandung, Calcutta or Cairo, nothing need hold us back from proclaiming the good news to friends, work associates, neighbors, and so many we meet on a daily basis.

A good question for us is What kind of evangelism *directly* leads to church planting? First of all, there are two kinds that do not. "Pre-evangelism" usually refers to the broad influencing of society, hoping to make people more receptive to the gospel in general, to create a greater openness to Jesus. There are perhaps other definitions of pre-evangelism, but I'm using the term in the sense of creating a more positive impression about Christ over time, as opposed to the direct preaching of the gospel in its central components (i.e., Christ's atoning death on the cross and every person's need to take Him as Lord and Savior) and calling for a decision. This has been the aim of certain publications. I also know of particular music projects having this broad goal.

Likewise, "broadcast evangelism" aims to sow the seed widely, through media such as radio, TV, correspondence courses, and the Internet. The hearers really do hear the *evangel*, and there are countless testimonies of how God has powerfully used a TV program or gospel portion to open someone's eyes. As we will see below, when broadcast ministry funnels into on-the-ground follow-up, the contribution to church planting can be direct; otherwise its contribution is more general. Both of these types of evangelism are very valuable, and I thank God for every single effort made along these lines to reach the unreached for Christ.

It is powerful when church planters *on the ground* can link up with broadcast-type ministries, who are often out of the country. In the early 1980s Joseph was an official in the outlawed Communist party in a certain African country. He was in charge of finances and of organizing clandestine meetings. He was burdened for the plight of the poor in his country, and wound up in jail for his activities. During his incarceration, his younger, illiterate brother Idi began listening to Christian programs from TransWorld Radio (TWR), and had a friend write away on his behalf for a Bible correspondence course. When Joseph was released from jail, his brother begged him to do the Bible study with him, since Idi could not read. Joseph didn't want anything to do with something else that might land him in jail. Yet, after persistent badgering, Joseph relented and not only did the initial study with his brother but the subsequent study as well. A ministry team received Idi's name and address from the correspondence people to follow up with him. A member of the team made contact and soon Joseph's entire immediate family came to faith, along with much of his extended family. In the fourteen years since, the team leader has been heavily involved and about five fellowships or churches have sprung up from this fruit of cooperation between broadcast evangelism and church planting.

Church planting teams need to major on evangelistic activity that can *directly* lead to church planting. For this to occur, it seems to me that two things need to be true:

1. Workers are able to personally lead local people to faith, and to confirm their new relationship with Christ in prayer and perhaps in confession to others.

2. Workers are able (eventually) to *baptize* the new disciples and to *teach them to observe all that Christ commanded* (Matthew 28:19–20), which generally includes helping the new believers become part of a fellowship.

Friendship evangelism (personally sharing the gospel with one's friends and contacts) meets these criteria. Many kinds of *apostolic evangelism* (projects aimed at wider sowing; see below) can also lead directly to church planting.

ARE CERTAIN CULTURES TRULY RESISTANT TO THE GOSPEL?

The lessons in this section apply to all of the major unreached contexts: Buddhist, Hindu, Muslim, and tribal. As an example of facing resistance, Kang-San writes: "Christian missions have been active in Buddhist heartlands for centuries. Despite the relative freedom (compared to missions among Muslims) given to Christian missionary work, we have not seen major breakthroughs of Chinese Buddhists coming to Christ. Various approaches and strategies have been developed, mostly on how to penetrate the Buddhist world as people groups."[2] Likewise, Japan still today is considered one of the most resistant countries in the world, with hopes for a church planting movement only faint.

Regarding the spread of the gospel in Muslim countries today, we have a good news/bad news situation. The good news is that Muslims are turning to Christ all around the world literally like never before. Patrick Johnstone, coauthor of *Operation World*, estimates that around two million Muslims may have come to faith in Christ in recent years.[3] David Garrison writes: "More Muslims have come to Christ in the past two decades than at any other time in history. In North Africa, more than 16,000 Berbers turn to Christ over a two-decade period. A Central Asian Church Planting Movement sees 13,000 Kazakhs come to faith in Christ over a decade and a half . . . In an Asian Muslim country, more than 150,000 Muslims embrace Jesus and gather in more than 3,000 locally led Isa Jamaats [Jesus Groups]."[4] Somewhere between 30,000 and 100,000 Iranian Muslims have trusted Christ. Many gospel workers in the Muslim world today feel that they are now firmly on the reaping side of John 4:35–38, whereas laborers only twenty years ago had only to sow, seeing little or no fruit.

The bad news is that all those who have come to faith in Christ in recent years are still a drop in the bucket compared to the 1.2 billion Muslims worldwide; and the same could be said about most other unreached contexts as well. The vast, vast majority of men, women, boys, and girls living in unreached people groups have still never heard the true message of Jesus and are trapped in a belief system which prevents them from ever hearing it or giving it serious consideration. While many workers are actively discipling believers or involved in forming or multiplying churches, many are not, and their entire "church planting ministry" is still one thing: evangelism. Many without fruit already feel like failures in their ministry. They would love to be able to report of believers and groups and movements like their colleagues, but so far cannot. Fruit is still quite scarce in the Middle East and North Africa. I know a number who have labored in particular areas for fifteen or more years of patient ministry who have yet to see one person come to Christ. Some have not yet even had the privilege of working with one keen seeker. I have no doubt that when we are celebrating at the Wedding Supper of the Lamb, the Lord will have special commendations and rewards for those who have worked so long and so hard at proclaiming Christ without the encouragement of fruit. What a uniquely challenging task in that context to keep pressing on, sharing Jesus with expectancy and not allowing yourself to be diverted into other "more fulfilling" tasks.

In the late 1870s a French consortium won the rights to build a canal in Panama and soon raised the money to begin. But all their efforts ended in total failure. They lost 25,000 lives, mostly due to malaria and yellow fever, and $280 million—the single biggest business loss to that point in history. This French company that went bankrupt was the Microsoft of the day, and its sinking sent shockwaves throughout the global economy. My point is that what we are called to is so much more important, and is not a failure. Anything so biblically crucial as attempting to fulfill the Great Commission among unreached people groups is worth it, whatever the cost. Even when our sowing in hundreds of places is not yet bearing fruit, it is absolutely precious in His sight and will be deemed in eternity for what it is: a wonderful success of obedience. As the adage goes, "Evangelism is sharing Jesus Christ, in the power of the Holy Spirit, and leaving the results to God." That is *never* failure.

Why is it that certain people groups remain to this day so very, very resistant to the gospel? The reasons vary, but here are the usual suspects:

The Normal Spiritual Stuff

Like all of us, our local friends are sons and daughters of Adam, born under the control of "the prince of the power of the air, of the spirit that is now working in the sons of disobedience."[5] Add to this the fact that people in general have a built-in inertia against considering a radical spiritual change. We're not asking people to change their cell phone service. We are beckoning them to take Jesus as Savior and Lord, and that decision might cost them everything. As with every human being, it takes a sovereign work of the Spirit for our friends' eyes to be opened to the truth of Jesus. They need a personal encounter with God.

Barriers to Hearing

Many governments in the 10/40 Window erect all kinds of obstacles to evangelism. Foreigners are not allowed in the country if their intent is to preach the gospel. Local Christians are prevented from evangelizing by law. Believers often face the severest of repercussions if they widely proclaim Christ. Once or twice I have asked my local friends this question: "Evidently your government thinks you should not have a choice regarding religious matters, since they restrict you from hearing more about Jesus. Why is that?" However, sharing one's personal testimony one-on-one in the context of a relationship is permitted virtually everywhere. And most of us would agree that any legal restrictions to sharing the gospel anywhere is one of those few things we must disobey.[6] We are to proclaim the message even if it means expulsion, prison, or death.

Theological

There are several countries where the legal and structural barriers are decreasing (e.g., India, Turkey, Tunisia), but there is still no widespread embracing of the gospel. We must remember that our friends don't hear the gospel in a vacuum—with a clean slate, as it were. For example, in most Muslim cultures people from childhood are told three significant untruths:

1) Jesus did not die on the cross; God put Judas in his place. And Jesus could not pay the price for anyone else's sins. No substitutionary atonement is possible.

2) While the New Testament was originally from God, it has since been changed and corrupted—by corrupt Christians.

3) God rewards a person with eternal life only on the basis of his or her works. While Allah is the Merciful and the Forgiving, He grants heaven only to those who have earned it. (Such teaching, of course, is incompatible with justification by grace through faith in a Savior; and this is also why the message of grace is often strikingly attractive to Muslims.)

As emissaries of the gospel, we must be prepared to deal with each of these primary objections our friends might raise.

Complacency

I've come to believe in recent years that the biggest reason a person typically doesn't seriously consider the message of Christ is that he feels he doesn't need to. Based on what he has been taught by his religion, he will be just fine—"Thank you very much!" This would explain why the Arab Gulf, for example, is the most resistant, the least penetrated region. Priding themselves on their religious orthodoxy, the people feel no vulnerability regarding their fate after death. Likewise, because of oil wealth so many are without needs in this life, quieting any concerns about safety and security. Few are willing to consider that they have an unresolved need regarding sin, guilt, and eternal destiny. Compounding this is a widespread belief in a form of purgatory that assures the less-than-good person that he too will eventually make it to heaven. Proportionally, people in resistant environments fear hell probably even less than Westerners do.

Bob, a friend of mine in Turkey, shared the gospel with a fellow on a bus who said he would just pay off all of his sins in purgatory. Bob asked him how long he estimated it would take to pay them all off. He said he would probably be there for several hundred thousand years! When Bob told him about the free gift of salvation and asked if it wouldn't just be easier to accept what God was offering through Jesus Christ, the reply was, "Oh, no thank you! I'd rather work it off myself."

To Become a Follower of Christ Is Too Costly

It seemed that the biggest hurdle in the hearts of many of those I have spoken with was not believing, but rather that they were put off by knowing what a high price they would have to pay. We have spoken elsewhere of how believers face persecution, ridicule, arrest, imprisonment, and sometimes even death. Add to this that so many have taken Christ as their Savior and Lord but are blocked from following Him more earnestly and witnessing to their families because of further threats and fears.

Though these factors remain a tremendous challenge to the church of Jesus Christ today, we serve a living and powerful God who is moving throughout the unreached world like never before. There has never been a more exciting time to be bringing the truth to the sons and daughters of Ishmael, as well as to Buddhist and Hindu societies. Because of what the Spirit is doing, there is now no place where His "sent ones" cannot proclaim Christ with a strong sense of expectancy.

Even in places like Cambodia, Kuwait, and Assam, wonderful new things are taking place.

THE GOOD NEWS ABOUT SHARING THE GOOD NEWS

It has been suggested that the ministry of evangelism on the field is really three things: 1) sharing Christ; 2) keeping a discovering eye open for those who might already know the Lord; and 3) constantly praying for God to fill you with power and boldness, to sovereignly lead you to His contacts, and to open up their eyes. I like this threefold model.

People debate whether or not there is a *gift of evangelism*. There were "evangelists" (Acts 21:8; Ephesians 4:11) as well as those notably called to "do the work of an evangelist" (2 Timothy 4:5). Regardless, experience tells us that some are eagerly and constantly drawn to share Christ with nonbelievers, and seem to be good at it, while the rest of us approach evangelism with some trepidation. Those of you who are gifted evangelists can almost skip the remainder of this chapter. In this section I would like to offer up seventeen encouraging perspectives and helpful tips aimed mainly at the rest of us, some of whom may be feeling discouraged or ineffective. Regardless of your gift-mix, God has brought you to the country you are in, and He wants to use you to bring people to Himself. It is my desire that these seventeen tidbits inject you with hope that fortifies faith.

1. Pray. The whole Christian life is to meet challenges firstly in prayer. To knock, to seek, to ask. And then to go for it. God loves to use the weak, and He loves to answer their prayers. Every pioneer team—especially those in Phases II, III, and IV—should regularly take time in team meetings to pray for each person's key contacts. And every team member can begin each day with, "Lord, I'm available. Use me to set one of the captives free. Make me sensitive to your leading."

One team in Kazakhstan launched "Operation Three" (*oosh* in Kazakh). Each team member was to pick three friends for whom they would purposely and earnestly pray for salvation. They prayed for them in times of individual prayer as well as in times of team prayer. Remarkably, in less than six months something like 60 percent of those prayed for came to the Lord!

We also need to pray for our whole country or people group. Some apostolic workers have launched global prayer projects for their country with amazing results, by the grace of God. Up until 1998 there were only about thirty known active local believers in one North African country, of whom only about ten ever met for fellowship. That year the Spirit led key leaders from all the groups working in the country to embark on an intensive year of united effort which would include mobilizing world-wide prayer focused on the country for the whole of 1999, along with special evangelism and training in the country. By the end of 1999 there were over a hundred new believers, from all sections of the country, formed together into some six fellowships. Today growth is continuing.

2. Remember God's elect in your city. As the Lord assured Paul in the daunting early days of breakthrough in Corinth, "I have many people in this city" (Acts 18:10), I have no doubt that Jesus' words in John 10:27, "My sheep hear My voice, and I know them, and they follow Me," are true of every city in the world—whether Guangzhou, Lahore, or Bhopal. Take hold of this truth about your city.

3. It's not taboo to talk about spiritual matters. Not being a strong people person, I have found it difficult to bring up spiritual issues in conversations with other Americans. When I moved to Arab countries, I was delighted to discover that people are much more eager to discuss spiritual matters. The Western notion of "Don't discuss religion" is absent in many places we work, and so is that awkward barrier.

4. Seek the Spirit's guidance. The Spirit can sovereignly lead you to individuals who are open. On a recent trip to India, one of my fellow workers went out walking in the evening's cool air. The Spirit drew him to approach a young man, Irawati, and after a short conversation this man took a Gospel portion. Two days later this worker met Irawati again, who told him, "When I met you, God told me you had something spiritual for my life and that you are the man I have been waiting for." By the end of the week, Irawati entered God's kingdom through Christ, becoming the first known believer in the region. He eventually led others in his footsteps.

5. Be bold! Bolder, more "prophetic" type witness will be more effective than cautious, indirect approaches. Because we feel we're guests, and because we want to build and not spoil relationships, we're sometimes "wimpy" in how we present Christ: "Oh, would you mind maybe considering Jesus? He's really a nice guy. And the New Testament is fairly interesting too. Would you? Could you?" Folks, we are talking to people headed to an eternity cut off from God and from all that is good. If we love our friends, we will grasp how they need to be shaken from a complacency that guarantees their lostness—unless they are freed. It's good to speak to people's heads; but we must also speak to their hearts, and to their wills. The element of *warning* was a big part of New Testament preaching. Have we lost that? Greg Livingstone writes, "My goal, then, is to have my Muslim friend feel that if the Christian's gospel is true, and he takes advantage of it, that would be good news indeed. And conversely, if it is true and he turns his back on it, there could be terrible consequences for him."[7] Remember, you are sent out with the truth and with full authority as God's ambassador. Do you believe that?

6. Try different ways to share Christ. There can be a wide variety of ways in which we personally participate in sharing the gospel. Consider these different facets: Meeting new people and forming relationships. Cultivating relationships longer term. Turning discussions to spiritual, heart matters. Skillfully sharing the gospel and handling questions, objections, or apologetics. Hospitality. We all have differing strengths and weaknesses, and our evangelistic roles can vary. I know of one team where a couple had an endless supply of relationships, but desperately needed help with hospitality and logistics several times a week. Others on the team jumped in. Another team had a wonderful "relationship opener," who was not good at explaining things, while another on the team was hopeless at meeting new people but an artist at work in explaining biblical truth to those keen to hear. It's good to major in what you're best at.

7. Work in your particular giftings. If you don't have a *gift of evangelism*, use what gifts you do have *evangelistically*. For example, though I am weak in personal evangelism, I do have a Bible-teaching gift. By the grace of God, I have seen the Lord use this gift in a variety of ways to lead people to Himself.

8. Get prepared. "The horse is prepared for the day of battle, but victory belongs to the LORD" (Proverbs 21:31). Note that the text doesn't say that since victory is in the hands of the Lord the horse doesn't need to be prepared. It should go without saying, but gospel workers in resistant societies need at least some minimal training in sharing the gospel in that context. Excellent courses are continually offered around the world, both on the field and in workers' home countries. At least three or four books ought to be read thoroughly, and there are many excellent ones out there. This will build confidence and faith, and help you to "always [be] ready to make a defense to everyone who asks you to give an account for the hope that is in you" (1 Peter 3:15). Kang-San writes, "In mission preparation, for missionaries working among Buddhists, there are many gaps to be filled, particularly in understanding Buddhist beliefs and practices."[8] Livingstone has two very helpful chapters on cultivating relationships and being effective personal witnesses.[9] And while some will want to become skillful in apologetics, all of us should be ready to give at least a brief reply to the main objections to Christ that people hold.

John Stott, the famous British theologian and evangelist, writes, "Some say rather piously that the Holy Spirit is Himself the complete and satisfactory solution to the problem of communication and indeed when He is present and active, then communication ceases to be a problem. What on earth does such a statement mean? Do we now have liberty to be as obscure, confused and irrelevant as we like, and the Holy Spirit will make all things plain? To use the Holy Spirit to rationalize our laziness is nearer to blasphemy than piety."[10]

9. Share in different contexts. Some believe that to witness to someone, let's say a friend or neighbor, you must first carefully cultivate a relationship over a long period of time so as to eventually "win the right" to be heard. While it may be this way with a few relationships, to think it must always be like this is unbiblical and would shackle us. This "win the right to be heard" idea generally is a myth that must be dispelled. You never see Jesus or Paul or others spending time with someone *before* sharing something of the kingdom with that person.

10. Grow in the language. At the risk of stating the obvious, a weak faculty of the local language will be a large obstacle to effective evangelism, while a strong proficiency will greatly boost confidence, faith, and relationships. There are a few who have been fruitful without language proficiency, operating only in English or through interpreters, but they are usually the exception that proves the rule.

11. Don't limit yourself relationally. One of the biggest mistakes us "non-evangelists" make is to stop with two or three friends, investing all of our time and witness only with them. Instead, we need to find ways to continually meet new people and discover who might be open, who the Lord might be speaking to. Join a club (e.g., a computer club, a tennis or sports club, a businesspersons club, etc.), find a coffee house to hang out in, get a part-time job that opens up many relationships, meet parents through your kids' activities, and so on. Most of us will do best, if possible, to seek out those who are most like ourselves. For example, if you are a formally educated thirty-year-old mother who likes to be active outside the home, then find women who are at a similar place in life.

Westerners, if they are married, often like to socialize couple-to-couple. But this is not the case in many of the cultures in which we live and work. Discover how relationships form in your setting.

12. Men work outside the home. As mentioned previously, I strongly urge male workers to establish a place, such as an office, *outside the home* to base your activities during the day. Not only do men spend time with other men mainly in the workplace, but spending all day at home will seem strange in most contexts.

13. Use the "Discovery Course" or other investigative Bible study. The Discovery Course (see http://www.rmuller.com/discovery.pdf) can be a useful tool in a wide variety of unreached contexts. It is surprisingly easy to ask this question: "Rajah, I know you are a man who loves God and continually wants to learn more spiritual truth. As I have read your holy book, I know you are also open to the New Testament. Would you join me for a six-part study of the most important things about al-Masih [Arabic for *Christ*] from the New Testament? How about getting together every Tuesday after work?" You don't even have to know the person very well to make this invitation. Our experience is that people say yes most of the time. And if they decline, even the proposal was a good witness.

This simple course has been instrumental in leading many to faith. It has been translated and used in around twenty countries and has even been made into a dramatized video in Arabic. Mike, a friend of mine in the Middle East, recently got a copy of this video and decided to try it out. He told a local friend who sold ice cream from a van, and whom Mike had talked with for years, about the video. The man said he'd be around the next morning to watch the first of six parts. After watching Part 1, Mike asked, "Do you want to come next week for Part 2?" But his friend insisted, "No. We must continue to watch the rest right now!"—which they did, without breaks. Hours later, at the end of it all, he gave his heart to Christ and was burdened to help the rest of his family find the way to heaven.

14. Pray for the sick in Jesus' name. Many people movements have begun with people seeing Jesus first as healer and then as savior, as among the Bhojpuri of India.[11] Here's something any of us can do: Simply say to your friend, "When Jesus was on earth, he very often miraculously healed the sick, right?" "Yes." Then ask, "Where is he right now?" "He is alive, with God in heaven." Then you can say, "Jesus instructed his followers to pray for the sick in his name. Do you mind if I pray right now, in Jesus' name, that God would heal you?" "No, please do." Of course, we can pray for other personal or family concerns as well (employment, broken relationships, etc.).

15. Bring up Jesus in the first thirty minutes. A close friend of mine, who *is* an evangelist, advises all gospel workers to somehow bring up Jesus with every new acquaintance in the first thirty minutes of conversation. Why? Sociologists say that we share virtually all the things that are most important to us with a new relationship within the first half-hour of total talk time. In other words, if you speak to a neighbor six times for five minutes per conversation over the period of a month, you will have most likely told him most of what is most central in your life. So if Jesus is somewhere in the list of the top ten most important things in your life, then at least one reference to him should come out of your mouth in some way early on in the relationship. Veteran workers know that if you don't bring up Christ early on, it becomes harder and harder to do so later.

Here is a typical example of being up-front about Jesus, from a team in Asia:

> There was some exceptional news this last Friday. A guy that Rob became friends with over a year ago brought a friend of his to the bookstore on Tuesday; they talked at length and were given materials to read. The friend of the friend came back, and he brought his wife. With ready hearts, through tears and thanksgiving, they have joined "the family"!! You'd be amazed (maybe, maybe not) at how the conversation went, the questions asked about "Now what do we do?", etc., etc. Pretty cool stuff. Though there have been "ups and downs" for us this year and last year, these kinds of "ups" sure make it worth it all. At least these kinds of things are affirming to us when we sometimes feel like others would rather us "not be so visible or up-front with the good news." There have been numerous times that people have come because they know where to come and who to come to. Sure, there are down sides, and we know the Lord uses other approaches, without a doubt. But we know there are several now in the kingdom because we not only have the opportunity to be more open, but are willing to do so even if there is a cost.

16. Four doable steps. Even if you feel you are the most non of all non-evangelists ever to hit unreached soil, here is a sort of minimal "easy plan" that *anyone* can follow: 1) Pray for opportunities at the beginning of each day; 2) Spend time with people, or at least spend time trying to meet people (see Point 11 above); 3) In conversations, try to ask questions that help you get to know the person and that get to real life, or heart, matters; 4) Don't be surprised if God answers your prayers. I'm not trying to promote an easy path; I'm merely offering this to those who may feel defeated or frozen. Anyone can do those four things.

17. Rejoice that the results are in God's hands. Rejoice in the knowledge that you will sow many seeds and probably won't see all the results. In other words, just because you aren't seeing direct results doesn't mean that there aren't any. This was driven home to us between the time of being in Egypt and going to our next country. We were in the United States, and Liz was eight and a half months pregnant with our third child. She was uncomfortable, and we had a bad argument about something (my fault, no doubt), so she went out for some retail therapy. As she went down the aisle, leaning on her cart, a voice called out from behind, "Liz. Liz. Do you remember me?" Fayza was an Asian gal whom Liz had befriended in our college ministry years earlier, before we had embarked to Egypt. "Let me show you something." She pulled out a fully worn New Testament. "Remember you gave this to me? After you moved away I read this and believed. Then I told my whole family here about the way of salvation, and many of them also believe." Liz might have gone the rest of her life without knowing this, except that God decided to bless her in this instance. But many times we won't learn about the fruit until we arrive in heaven.

APOSTOLIC EVANGELISM

A pioneer evangelist friend of mine brought to my attention the fact that "friendship evangelism" (building relationships one-on-one and *then* sharing Christ) was *not* the model of the apostles in the New Testament. When seeking a breakthrough for the gospel among an unreached people group, the apostles generally reached out to large numbers at a time, preaching or using other methods to cast a broader "net." Even when individuals were involved (e.g., Lydia in Philippi), it was not after a lengthy personal relationship, and invariably involved their wider network of relationships. Thus, this approach in evangelism was a vital building block in the early church, even as it must be today in pioneer church planting.

In our organization, experience has born this out. The teams I have led have seen several come to faith, but almost none of them were our close friends or neighbors. One of our most effective church planters once lamented to me how they had lived in the same neighborhood for eight years and had shared Christ with virtually everyone. They lived at the level of the people and adapted very well culturally. They had even prayed for physical healing for several and had seen some remarkable answers to such prayers. But none of these neighbors had come to faith. All of their fruit, rather, had come from outreaches further afield. This is not uncommon.

So what is apostolic evangelism? It is the exposing of many to the gospel in order to find the few who are spiritually responsive. A sister organization defines it as "any bold evangelism outside your neighborhood." A friend defines it as "evangelism by a group, to a group, to win a group." Usually apostolic evangelism involves a program, plan, or event. Examples would include following up people from radio broadcasts, hosting an event with a speaker, holding a party for many guests (for example, around a Christian holiday), hosting an event where you pray for the sick, canvassing an area with a spiritual survey and praying for opportunities to present Christ, and so on.

In one instance I was with a group in Sri Lanka and the plan was to do servant evangelism by picking up the trash scattered around a large neighborhood field. I bought a roll of bags and away we went. As I went into a bush area to clean up, someone grabbed my arm and advised me not to go in there, as the local people knew there still might be mines there from a recent conflict! Soon many were joining us in the cleanup and our efforts opened up dozens of warm relationships. Finally, one in our group had the idea that with a bulldozer and some minimal equipment we could give the neighborhood a good volleyball court. The local people received this proposal with enthusiasm and appreciation. The next week saw the first volleyball tournament between our team and a certain unnamed-but-famous political group! All this has since opened up a wider and somewhat fruitful church planting effort in that part of the city, so needy for the gospel.

I personally find this approach to evangelism among resistant people to be quite reinvigorating for several reasons. First of all, I have no doubt that the Lord is stirring the hearts of some in the particular city where I am laboring. There are His elect here. There are sheep who will hear Christ's voice. But I'm not so confident that I could find them with a slow friendship evangelism only approach. Let's say the Spirit is stirring and opening the hearts of 1 percent of the population. But if I have put all my eggs in one basket of a handful of friendships, then what is the chance that they are part of that 1 percent? Broader "nets," or "filters," are essential. Secondly, wide evangelism among a people is essential for a church planting movement. David Garrison places "Abundant Evangelism" in the category of "ten universal elements at work in every Church Planting Movement."[12] He writes, "Essential to every movement is the principle of over-sowing. Just as nature requires a tree to drop thousands of seeds to produce a single sapling, or a human body to generate hundreds of eggs to yield a single baby, so it is with evangelism."[13] And thirdly, this opens up many doors of effective ministry for those who may not be gifted personal evangelists.

Does this mean that apostolic workers need no longer bother with personal evangelism? Certainly not! For one thing, the love of Christ compels us to share Christ with whomever we can, including our friends and neighbors. Most workers will not be equipped for apostolic evangelism until they have learned the language *and the culture* very well, including having communicated the way of salvation many, many times one-on-one with people. Most should focus on friendship evangelism for the first four years on the field. And modeling one's personal witness will continue to be a priority in our discipling of believers.

Now, I know what you're thinking: How can you promote bold, possibly public forms of evangelism for some of our most hostile contexts? Arrest, jail, expulsion, or worse may result. Biblically, of course, those are not reasons to not proclaim Jesus. There certainly may be strategic or tactical concerns that limit what kinds of apostolic evangelism you should do. God will give you the wisdom and the boldness you need for these matters, as you seek Him. Nonetheless, I do know that all across the 10/40 Window teams are carrying out various forms of apostolic evangelism, even in places you would not expect.

Evangelism FAQs

1. Do I need to be experienced and adept at ministry in the supernatural to be effective?

Answer: I hope not, as that would disqualify most workers. There is no question that many today are coming to know Christ after a healing, a deliverance, a dream, or a vision. However, I personally hear of more people putting their faith in Christ as a result of reading the New Testament than from instances of the miraculous.

2. Should I only share Christ in the context of witnessing to a whole group, such as an extended family or social network, in the hope that all will come to Christ at once—i.e., a multi-individual, mutually interdependent decision and consensus to follow Christ? Isn't *net fishing* better than *line fishing*?

   Answer: I rejoice over any kind of witness. So if you feel called to pursue a whole clan rather than witness to individuals, God's speed. However, there is one factor that I think some miss in the ongoing debate about hoping a whole group comes to Christ together: if an extended family has been won to Christ, it almost always first started with a key individual believing and following Christ *for a period of time*. I can think of countless examples. Call it the "Gideon factor." First Gideon had to risk all in order to follow Yahweh alone; then his family and later the nation were won as a result of his tested and persevering faith. After twenty-eight years in this sort of ministry, I cannot think of one example of a whole group or extended family embracing Christ all together at once without one or two key individuals doing so first. I'm not saying such examples don't exist—just that I don't know of one. I'm convinced there is still a role for seeking to win individuals (and then working with him or her to win their wider network)!

3. Is it essential that our witness be coupled with humanitarian work?

   Answer: I believe this really depends on your context and your calling. I don't believe it is an "absolute must," either biblically or strategically. But showing the compassion of Christ in meeting urgent physical needs of local people may be the Lord's leading in your ministry, and God has certainly used such demonstrations of practical love around the world to move people's hearts.

4. Is there a place for a critical witness, for example, highlighting problems in the local people's holy book?

Answer: Yes and no. There are people who come to a place in their lives in which if they are confronted with difficulties in their own religion they will consider Christ with an open mind. But generally speaking, majoring on a negative approach will be counterproductive. As Livingstone writes: "To decry Mohammad for his failings is to forget his heroism, and the merit of his efforts in calling Arabs to seriously obey the one true God. To focus on Koranic contradictions and errors is to miss its teaching about God's activity in nature, or the ethical duties of mankind. To attack Islam because of what it has failed to do, is to forget both its contributions to European culture and Christianity's failure to change its own societies."[14]

5. Should I quote verses from the people's holy book in my witnessing?

Answer: You should certainly use verses from the Bible, but whether or not to use their holy book is a trickier question. Those who say yes point out two vital facts: 1) If you start with their book, you are starting where your friend is at, with what presently has credibility and authority in his or her life; and 2) Their book may contain many positive statements about Jesus, the New Testament, Christians, and even concepts of salvation. Those who respond in the negative point out that by quoting their book you might be inadvertently communicating that you see it as authoritative. And if you just stick to presenting Jesus and the truth as it is in the Bible, you will lack nothing in witnessing to the spiritually receptive. Personally I think both sides have it right, and that it sort of depends on your gifts. Certainly to use their book well and to avoid mistakes and pitfalls requires lots of skill—but some do have those gifts.

CONCLUSION

"Ask, and it will be given to you; seek, and you will find; knock, and it will be opened to you. For everyone who asks receives, and he who seeks finds, and to him who knocks it will be opened." (Matthew 7:7–8)

I used to think Jesus was just talking about prayer in this passage, but He's not. He's talking about a whole approach to life. It is about the person who knows what should be done, what can be done, what is the right thing, and what is possible, and that person *going for it* even when the obstacles are huge and the reasons for stopping are manifold. Examples of this "go for it" faith abound on the pages of Scripture: The leper who pushed through the crowds to brashly say to Jesus, "Lord, if You are willing, You can make me clean" (Matthew 8:2). The guys who took their paralyzed friend and cut a hole in the roof above Jesus while he was preaching (no doubt releasing chunks of clay and dust on Jesus' head in the process), because going through the door was a closed option (Mark 2:1–12). Jesus telling the presumptuous centurion, "Go! It will be done just as you believed it would" (Matthew 8:13; NIV). Jonathan to his young apprentice in faith: "Come and let us cross over to the garrison of these uncircumcised; perhaps the LORD will work for us, for the LORD is not restrained to save by many or by few" (1 Samuel 14:6).

A friend of mine was given a large tent (think circus) in a very unreached country. So he and his team pitched that tent in town after town, filling it with hundreds of people from the majority religion at a time. They all heard the good news, and those needing healing were prayed for. A large number were saved. When the team was threatened with death by scary guys carrying machine guns, they talked with them and pacified them. When hard rain made the ground impossible for a tent meeting, they requested—and received—permission from the regional cleric to use a community center. Somehow in our pre-field training we forgot to tell this team leader that this sort of thing is impossible in that part of the world, or that you can't do such things because of security concerns or excessive dangers. In fact, he and his family remained and ministered in that country for many more years.

When most people are moving forward on something and encounter an obstacle or something frightening, they stop. But perhaps God is teaching you to react differently. It's not that we are strong; rather, we are weak and faltering. Hopefully we are learning the lessons of pressing forward by faith, of how God loves to use the weak, and of how He rewards prevailing faith. As you willingly say yes to moving out of your comfort zone, may the power of God the Holy Spirit rest upon you in order to win a harvest for Christ, especially where the ground has been hard and barren for so very long! By the grace of God, the time of harvest among all peoples has arrived.

9
Discipling Local Believers

"Go therefore and make disciples of all the nations,
baptizing them in the name of the Father and the Son
and the Holy Spirit, teaching them to observe all that
I commanded you; and lo, I am with you always, even
to the end of the age." (Matthew 28:19–20)

Making disciples is at the very heart of the Great Commission. As a disciple (i.e., one who believes in Christ, follows Christ, and is eager to obey Christ), I "go" with the objective of making other disciples. That will involve leading people to Christ, helping them get established in their faith, and helping them to grow and to be *disciples* themselves. When that person is a disciple, endeavoring now to serve and obey Christ, he or she will also want to make other disciples. And the process goes on and on—a never-ending chain reaction.

Disciple-making is essentially this: influencing another believer over time to think like me and act like me, for Christ's sake. That might sound terribly presumptuous, and a humble response suggests something like, "My understanding of God and of life is flawed and my behavior is worse. So why would I want to do that?!" But that's exactly what Jesus calls us to do. Paul wasn't saying anything too unique when he wrote to the Philippians, "The things you have learned and received and heard and seen in me, practice these things, and the God of peace will be with you" (Philippians 4:9). Rather, this should be normative for all disciple-makers.

Please don't take this chapter on "discipling local believers" as in any way paternalistic, as if the expatriate worker has all the maturity and knowledge and the local believer has all the immaturity or problems. It's never a one-way street. The discipler is always stretched and learns from the disciple. These precious brothers and sisters from Hindu, Muslim, or Buddhist backgrounds (HBBs, MBBs, and BBBs, respectively) are equals and peers. Indeed, as they grow they will no doubt show us up in many areas of faith. Numerous times I have seen local believers also pastor or counsel and help many expatriate workers. Discipling can go both ways. Many of you reading this book have had the wonderful blessing of being discipled or mentored in your Christian life. Shouldn't you turn around and give the same gift to others? We all need to grow, and we all need to spiritually reproduce. Discipling younger followers of Christ cross-culturally is a key way to help them on that road.

What Is Discipling?

What we mean by *discipling* is simply this: one who is more advanced in the Lord coming alongside a brother or sister for a few years, to very intentionally befriend them, support them, and help them grow in Christ. Though others are involved, this mentoring relationship is primarily one-on-one. There is a deliberate commitment to the discipling relationship from both sides. It is said that when you disciple a younger believer you are reproducing yourself. That can be a little daunting. But we need to remember that even in physical reproduction we are not creating clones. Our kids are special and unique—not carbon copies of ourselves. Nonetheless, in discipling, as in physical reproduction, we have the tremendous opportunity to bring up another, and to pass on knowledge, wisdom, values, training, and strengths, so that the next generation moves that much further ahead. As Jack Welch, the famous former CEO of General Electric, once said, "Before you become a leader, success is all about growing yourself. When you become a leader, success is all about growing others."[1]

Discipling has been likened to training someone to pilot an airplane. That person can study aviation, wind patterns, and navigation in the classroom. But at some point the student only moves forward with the benefit of hours and hours of one-on-one personalized training. The flight trainer takes the trainee up in the air and demonstrates various flying techniques as the learner looks on and takes notes. At some point the trainee takes the yoke, but only with the trainer right there to guide and correct and prevent crashing into a mountain. This phase goes on for some time. Then eventually comes the day of the first solo flight! After more hours of supervised solo flying, the trainee is licensed as a pilot. Eventually, the new pilot might become a trainer. If this long process is essential in learning to pilot an aircraft, how much more valuable it is to progress in all aspects in Christ, and to mature as a minister of the gospel.

Fortunately, Scripture provides innumerable examples of one-on-one spiritual mentoring: Moses with Joshua, Elijah with Elisha, Jesus with the inner circle of Peter, James, and John, Barnabas with Saul/Paul, Paul with Timothy, and many others. Indeed, when we look at all of the various names of pioneer gospel workers associated with Paul, especially during his lengthy Ephesus stay, it becomes clear how high a priority it was for Paul to reproduce new workers. It has been said that Paul's teams were *reproductive machines*! So when we look at the challenge of somehow creating church planting movements among all unreached peoples, can there be anything more crucial than developing leaders by discipling faithful believers?

While there are certainly unique aspects to discipling a believer from a Buddhist, Hindu, or Muslim background, the process is much the same as discipling any other brother or sister. When workers have discipling experience in their home country before heading to the field—both as the discipler and the one being discipled—it will greatly help them when it comes to mentoring disciples. In addition, some of the old tools of discipling, such as *The Lost Art of Disciple Making* by LeRoy Eims[2] and *Disciples Are Made, Not Born* by Walter Hendrickson,[3] still remain tremendously helpful.

EIGHT KEYS TO EFFECTIVE DISCIPLING

1) Don't fear failure. When we start off mentoring a younger brother or sister we can tremble at the thought of steering them wrongly. Will they be ruined if I don't do it just right? Will they

face harder troubles if I don't prepare them well? Relax! Share your life, Christ's love, and the Word of God. Learn by doing. Even if you aren't the world's best discipler, God is sovereign and He will use you because your heart is willing.

2) Disciple as Jesus discipled. Did he suffocate the Twelve with the mother of all teaching programs? No. Here is what He did: He called them to relationship and to a commitment to grow; He spent lots of time with them; He taught them and then gave them opportunities to obey and "practice" what they were learning; He at times corrected them; He sent them out in ministry; He encouraged them to work as a group, and He gave them a vision for how the Father would use them in extraordinary ways to change the world. Simple!

In this kind of discipling, which is more important: relationship or teaching content? The answer to this question is similar to the answer to the question of which wing of an airplane is more important: the right or the left! Both are absolutely indispensable. As Paul said to the Thessalonian believers, "Having so fond an affection for you, we were well-pleased to impart to you not only the gospel of God but also our own lives, because you had become very dear to us" (1 Thessalonians 2:8). It is never just teaching and training, but rather it is life-to-life. We spend time together in all aspects of life: in my home, in his home, on the job, in sports or recreation, in the market, with our families, time together with the Lord, and so on.

Not only do we soon get to know them quite well, but they come to know us well too. They see our flaws, our sins, our struggles. No one expects a perfect discipler. They can encourage us, pray for us, even challenge or admonish us where appropriate. They get to see the grace of God at work in us, as we too repent and grow.

3) Nonetheless, what we teach is so very vital. Learning and ministering the Word of God is at the heart of discipling: "The things which you have heard from me in the presence of many witnesses, entrust these to faithful men who will be able to teach others also" (2 Timothy 2:2). There is no greater ministry of the

Word of God than ministering it to those we are discipling. We teach them to live life by the Word of God. They learn to draw on it daily as spiritual milk and solid food. They grow in their understanding and grasp of the Scriptures. They learn how to read and study for themselves. And they learn to apply it and minister it to other believers.

4) While it is important that they grow in understanding the Bible, their learning to obey Christ is even more important. Bible content without challenge to obedience and application is hollow. But continued calls to obedience without growing spiritual understanding and context can be haphazard. Yes, Jesus said in the Great Commission that we make disciples by teaching them to obey Him. But notice this does involve *teaching*; and it is teaching them "all that I commanded." As Paul said to the Ephesian elders: "I did not shrink from declaring to you the whole purpose of God" (Acts 20:27).

Obedience-oriented discipling is core. I obey Him because of His love and because I see it as in my best interest. But when I am not fully persuaded that His way is best, I still need to obey Him, because He is Lord. The gospel enters the mind. It touches the heart. It must also change the will and *heart motives*. As disciplers, we are in the business of life transformation involving the will and heart. Around the world, far more fellowships in pioneer contexts have been ruined by obedience-to-Christ issues and character issues than by persecution.

5) Since discipling is inherently reproductive, help those you disciple to understand from early on that the two of you have embarked on a road that will lead to them discipling others. They are not an end node. They are a link in God's redemptive plan.

6) Discipling believers in hostile contexts usually calls for special perseverance. Most followers of Christ from a Muslim background, for example, face unusual problems and threats. There is fear, persecution, emotional struggles from leaving one's religious heritage, heightened tensions or ruptures in the family, and so on. As a result, especially with younger ones, they may not be as faithful and teachable as we might want. You may have

more appointments broken than kept. You might think things are going great, only to be shocked by Mahmoud's actions all of a sudden. There may come a time to stop discipling Mahmoud, if he isn't serious about growing. But you probably have to stick with him a bit longer than your first inclinations. I am certainly glad my past mentors stayed with me even when I was more than a little flaky.

7) Make your discipling multidimensional. Don't just settle on one or two areas. Rather, over time make sure you are helping those you disciple in all areas, particularly in:

    a. Their walk with God.

    b. Their family life: their relationships with parents and siblings, as well as their spouse and children, if they are married.

    c. Their work life.

    d. Their life in the body of Christ: relationships with other believers; their role in the fellowship.

    e. Other matters of personal character: for example, overcoming "the deeds of the flesh" (Galatians 5:19–21) and growing in "the fruit of the Spirit" (5:22–23).

8) We disciple them into community. Even though a mentoring relationship is often largely one-on-one, it is crucially important that those we disciple link with others in the body of Christ as soon as possible. Often we don't see who are the most faithful, those committed individuals whom we should really invest in, until they emerge out of a group. As a fellowship group emerges, local believers should be in the middle of it, committed to the Lord's mandate for community. We are not to grow in isolation, but rather "we are to grow up in all aspects into Him who is the head, even Christ, from whom the whole body, being fitted and held together by what every joint supplies, according to the proper working of each individual part, causes the growth of the body for the building up of itself in love" (Ephesians 4:15–16).

A discipler is not a substitute for the body of Christ. A vital component of a new believer's growing in obedience to Christ is obeying Him in regard to His teachings on the community of faith. Over the years I have observed discipleship plans that involve working one-on-one only, keeping believers isolated from one another. I have never seen that approach succeed.

How to Disciple

So, pulling all these things together, how does it work? Most of us need some simple, straightforward steps for starting out on something like this—some rails to run on. Let's say you have met Ibrahim, a believer who has known the Lord for a year or so but who, due to isolation, has not yet grown up in Christ very much. You would like to come alongside him and help him mature in the Lord, and also help him become part of the church you believe by faith will emerge. We can think of your discipling relationship with Ibrahim as more or less consisting of four steps:

1) Propose the discipling relationship to Ibrahim. Share from the Word how Jesus formed committed relationships with twelve disciples. He first called them to spend time with him (John 1:35–39), and a bit later on to be trained for fruitfulness (Matthew 4:18–20). While Ibrahim will be Jesus' disciple—not *your* disciple—the discipling process is still much the same. Explain what you are proposing and ask Ibrahim for a clear yes or no decision. Something like this: "Brother Ibrahim, my affection and respect for you continues to grow. I propose that you and I embark on a discipleship relationship. This means we will be even more intentional in our friendship and the time we spend together. We will regularly spend time together in prayer and in the Word, with the goal of your growth in Christ. I will grow through our relationship too. There is also the goal that you will be able to disciple others, too, eventually. Would you pray about this proposal and then give me your decision?"

2) Begin investing in the relationship in earnest, as explained in the second of the eight "keys to effective discipling" above. Become friends. Pray for each other. Become more and more trusting and

transparent with each other. Spend time together in all aspects of life. And let accountability begin.

3) Make sure you have focused times of being in the Word and prayer together at least once a week. These don't have to be regularly scheduled times; but most people will be more consistent if they are.

What should be the content of your teaching? There are discipleship courses you can use. The Discovery Course is a good start for new believers (see chapter 8). There is the "SEAN" course.[4] Organizations like the Navigators or Campus Crusade for Christ have good material. Or you may feel more comfortable simply coming up with your own stuff. And last but in no ways least, it is always an excellent option simply to work through key passages of Scripture together. Indeed, one very important objective in your discipling of Ibrahim will be to train him how to study passages in-depth on his own. As early as possible, ask Ibrahim to be responsible sometimes to prepare and lead your study together.

Any Bible studies you present should be simple and practical, and hopefully Ibrahim will say to himself, "I could also present that study or a similar one to others." At some point you will want to give Ibrahim assignments to complete on his own. If Ibrahim is not literate, this obviously changes things. See appendix 4 on Orality and Steve Evans' excellent work in the area of "biblical storying."

Finally, if you are discipling others, make an effort to come together as a small group—in addition to your one-on-one times. This can greatly accelerate Ibrahim's sense of growth, as he becomes excited to be following Christ with the support of two or three others who are committed to him.

4) Early on you are going to want to remind Ibrahim of the biblical concept of reproduction, and that the goal is for him to become a "discipler" himself. This will probably surprise and frighten him at first. But over time he will realize that he too has something to offer younger believers, and this can become a strong motivator

in his walk with the Lord. When the time is right, work with Ibrahim to make this goal a reality.

SPECIAL CHALLENGES

As mentioned earlier, discipling cross-culturally is similar to discipling a believer from our own culture. However, there are some significant differences and hurdles, especially in resistant or hostile environments. We have to be prepared to help our dear friends face these unique difficulties, as much as we are able. Here are some of these unique challenges:

Rejection by Family and Society. In India, for a Hindu to become a follower of Christ often means being forced out of one's caste and grafted into a low "Christian caste." Here the point of crossing the line is not so much baptism or praying to Jesus as Lord as it is becoming an active member of a "Christian" church.[5] In many Arab contexts, dabbling in church attendance or reading the Injil (New Testament) is usually not an insurmountable problem, but rather the issue is brought to a head at baptism. The point is that church planters need to understand the culture they're in and work hard to help new believers remain in their families and heritage, for Christ's sake, to whatever extent possible.

Self-identity. Now that they are believing in and following Christ, how do converts identify themselves to others? How do they wish to be perceived by Christians? By friends or family in the majority religion? By the government? When new believers first come to faith, there is usually a brief period of time when the discipler encourages them to simply "keep their head down" and not provoke attention to their new faith. They first need to grow and become more grounded in the gospel, hopefully, before having to explain or defend what has happened in their lives.

For this reason the self-identity issue may not have to be resolved right away. Teach new believers about being respectful of their parents and other older family members. Explain to them that their parents or siblings will be much more open to finding out about their new faith if they first show themselves to be changed people in terms of family relationships: more obedient children, more loving husbands or wives, more willing to confess when they have been wrong and to ask for forgiveness. Many young believers have led their spouses or family to the Lord by slow and patient witness through changed lives and by using the opportunities to witness verbally as they have learned more.

But sooner or later each new follower of Christ needs to be able to answer the question, "What are you? Hindu [for example]? Christian? Something else?" Those who haven't thought this through and are unprepared will simply make matters harder for themselves. Around the world, believers from Muslim background answer this question in different ways. In a few places the MBBs say they are now "Christians," usually using the Arabic word *masihiyiin*. This might be due to the philosophy of the expatriate workers among them, or the believers themselves may feel a strong urge to move away from their former religion as they embrace Christ. However, this approach is probably used by only a minority of such disciples around the world, as taking on the label *Christian* conveys not just turning to Christ as Savior but connotes unwanted cultural or even political baggage as well, which is definitely not desirable. In Central Asia, for a Muslim to say he or she has become a "Christian" can suggest that they have become somehow Russian and a traitor to their people. At the other end of the spectrum, in many places MBBs continue to call themselves Muslims. Indeed, in contexts of C5 type contextualization,[6] this is the norm, as MBBs continue to fast during Ramadan, pray five times a day, and attend the mosque. They wish to follow Christ without risking cutting off relationships or their cultural heritage. In the middle of these two approaches are disciples who simply call themselves *mu'miniin* ("believers"), leaving the issue somewhat open. When pressed to be more specific, they might answer the question in different ways, depending on who is asking and why. We recall how believers in the New Testament were simply designated as belonging to "the Way" (Acts 9:2; 19:9, 23; 24:14, 22).

This question of self-identity is usually not an individual decision, but one determined by a community of believers. Of course, if a believer is part of a larger group it makes resolving this issue simpler, as "strength in numbers" makes it easier to take on a particular identity. For example, "insider movements" refer to movements of new believers and fellowship groups that remain inside their original community of faith (e.g., Hindu community, Muslim *umma*), even as they follow Christ. This connection is perhaps easier to maintain if there are hundreds of such believers doing it together.

Fear. As described earlier in this book, many believers face an assortment of dangers and threats as a result of their determination to follow Christ: from immediate family, other relatives, the police, the courts, extremists, employers, and so on. Therefore, it is perfectly understandable that they will experience great struggles with fear, and this may cause their growth to short-circuit. We must meet this struggle with them with great empathy and support. While expatriate workers also face special threats (e.g., the unique struggles of living as a Westerner in many politically troubled countries; and the fact that more expatriate gospel workers have been martyred in recent years in the Middle East than have MBBs), it generally won't be helpful to try to compare situations. Rather we must impress upon them how the Lord understands their circumstances and stands with them. Their trials for His sake are precious in His sight. Nonetheless, "Do not fear" is probably the most repeated command of Christ. The last thing Paul and Barnabas did with the believers from their first journey was to prepare them for suffering: "Through many tribulations we must enter the kingdom of God" (Acts 14:22).

In my experience, as new believers in hostile environments walk along the pathway of growth in Christ, fear can stand in that road like a growling lion. Until the believer gets past that lion, he or she will likely not develop further. Growth will stop until they get around that lion. Some measure of victory over fear is essential to further progress. The discipler can patiently minister the various teachings of Christ about the Father's sovereign love and care.

Employment (or Lack Thereof). The economies of most of the developing countries that pioneer church planters work in are not good. Unemployment rates of 20 percent or higher are common. Many of the disciples we are wanting to help are unemployed or doing only unskilled labor; and if they are working, they're swamped with a sixty-hour workweek. In this environment, the expatriate is tempted to jump in and help by offering jobs. But that is almost never a good idea (see *Employing Local Believers* below). What *is* often beneficial is helping them receive vocational training.

Legalism. Islam as a system is unabashedly religious law oriented. Followers gain "points" by all manner of works: praying five times a day, regularly going to the mosque, dutifully fasting in Ramadan, and so forth. There are even extra credit schemes for receiving double points or ten-times points for the sinner whose *hisab* or "account" is especially low. Children are taught from the earliest ages that Allah will decide their eternal destiny simply by means of the two-sided balance scale: good works on the right, bad deeds on the left. Favor with Allah is *earned*. There is no other way. Hinduism has similar avenues to merit with the gods: for example, fasting and keeping vigil in *Yekadasi* or a variety of arduous pilgrimages.

Because of this, those discipling in these contexts must not assume that because he or she taught about grace in week 3, Ibrahim now gets it. Ibrahim or Farida will have grasped God's forgiveness in Christ; but there will always be enormous gravity pulling their mindset back to the god of works. We must instill grace over and over and over. We must find all kinds of ways to instruct them in God's acceptance of them on the basis of Christ's atonement alone and all the implications for that throughout life, rather than focusing only on the initial forgiveness of one's sins. And not only does Christ's sacrifice remove my guilt, it also takes away my shame—a much more important concept in most Eastern cultures than in the West.

Children. Children belonging to our brothers and sisters under persecution are precious; and they are the next generation of the church, even as they bring a reality and depth to that church now! In some contexts I've worked with, nearly half the believers are kids. Praise the Lord! They will be the first in their families to be raised under the freedom of the good news. Despite this heritage, they also face special pain. Uncles, aunts, and grandparents can pull them away from their parents' faith, either overtly or subtly. At school and in their neighborhoods they become the objects of rejection, ridicule, abuse, or worse. There have been too many stories from our fields of believing children even being martyred as punishment for their faith or their parents' faith. Are you prepared to help the one you are discipling get ready for this?

Surveillance and Interrogations. Probably the majority of persecuted believers around the world are watched closely by the authorities. This is a steady, unremitting pressure. Periodically many are called in to the security offices (or "secret police") for interviews. This always means threats, lies, coercion, and pressures to renounce Christ or stop involvement in a believing fellowship. The only antidote is to anticipate it, prepare for it, and be spiritually ready for it. If there is a group of mutually supportive believers, they can teach each other what to expect and how to overcome. It is common that when one is called in to the secret police, word quickly goes out to dozens to fire up prayer. As a result, some have even looked forward to being called in!

Secret police units routinely employ two special tricks of their trade: Firstly, they will often lie about what other believers have said or done. They will insinuate that so-and-so has informed on them or is secretly working for the government. Their aim is to divide believers and break up fellowships. Secondly, they can threaten the frightened follower of Christ with such things as getting fired from one's job, torture, serious criminal charges leading to prison, or breaking up one's marriage. Usually these threats are exaggerated. The aim is simply to get the believer scared and shaken up. Such a person is then more pliable for information or for doing the police's bidding. Disciples have to be ready for these two tactics!

Rejection from CBBs. I hesitate to bring this up, because all around the world many national believers from Christian backgrounds are showing immense love and courage in reaching Hindus, Buddhists, and Muslims for Christ and serving those who respond to Him. Many have taken huge risks and made great sacrifices to help new believers be built up in their faith. But there are some individual CBBs and churches where this is not true. There are too many stories of believers starting to attend a particular church, only to be told after a couple of months that some church members would actually prefer that they stopped attending. These church members may fear that the HBB's or BBB's or MBB's presence brings danger on them. Or they may doubt the genuineness of, for instance, Ibrahim's faith. Or they may fear that Ibrahim will seek one of their CBB daughters for marriage. The fact is that while many CBB churches are working through these problems, this sort of rejection still occurs all too often. Added to this is the differences of culture (e.g., in vocabulary, women's dress, etc.). Either the new believer from the other culture will not fit in and hence feel rejected, or else he will try to conform culturally—thereby cutting himself off from his family and friends. Personally speaking, I believe that while such believers can certainly gain encouragement from CBB churches, it is usually best to make the special fellowship (e.g., HBB) one's "church home."

Second-guessing Their New Faith. Imagine being raised from birth in a particular religion, indoctrinated in it every day of your life—at home, at the temple or mosque, and at school in religion classes. Then you come to know and accept the truth of Christ, give your life to Him, and personally experience His love and grace. But you are still surrounded by everyone and everything that tells you consciously and subconsciously that you have made a terrible mistake, you've been deceived, your old religion is the only right way, and you are apostate! These disciples need strengthening in their faith in Christ daily, and the most powerful reassurance will come from other believers from the same background.

Lack of Biblical Heritage. When a Western unbeliever comes to faith, he or she will already be aware of some biblical stories and teaching. It is part of our cultural background, whether or not we were "raised Christian." As a result, expatriate workers in developing countries can sometimes take for granted a minimum biblical understanding. That, of course, is a mistake. We mustn't assume anything. For example, according to Islam Abraham's most important son was Ishmael; people don't sin, they just make mistakes; there was no "fall," but rather man has always been immoral (no pre-fall sinless Adam and Eve); blood sacrifice is only a ritual with no atonement meaning; Jesus did not die on the cross; and no man—even al-Masih (Christ)—can pay for the sins of another. The point is, every important truth must be explicitly taught from the Word.

Disunity. In many cultures, group unity, cooperation, compromise, and easy correction of offenses are rare or nonexistent. Schisms, disunity, and irreparable relationships are the norm. Though it may not be difficult to pull believers together into a good fellowship group in some countries or cultures, in environments where persecution persists it can seem impossible. Attempts to unify believers break up more often than they succeed and last. Church growth will only occur when believers work through these things and where group splits become rare.

MONEY ISSUES

This is a bit of a minefield, but it would be almost criminal for me not to deal with this a bit. I cannot think of a single church planting ministry among unreached peoples, or a discipling ministry with HBBs/MBBs/BBBs, that didn't have to grapple at least a little bit with money matters. Is this because our local brothers and sisters have a particular problem with money or wrong motives? Certainly not! So many times they are better than their expatriate CPer friends in terms of not being money-oriented and being able to trust God with their needs. Nonetheless, tensions over finances too often threaten to divide believers from the apostolic workers who are ministering to see Christ made complete among them. By touching on these issues, my aim is not to create a "we-they" division, but rather to help us all prevent such moving apart from taking root. We don't prevent these kinds of potential rifts by avoiding unavoidable issues.

Consider these three areas:

- Those who have particular needs and want some help.
- Expatriate workers employing believers.
- Believers who enter vocational ministry.

Let's try to tackle these one at a time.

People with Needs

Generally these are urgent needs, rather than just the brother who wants to upgrade his cell phone. Local believers are oftentimes truly in difficulty: loss of employment, urgent medical needs, even being unable to provide food for one's family. Let's say Ibrahim has a "discipler" from America or Holland or wherever, who may not be rich by Western standards but is certainly rich by local standards. Ibrahim's daughter needs urgent surgery, which will cost $100, but he doesn't have it. What to do? Isn't a friend supposed to help a friend in the local culture? Doesn't 1 John 3:17 say, "Whoever has the world's goods, and sees his brother in need and closes his heart against him, how does the love of God abide in him?" The CPer's family might not mind at all the loss of $100, but it might make all the difference in the world for Ibrahim, who desperately needs $100 for his daughter's urgent surgery.

So it's easy, right—just give to those in need? But wait! Local followers of Christ who are known to have received money from foreigners might have their witness totally discredited. Ibrahim could be accused of "selling his religion." Plus, if the foreigner is always there to help, will the local believers learn to count on God and see His sovereign provision for their needs? Will the relationship between the worker and the believer become increasingly strained over financial questions? Will the motivations for "discipleship" become confused? How many times I have heard workers tell me that when they made it clear they weren't there as a source of finances, suddenly people weren't so interested in their Bible studies or even in Christ. And finally, the foreign worker being the source of funds for people's needs is inherently irreproducible. In other words, in a growing movement of fellowships people cannot be dependent on expatriate subsidies, but must see God as provider for themselves.

So that's it, then—don't give a nickel? Well, I'm going to have to frustrate the reader and say I don't think there is one simple answer. Every situation will require "wisdom from above" and should drive us to our knees. Generally, if not giving requested money will kill a relationship, then it is probably not a good relationship. We can also ask for counsel from locals. When there is at least a small group of believers from the unreached people group, it is essential that you or they establish a fund for helping out those with urgent needs. Then the group can insist that those with needs go to the local believers who administer the fund and not to the foreigners. Let two or three hear "cases" and disburse help as appropriate. Let whoever wants to give to the fund give in secret, including the foreigner. And let all believers be taught the stewardship of giving.

A close Egyptian friend once asked me for a $300 short-term loan. It felt a little awkward, but I decided, "Sure. Why not?" Not only did he pay it back promptly, but he moved to the United States, eventually gave his heart to Christ, became a huge success in business, and also became one of our ministry's financial supporters! He and his family are dear friends to this day. That is sort of an unusual story, and too often things like this don't turn out well at all.

Employing Local Believers

First of all, there are many reasons for expatriate CP workers to employ local believers they may be associated with in ministry. As Jesus said, the worker is worthy of his wages. Many expatriate workers have tentmaking businesses, humanitarian enterprises, translation projects, or are in need of language tutoring. Being in the workplace together can provide more opportunities for fellowship and discipleship. Local believers can have a witness in your business among the unbelieving employees. And what local people are going to be more reliable, honest, and understanding than those who are following Christ? Likewise, as has already been noted, believers usually have an urgent, legitimate need for decent employment.

So that's it, right—go for it? Well, were it that simple! Some are adamant that when you mix employment with discipling both get hurt. What if Ibrahim is a model employee, but is now backsliding away from Christ? Or not obeying the Bible in how he treats his wife? Or what about the opposite: What if he is a faithful disciple but a lousy employee, and you are inclined to fire him? And what about all the other believers in the fellowship group who need work but you haven't hired them, so there are hurt feelings? Is it really possible to plant a healthy church that is on its own two feet if from the start all the leaders are on your payroll?

In my observations, maybe nine times out of ten employing local believers doesn't work out well. There are tensions or demands over the level of pay. Motives are mixed. The church can crumble when you stop employing certain people. The believers' relatives view them as on the foreigners' payroll—"and so of course you're a Christian."

In general I counsel that if a local disciple is to be employed in a worker's business or NGO (nongovernmental organization) that discipleship not be mixed with employment. In other words, let's say there are two or three separate expatriate teams or ministries in the city. If Sok is active in the ministry Team A is leading (e.g., a young church plant), it is probably not as much of a potential problem if he's working for Team B's NGO (and hopefully Team B respects that Sok is part of Team A's church plant and will not interfere with that relationship.) Of course, none of these recommendations are firm rules. May the Lord give you wisdom.

Local Believers in Vocational Ministry

As pioneering ministries develop, questions like this inevitably arise, "Seng is a faithful man whom God is clearly using. Should he be encouraged to somehow be in the Lord's work full-time?" Sometimes the initiative for this comes from the church planters and other times from the individual believer. At other times it might arise from unhelpful interference from outside ministries: for example, some ministry that is not involved with Seng nor discipling him comes along and offers him a job and salary to follow up on Bible correspondence courses. Because I will be dealing with this whole area later in the chapter on church planting movements, I won't go into it more here.

CONCLUSION

To be placed by God into a discipling relationship with a follower of Christ from an unreached people group is an incredible privilege indeed! What an honor and joy it is to spiritually reproduce one's faith with those believers on the frontlines of the expansion of the kingdom of God. Disciple-making in pioneer work probably will not be as glittery as large-scale evangelism or as recognized as certain leadership roles. The worker may simply labor in obscurity for years. But nothing else is as strategic for the kingdom of God. I think of some leaders from unreached peoples who are now powerfully changing their whole countries for Christ. In each case, behind them were patient workers who poured their very lives into them over many years. Isn't the diligent and skillful discipler worthy of double honor?

10
Leadership in the Apostolic Task

A colonel gets a big promotion—a new position in the Pentagon. On his first day he is quite pleased with his large oak-paneled office. Feeling a bit insecure, he is more than a little eager to impress people. Around ten o'clock that morning, a sergeant knocks on the door. As the colonel barks out "Come in," he picks up the phone and says, "Yes, General, I have completed the report for the President, and I'll send it right over." He hangs up the phone and says, "Yes, Sergeant, what is it?" The sergeant replies, "Nothing, Sir. I'm just here to install the telephone line."

As Christians, we realize that leadership is not about being a big shot. It's not about somehow enhancing the respect people might have for us or about enjoying the perks of position (which are almost nonexistent in this work of pioneer church planting anyway). Rather, it's about gifts and calling, and a willingness to take initiative and responsibility, to shepherd, lead, and feed God's people in a way that hopefully makes good things happen for Christ's sake. Leadership is servanthood—for Christ and for His body. Men and women called to the pioneer church planting task invariably pay a high price. Apostolic leaders pay an even higher price.

All the books written on "Christian leadership" could fill a gymnasium. This is not an attempt to compete with them. Rather, we will focus specifically on leadership in the apostolic task, on the pioneer church planting team. We want to look at the nature of that task, the challenges to good team leadership, biblical principles underpinning our understanding of accountability and oversight, and certain practicalities on the field.

Anything important, anything worthwhile, should be led well and managed well. The consistent testimony of Scripture is that the right leadership in the work of God is critically important. Our organization has been accused of being "team leader-centric," and I suppose that is true. Working in teams is one of our six foundational principles (sometimes referred to as our "nonnegotiables"). Effective leadership of those teams is essential if the team is going to have clear vision and direction, carry on well spiritually over time, and be able to stay on task all along the way. Our *Ethos Document* contains the following: "Leadership is done by those who are spiritually qualified, servant leaders, and who are, in fact, being followed. Individual team leaders may design the decision-making process of their teams, but the International Office holds the team leader responsible for final decisions." Because team leaders bear this weighty and sacred responsibility, team members are aware that they are under the spiritual and organizational authority of the team leader, who oversees them and their ministry.

Our teams are not dictated to from "headquarters." We believe our teams and team leaders should have lots of entrepreneurial freedom in how they go about pursuing the church planting goals God has put on their hearts, within our organization's "nonnegotiables" and the team's own stated vision. This freedom can even add to the team leader's independence and our overall "team leader-centricity." Therefore it is also a big part of our thinking that our teams are "semiautonomous." Though there is considerable latitude given to our teams and team leaders, the team leaders themselves are also under authority and oversight, and all are supposed to be "eager for coaching and committed to accountability." We have also tried to build in a few other mechanisms so that the team members are heard and have recourse when communication between them and the team leader is not going well.

This is perhaps not a perfect setup, but it's the best we've developed so far in trying to stay true to our principles of apostolic team church planting. It all combines to make us quite sober regarding the special role the team leader has before God, his team, and the people the Lord has called them to reach.

What's a Team Leader to Do?

I was recently training a group of around thirty new team leaders, and being the sneaky person I am, I threw out the question, "What are the responsibilities a good team leader should undertake in order to be effective?" Hands went up and these new leaders eagerly jumped into brainstorming on such a pertinent question. There was not a person there who did not have strong opinions on what is really important, such as:

- Meet regularly with individual team members to review life and ministry.
- Help team members set up their housing and logistics.
- Maintain a strong walk with God.
- Be a strong, charismatic leader.
- Pray a lot and have spiritual retreats.
- Consistently provide vision for the team.
- Recruit just the right new team members.
- Be an example in language learning.
- Report regularly to your overseer and get help.
- Lead team meetings.
- Host important visitors.
- Be a good listener.
- Make sure the team is well-run, well-administrated—having clear team policies and efficient logistics.
- Communicate well with the sending bases and churches.
- Be a diligent evangelist and disciple-maker.
- Study and teach the Bible effectively.
- Organize fun and profitable team retreats.
- Meet the pastoral needs of the team.
- Be a good example in your own tentmaking (whether it be a business, humanitarian project, or whatever); maintain solid residency and viability.

- Be an apostolic, "make things happen" church planter, enabling the new fellowship to go from strength to strength.

- Develop strong relationships with other workers in town, as well as with leaders of the national church.

- Stay up on your e-mail, including participation in organization-wide discussion groups.

- Maintain a vibrant and healthy marriage, and be a strong example of good parenting.

- Keep your financial support healthy.

- Attend all leaders' conferences and regional conferences, as well as participate in special training opportunities.

- Keep everyone's computers current with the latest software. (OK, this one wasn't mentioned. Just seeing if you're still reading!)

By the time we had filled up several flipchart sheets, most had slumped into their chairs about half of a foot. So I asked a second question, "OK, who wants to quit right now?" All hands went up! Not wanting them to wallow in despair too long, I offered this hope: "Folks, you cannot do all those tasks. You have no choice but to *triage*. In other words, take all the expectations on you as team leader—whether they be from the organization, from your team members, from your church back home, from yourself, or wherever—and divide them into three categories: What you must do, what you must delegate to others, and what will simply be left undone." Hope levels rose a bit in the room.

It's so very easy for us to get our priorities messed up. The story goes that a man who was at the Super Bowl (the championship game for American football) spied an open seat in a better section, right on the 50-yard line, and decided to move down there. After a few plays he asked the man next to him why the seat might be empty in the sold-out stadium. His neighbor explained how the ticket had belonged to his wife who had passed away. "Oh, I'm very sorry to hear that. But don't you have any family or friends you could have given the ticket to?" the man asked. He replied, "Sure. But they're all at the funeral." Confused priorities!

Here are the six responsibilities that I believe are essential for every team leader to personally maintain, even if other things may suffer.

1. Be Spiritually Healthy

This may be stating the obvious. But what could be more important? If the leader is not "in the Spirit" in his life and ministry, he may be working eighty hours a week and doing all sorts of tasks, but it will all be without spiritual profit. Daily "quiet times"—times in personal prayer and Bible reading and/or study—are not a luxury. Confessing sin and not allowing any area of disobedience to persist are essential if one is to be in "fellowship with God" and "walking in the Light" (1 John 1). Cooperating with the Lord in His plans to work in me for growth are part of the picture, as well as not allowing broken relationships with others to fester and spoil my relationship with God.

One of the biggest threats to the leader's walk with God is the proverbial *tyranny of the urgent*—where urgent tasks prevent important matters from getting oxygen, as it were. When there are so many tasks "that I absolutely must get done by two o'clock," how easy it is to let our quiet times be the first casualty. We give in to this, and pretty soon it becomes a lifestyle. The Lord calls us back, "Dan, you are worried and bothered about so many things; but only one thing is necessary" (Luke 10:41–42, without the *Dan*).

In the Bible, leadership is almost synonymous with wisdom. "Who among you is wise and understanding? Let him show by his good behavior his deeds in the gentleness of wisdom . . . The wisdom from above is first pure, then peaceable, gentle, reasonable, full of mercy and good fruits, unwavering, without hypocrisy" (James 3:13, 17). Only by the Spirit of God can we leaders operate in this kind of wisdom.

2. Cultivate Vision and Faith

An advertisement in the Wall Street Journal says, "Vision is having an acute sense of the possible. It is seeing what others don't see, and when those of similar vision are drawn together something extraordinary happens." When God raises up an apostolic leader, He gives him a burden and a vision for what He will accomplish through the team. In a sense, the team leader can see it, touch it, and smell it, even though it does not yet exist in time.

Unfortunately, we often confuse this endowment of vision and faith with personality. We think someone is a visionary leader if they are charismatic, if they sparkle and glitter. It is true that leaders have to be able to lead. Are there people following? But from what I have seen, those who have this sort of vision and faith from the Lord for a particular apostolic ministry are able to make sure that the team catches it—and this ability does not come in only one personality package. The key is that the leader's vision will be infectious.

A few years back a member of a rather new team wanted to encourage his leader, "I want to commend you for how much you've fueled the team with *vision*." This sort of caught the team leader by surprise, as the team leader didn't have a particularly "visionary personality." So the team member clarified, "It's not that we have had vision meetings or something like that. It's just that everyone on the team sees clearly what we are going after, because you see it so plainly. We have often talked about where we are going, and how the Lord is going to get us there. So it's palpable. You won't be deterred, and you won't let us be deterred either. We've all caught the vision as a result, and that is really motivating."

3. Be Significantly Involved in Church Planting and Set the Overall Direction

I made a strategic mistake in my first leadership assignment in Egypt. As we were a team of fifteen adults, there was always lots to do in terms of meetings, planning, communications, problem-solving, and administration. I allowed "team management" to become a full-time job, and as a result my learning of Arabic really suffered. Pretty soon a handful of men and women came to faith, and I found myself "on the outside looking in" in terms of my personal involvement in discipling and gathering. Now I am not saying that the team leader should always be in the middle of everything related to church planting. But I do believe he should be significantly involved, as this is the main purpose for the team being there.

I sometimes wish we had a title other than "team leader" for this role. Why? Because it subtly implies that the main role of the leader is to lead the team and take care of their needs. That is not the case. Rather, the main role of the team leader is to get the church planted, and providing effective leadership of the team is a means to that end. Sometimes we get the *em-PHA-sis* on the wrong *syl-LA-ble*.

A number of times there has been a person on the team who is clearly the most gifted leader and church planter. But that person says he wants to let someone else be the official team leader so that he can major on church planting. Invariably the reason given is because of the many burdens of being the team leader, such as reporting, organizing, and pastoral care. In these situations I normally advise that this is the right response to the issues, but the wrong solution. It is generally better to have this person remain as the team leader, in order to set the vision, direction, and spiritual environment, but to call another leader on the team to serve as "chief of staff" or "associate team leader." Ideally, the most apostolically gifted person on the team should be the team leader.

4. Listen

We all know how good it feels when we are with someone and they really focus in and listen to what we have to say. Team leaders, ask yourselves: What is it that team members want more—to be heard, or to always have their way? Most people, if they know that they can give their input and it will be respected and considered, will not insist on matters going their way. They understand that sometimes decisions will go a different way, as the team leader has to juggle other factors and other people's feelings. But as long as they know they have participated and have been heard, they can still own those decisions.

5. Oversee Individual Team Members

A good friend of mine who has a very magnetic personality was a team leader for several years. People would excitedly catch his vision and join him on the field; his team grew to nearly thirty members at one point. I remember my first visit there. One after another, all the team members told me the same story: They were thrilled to join this team, but after six months they had become frustrated, almost disillusioned. "We're not being given any direction. We don't know where we fit. Day to day we're not sure what we're supposed to be doing" was the repeated refrain. Steadily team members moved away or joined other teams.

Team leaders have a special opportunity and a special obligation. The team leader is the one person on Planet Earth whom people *expect* to oversee the team members' lives and ministries. The team members themselves, the organization, and all the senders and churches back home assume their people will be looked after and their work guided and kept accountable; and that falls squarely on the team leader. For team members on financial support—which are the majority—this means the team leader is also their supervisor vocationally or professionally. Here are four mechanisms that make up a reasonable oversight package: 1) Weekly activity reporting (usually using some simple form); 2) One-on-one reviews every other month; 3) Setting and revising of "hard targets" (see below) every six months; 4) One of those times—once a year—reviewing performance and attainments, as well as setting out new goals. Of course, the nature of your oversight will have to be adjusted for those who are not full-time in the work (e.g., some mothers of young children).

The issue of pastoral care often arises. See below for more discussion on this. We expect the team leader to facilitate growth and be responsible to help the team members find resources for their personal well-being. But as many apostolic leaders are not strong themselves in pastoral care, this may need to come from others.

Your team members are going to need encouragement and affirmation. That which comes from you, their leader, has the highest value. John Robinson, former head football coach of the University of Southern California Trojans, said, "I never criticize a player until they are first convinced of my unconditional confidence in their abilities."

Team leaders have a special opportunity for the kingdom. If a team member can be 50 percent effective simply left to herself, she can be 75 percent or 100 percent effective if the leader spends just a minimal amount of time and energy giving encouragement and direction. This is truly *multiplying* your time.

6. Model Being Accountable and Teachable

We learn a lesson from the pagan centurion in Matthew 8:9: "For I myself am a man under authority, with soldiers under me. I tell this one, 'Go,' and he goes; and that one, 'Come,' and he comes. I say to my servant, 'Do this,' and he does it" (NIV). He recognized that just as he had responsibility and authority over the soldiers under him, so too he was responsible and accountable to the leader above him. In my ten years as field director I've observed a strong correlation here: Those team leaders who are faithful and responsive to the overseer over them generally are treated likewise by their own team members. Likewise, those who are evasive or consistently inconsistent in reporting are usually the ones who experience the biggest frustrations with their team members—people not listening, doing their own thing, making major decisions without consulting, passive-aggressive behavior, and even mutiny. The wise team leader will be very faithful in his own accountability, and will make sure his team knows it.

"Listen to counsel and accept discipline, that you may be wise the rest of your days" (Proverbs 19:20). Am I willing to accept correction and constructive criticism? Do I know I need coaching and seek it out, or do I feel that I've already got all the answers? How does my team perceive me in these matters? When was the last time my team heard me say, "I'm weak in this area, so I'm going to get training or take such-and-such class"? If we want hungry and coachable team members, we have to model it.

Unessential Tasks

So if these are the six indispensable priorities for the effective team leader, what are some responsibilities the leader can let go of? The following list is not meant to be complete. And it doesn't mean that you should stay out of all these areas. You can do some of them, depending on your gifts and what your team is like. But in general, delegate whatever you can avoid doing yourself and have handled reasonably well by someone else.

- *Leading all the activities and meetings of the team.* When the team has six or more members, I advise the leader to appoint a "chief of staff" or "associate team leader" who can carry many of these responsibilities. Also, some team leaders will form a small "leadership core" to help them with team leadership functions.

Not a pub ball thing (handwritten)

- *Being involved in **all** aspects of church planting.* (This is not a contradiction of the third point above.)

- *Being overly involved with e-mail.* Not long ago I was in the home of one of our most effective team leaders and church planters. Somehow it came up that he looks at his e-mail only twice a week (and *never* at the discussion groups, except for key announcements). Many of us go overboard on e-mail, and there's a significant price to be paid for it.

Someone else (handwritten)

- *Language learning supervision of the team.* (See chapter 6, where having a language supervisor other than the team leader is discussed).

- *Taking care of all the team logistics and administration.* Again, if you lead a large team not only are you able to delegate more, but you absolutely must to survive. It's common for me to see team leaders running around getting apartments ready for new arrivals, making countless airport trips, fixing computers, handling team finances, organizing functions, etc., all while their team members have the time and the desire to help. "But if I delegate it, it won't get done as well" a leader might object. A team leader friend of mine shared this rule of thumb with me: if he can delegate something and have it done even 75 percent as well as he would do it himself, he'll delegate it. He later told me he dropped the threshold to 50 percent!

- *Being the primary pastoral care provider on the team.* All leaders will want to be caring and encouraging concerning whatever coworkers are going through. There certainly will be needs. We have a wide spectrum of gifts in the pastoral area among our team leaders: from the "Barnabas" types to the "General Patton" types. As a leader you will need to know your own strengths and weaknesses, and lead with your gifts. If you are pastorally strong, then you will definitely want to make that a big part of how you lead the team. But if you aren't, you should probably look for other ways to have your team's pastoral needs met—either by others on the team or by someone outside the team. Some team leaders also feel strongly that it is unwise to invite people onto the team who are highly needy, either in terms of remedial work or ongoing pastoral care.

- *Obtaining your doctorate.* I'm going to get in trouble on this one. If God is calling you to be a missiologist or a seminary professor, then you definitely need a doctorate. But for those He has called to apostolic church planting where Christ is not named, *most* will not need this or want it. Perhaps getting a doctorate *is* the Lord's will for a portion of pioneer workers, but I can't imagine that this is the case for a large percentage.

- *Personally overseeing **every** member of the team.* (This is not a contradiction of the fifth point above.) On larger teams it is fine to have younger, greener members overseen by senior team members. Likewise, I generally advise leaders of larger teams to appoint a senior woman to oversee the ministries of the women on the team, as she will be able to do a much better job. I remember meeting with a single woman on our team in Egypt, who was a friend and respected coworker. I gently asked for some goals for the time period. When she burst into tears, I sort of knew I wasn't the best one for this oversight relationship!

One more thing: In view of all the responsibilities that the team leader *will* need to fulfill, it is important that he have a residency platform that is minimally demanding of his time. Let's face it: it's often easier to do "platform" work than church planting. It's easy to justify your time investment by saying, "I need to do this to be able to stay here." Platform work is immediately gratifying—you are often meeting physical needs and accomplishing something. You have something to show for your time. It's easy to get people back home to support your platform. I especially see this dynamic as a downfall for men, because platforms are tangible—and men like to build! Conversely, church planting work is often unrewarding. It's hard. It's uphill. It's not immediately satisfying. And it gets spiritually attacked! You have to really be focused to stay with it, because it can be so discouraging. Team leaders must set the pace on keeping the focus on church planting.

Accountability in the Apostolic Task

Oversight and *accountability* are two words whose meanings can be a bit ambiguous. When we hear these words, no doubt we all conjure up different concepts of what they mean. That's unfortunate, since their role in the apostolic task—especially if it is in any way on a team basis—is extremely important. The dictionary definition of *accountable* is "responsible to somebody or for something."[1] And to *oversee* is "to watch over, manage, and direct somebody or a task done by somebody."[2] But are these just Western concepts, perhaps born out of the management craze of the past two decades?

The story goes that a Huey Cobra helicopter, while practicing autorotations during a military night exercise, landed on its tail rotor, separating the tail boom from the rest of the aircraft. Fortunately the aircraft wound up on its skids, and slid down the runway doing 360s in a shower of sparks. As the Cobra passed the tower, the following exchange occurred: Tower: "Sir, do you need assistance?" Cobra: "I don't know, Tower. I ain't done crashin' yet!" That's sort of how we feel about the whole area of accountability: we're still trying to figure it all out. Nonetheless, we need to work hard to try to learn all that Scripture has to teach us about it, as this has a direct bearing on how we work together on the field in planting churches. A team leader who does not have a solid biblical framework regarding the spiritual exercise of authority will almost surely lead in a way that is vague or unsure, and that profits no one. Likewise, team members with a weak understanding will not know their biblical options and responsibilities, and may not always respond to their leaders in a Christ-honoring way. How much of the turmoil on our teams rises from a lack of understanding of what the Bible teaches?

More than once I've heard it said that we don't need another book on leadership but what we need is a book on "followership." We live in a day in which leaders are universally viewed with distrust, and this has carried over into the church. Dallas Willard writes, "The Western segment of the church today lives in a bubble of historical illusion about the meaning of discipleship and the gospel. We are dominated by the essentially Enlightenment values that rule American culture: pursuit of happiness, unrestricted freedom of choice, disdain of authority."[3] Similarly, Paul McKaughan writes, "We spend much time teaching leadership and assume that following is natural when our Bible and experience tells us that humans are basically anarchists not followers. We humans are sheep each going our own way. This is not just the tendency of those who won't follow our lead. It is as much our fallen human nature as it is theirs. Independence and self-sufficiency are never positive biblical traits. Almost every time we see it in scripture we note that bad things happen. Healthy dependency is a more biblical norm. We were created so as to need each other."[4]

I wish I could say that our shared difficulty in following leaders has not impacted teams, but that workers always selflessly serve the people and their coworkers. But let's be real. We are all products of our own generation to one degree or another. If "followership" has been a problem for us baby boomers, word has it that it is only going to be more pronounced with our Gen-X brothers and sisters. In Scripture godly leaders are spoken of as a means of grace, whether referring to godly kings, apostles, elders, teachers, etc. People who don't have good leaders are spoken of as "sheep without a shepherd," implying a certain harshness of life. So what does the Bible teach on these issues? Why do we need leaders? What is submission? What is authority? Why do we need "reporting"?

Leadership and Authority in the Body of Christ

Jesus taught his disciples: "But you are not to be called 'Rabbi,' for you have only one Master and you are all brothers. And do not call anyone on earth 'father,' for you have one Father, and he is in heaven. Nor are you to be called 'teacher,' for you have one Teacher, the Christ. The greatest among you will be your servant. For whoever exalts himself will be humbled, and whoever humbles himself will be exalted" (Matthew 23:8–12 NIV). Passages like this are foundational. All of our relationships in the body, in an ultimate sense, are "peer-to-peer." The backdrop for us is an equality of value, dignity, and heavenly citizenship. Jesus likewise taught, "You know that those who are recognized as rulers of the Gentiles lord it over them; and their great men exercise authority over them. But it is not this way among you, but whoever wishes to become great among you shall be your servant; and whoever wishes to be first among you shall be slave of all" (Mark 10:42-44). Whatever leadership is, it's essentially *serving*.

But are these the only relevant passages in the New Testament? What about these?

"The elders who rule well are to be considered worthy of double honor, especially those who work hard at preaching and teaching" (1 Timothy 5:17). One of the responsibilities of elders is to "rule" (Greek *proisteemi*); and it's hard work.

"But we request of you, brethren, that you appreciate those who diligently labor among you, and have charge over you in the Lord and give you instruction" (1 Thessalonians 5:12). Leaders are those who "have charge over" those in their care.

"We have different gifts, according to the grace given us. If a man's gift is . . . leadership, let him govern diligently" (Romans 12:8 NIV). Paul here speaks not only of elders, but of leaders in general. Jesus is our leader, but He has ordained a plan whereby He works through human leaders.

"Obey your leaders and submit to their authority. They keep watch over you as men who must give an account. Obey them so that their work will be a joy, not a burden, for that would be of no advantage to you" (Hebrews 13:17 NIV). Here again the writer speaks not only about our relationship with elders, but with our leaders in general. Leaders in the body have oversight responsibility and authority. They themselves must give account. (He doesn't say if this is to God or to the human leaders over them. Perhaps it could be both.) Their work could be joyful or burdensome, depending on how I respond. God calls me to *obey* and *submit*—not very politically correct words in today's environment.

Do passages such as these apply to leadership, oversight, and accountability on apostolic field teams—for example, in the team leader-team member relationship? I believe they do.

Spiritual Authority Versus Positional Authority

Positional authority is that which individuals have by virtue of their position or status in an organization, such as "team leader," "team leader overseer," "regional coordinator," etc. Irrespective of the person, because the position carries a certain responsibility and authority, people under them should cooperate with their leadership. Spiritual authority is different. It means that individuals may or may not have any positional authority or rank, but people respond positively to their influence and input because of the quality of their lives, accomplishments, experience, and wisdom.

Some say we need only respond to spiritual authority. Isn't that a half-truth? Indeed, character, true spiritual maturity, and proven experience are of huge importance in the Bible. But if we *only* respond to spiritual authority one can quickly see how that is a recipe for chaos during hard times and for things ultimately breaking down: at the end of the day, one responds to the spiritual authority of others only when one feels like it, according to how he or she perceives their authority at the moment. To only be willing to respond to *spiritual* authority, is actually to be unwilling to submit to *any* authority.

But what about a leader's *style*? We want our teams to be effective. But as humans we also have a desire to be liked. Should we be assertive, heavy-handed, controlling, and directive? Or should we be unassertive, neglectful, winsome, passive, allow the team or members to drift, and operate strictly in consensus-building? Of course, these aren't truly *either-or* matters. We mustn't allow ourselves to be trapped by emotive connotations of words. No two leaders' styles are going to be exactly the same. Let us seek God to be the leader He has made us to be, to be teachable, and to grow to maturity in that leadership calling.

Leader-to-Leader Accountability

Most pioneer workers are leaders, whether or not they are "team leaders." They were leaders back home, or else they probably wouldn't be out there in the apostolic task. On the field they are going to be engaged in such ministries as discipling, planning evangelistic projects, teaching, mentoring, and preparing local elders—in other words, *leading*. So when we speak of the team leader to team member relationship, the nature of it is really leader-to-leader. Once again, we're grateful for how Scripture speaks to this.

First of all, we are exhorted to always allow other believers to speak into our lives:

- "The way of a fool is right in his own eyes, but a wise man is he who listens to counsel" (Proverbs 12:15).

- "He whose ear listens to the life-giving reproof will dwell among the wise. He who neglects discipline despises himself, but he who listens to reproof acquires understanding. The fear of the LORD is the instruction for wisdom, and before honor comes humility" (Proverbs 15:31–33).

- "Listen to counsel and accept discipline, That you may be wise the rest of your days" (Proverbs 19:20).

- "Be subject to one another in the fear of Christ" (Ephesians 5:21).

There was a curious incident in the beginning of the church that gets little press. Remember *Peter's* "second apostolic journey" (Acts 9:32–10:48 [the first being found in Acts 8:14–25])? His travels took him to Lydda and Joppa, and then the Spirit called him up to Caesarea in a unique way, giving him the same vision three times. (Ever notice how often things had to happen to Peter three times? Hmmm.) Anyway, we're all familiar with how the Lord wonderfully advanced the gospel to this collection of prominent Gentiles—Cornelius, his relatives, and his wider sphere of relationships—thus inaugurating the third, "ends of the earth" phase of Acts 1:8. All of them heard the preaching, believed, received the Holy Spirit, spoke in tongues, and were baptized by these Jewish Christians who, a week earlier, wouldn't have bought a bagel from them.

Notice what came next: "Now the apostles and the brethren who were throughout Judea heard that the Gentiles also had received the word of God. And when Peter came up to Jerusalem, those who were circumcised [i.e., everybody who was anybody] *took issue with him* [emphasis added], saying, 'You went to uncircumcised men and ate with them.' [This sentence should probably close with a question mark. And then left out of the best early manuscripts was the likely next question: *"What were you thinking?!"*] But Peter began speaking and proceeded to explain to them in orderly sequence, saying . . ." (Acts 11:1–4).

This is Peter! The lead apostle. The great "Preacher of Pentecost." The Rock upon whom the church will be built. And who is this calling him on the carpet? I wonder if formerly the not-too-humble, hothead Peter would have said something like this: "Get off my back. God just did a great work . . . *through me.* Who are you? Did you somehow miss those Bible studies Jesus gave about the worldwide reach of the gospel? About all those prophecies in the Torah of the Gentiles coming in? About grace? About His *other sheep*? You can take your deficient soteriology and . . ." But he didn't. He denied his pride and submitted to his fellow apostles and other leaders. Instead of being aggravated by these Jerusalem elders, he respected their position, and he trusted the Spirit to speak to them. That must have been really hard.

It shouldn't surprise us that most of the examples in the New Testament of leadership on apostolic teams revolve around Paul. Numerous times we find Paul being directive to the others about where and when to go, what to do, what to teach and emphasize, character admonitions, and correctives of their thinking (cf. Acts 16:1–3; 19:21–22; 20:4–6; 2 Timothy 4:9–15; Titus 3:12–13). The three epistles specifically between apostolic workers[5] (1 and 2 Timothy and Titus) are written in the imperative voice to a large extent.

In 1992 I was a field team leader, and after being in the United States on furlough I made the mistake of going back to the Middle East by way of our international office in Europe. I had assumed I was more or less in good stead. (OK—so I only turned in monthly reports about once a year.) Besides, the directors and I were buddies. But guess what? They locked me in a small room with them, shined a bright light in my face (maybe my memory is exaggerating a tad), and *nailed* me about not reporting and not being accountable. What could I say? I was guilty. So I went back home (on the field), pulled out my calendar, and circled the fifteenth of every month for the next twenty-four months. One way or another, team reports were going to be done by the fifteenth. And, by God's grace, they were. By the way, the next two years were a particularly fruitful period of ministry.

A few years ago our general director voluntarily stepped out of that role and returned to the field, as a team leader. He also was in the role of team leader overseer, overseeing a handful of teams, and accountable to me as field director for such. This has always felt a bit odd: me—a younger, wet-behind-the-ears, green nobody—overseeing a respected veteran leader like this. On his way out the door he said, "The more you keep on my back, the better results you'll get, and the better TLOing they'll get. And you can quote me to the young fellers. I'm a man under authority."

The point is that leaders should be the best at submitting to the legitimate authority of other leaders. Why do we welcome accountability? Because we are passionate about *the task*, for Jesus' sake.

Bringing It Together

In the New Testament examples, people were free in the Lord to join a team or not join a team (e.g., John Mark, Epaphroditus, Timothy, Silas, Urbanus, Luke, Epaphras, Euodia and Syntyche, Barnabas). It was a voluntary linking together for the task. But once they were on a team, the principles of leadership, accountability, and submission applied. Likewise, people could decide to break off from the team and not be reproved or disciplined for sin (e.g., John Mark's premature departure, Paul and Barnabas' mutual separation). In a modality (i.e., a local church) there is an element of submission to leaders which is not voluntary. But in a sodality (i.e., apostolic band) the joining or leaving seems to be voluntary. When one is on a team, or likewise in a broader network of teams (i.e., field agency), one needs to obey the scriptural principles concerning accountability and submission.

What about working within the context of a field agency? First of all, I believe we see hints of such networks in the New Testament. In general, you get the sense that the various apostolic bands were in mutually supportive relationships wherever possible. During Paul's lengthy time in Ephesus there evidently were several church planting teams that seemed to be networked together. Does the New Testament teach that we must have organizations for sending out workers? No. But there is certainly precedent for pulling together, and God calls us to wise stewardship. If a broader networking and international joint effort results in synergy, and greater CP effectiveness, it makes sense to do so. "Two are better than one, because they have a good return for their work: If one falls down, his friend can help him up. But pity the man who falls and has no one to help him up! Also, if two lie down together, they will keep warm. But how can one keep warm alone? Though one may be overpowered, two can defend themselves. A cord of three strands is not quickly broken" (Ecclesiastes 4:9–12 NIV). Does an apostolic team (e.g., from one local church) have to belong to an agency? No. But if they do, they should abide by the biblical principles of accountability within the context they join.

As team leaders are recruiting and building their team, they will want to be able to communicate clearly to people what they are calling them to join. It is strongly recommended that they develop two vital documents: 1) A Vision and Strategy Paper, which describes what the team wants to accomplish in the Lord, and a bit about how; and 2) A Memo of Understanding, which goes into more detail about team life and policies, and life on the field. See appendix 3. These two tools will greatly help the team leader to communicate his heart and vision, including on the subject of accountability, as well as to minimize misunderstandings later on.

What Accountability Looks Like

A ministry oversight relationship (e.g., team leader-team member) generally means this is the primary oversight and accountability relationship with regard to ministry. It is vertical (à la 1 Thessalonians 5:12), not peer-to-peer. It pertains to spiritual matters, to ministry and occupational issues, and to personal matters as they affect the ministry. It is also usually, though not necessarily always, the primary coaching or training relationship. If I am accountable to you in a ministry situation, here are the consequences:

useful for MOU

- It does not mean that you, the overseer, can necessarily do a better job than me, the "overseen." Oftentimes the opposite is the case.

- It does mean that you are viewing my life and ministry, in a sense, from above—seeing the forest and not just the trees—and therefore are able to think of good ideas, to spot pitfalls, and to see clearly priorities that I might miss. You are in a good position to hold me accountable.

- You are watching out for me in the two vital aspects of thriving spiritually and working on task.

- I am regularly informing you of all key aspects of my spiritual life and ministry. I am not intentionally withholding any important information from you.

- I welcome the tough questions from you on a regular basis. I am allowing you to fully monitor my life and ministry. Where you feel you can oversee me better by *measuring* certain activities (e.g., language learning progress, sharing the gospel), I welcome that. As someone has said, "The leader cannot manage and motivate what he or she can't measure," and "Wise management must measure the right things."

- You work with me to set goals and "hard targets" (specific one-time goals, or ongoing objectives, such as "Study the Bible in Arabic three hours each week"). You follow up on my progress.

- If I get stuck in any unhelpful patterns of passivity, I welcome you pushing me out of those, getting me *unstuck*. The Bible speaks to such "sins of omission": "Anyone, then, who knows the good he ought to do and doesn't do it, sins" (James 4:17 NIV).

- You can challenge my preconceived notions. I welcome your input in general.

- You must remind me of things we have agreed on: goals, hard targets, team or agency ethos, etc.

- I gladly receive exhortation, admonition, even discipline.

Very practically, here is why all of this is important:

1) This active oversight and accountability lets the leaders know what is happening, and gives them opportunity to influence it (to improve, to add, to correct, to network, etc.).

2) It gives leaders the opportunity to provide pastoral ministry and/ or mentoring.

3) Leaders cannot affirm and encourage when they are uninformed.

4) If a team leader or team member is not reporting, then effectively they are independent and not accountable.

5) Most pioneer church planting organizations are strongly committed to the biblical principle of accountability for all their members.

6) In my ten years of experience as a field director, when a team leader is not reporting, around half the time something pretty bad is being hidden (e.g., severe discouragement, team mutiny, even adultery). When accountability is breaking down, a leader *must* "get in the face" of those they are responsible for.

7) Bottom line: Effective oversight means more fruitful ministry for Jesus' sake among all unreached peoples.

SOME CONCLUSIONS

Professor Bobby Clinton reflects: "Leadership is complex, problematic, difficult and fraught with risk—which is why leadership is needed. Leadership is complex. Paul deals with a whole range of problems including moral issues, philosophical issues, practical everyday issues, social issues, theological issues, conceptual issues, methodological issues. Problems in a leadership situation are a main reason for the existence of leaders. Leaders must see problems not as hindrances to leadership but as the warp and woof of leadership responsibility."[6]

Too often we leaders have overlooked this vital admonition: "If [a man's gift] is leadership, let him govern diligently" (Romans 12:8 NIV). Paul wrote this in the context of church ministry, where his overall exhortation was, "Having gifts that differ according to the grace given to us, let us *use* them." It has to do with the stewardship of what God has given us to do, individually, while on this planet. It is a major part of our life that will enable us to hear later on, "Well done, good and faithful servant."

Paul is saying that the role of leaders is very important. Leaders have got to lead. When they don't, the body of Christ and the cause of Christ suffer. When leaders do lead, according to the Spirit's work through them, it is tremendously life-giving.

Today, a writer might exhort "to lead sensitively," or "to lead with a servant heart," or "to lead by building consensus," or "to lead with vision." And yet Paul, speaking by the Holy Spirit, curiously puts his finger on leading with *diligence*! This might seem particularly odd to young apostolic leaders, for whom diligence sort of "comes naturally." But Paul has a real insight here. The natural tendency of leaders over the long term is not toward diligence, but toward passivity. Have you experienced this? Eventually gravity pulls us all toward avoiding the hard work of giving good leadership, toward slowness, toward a lack of caring or an unwillingness to confront, and toward methodical bureaucracy rather than giving energetic, proactive, and courageous direction. Human nature works against us.

A wise friend of mine once remarked, "Dan, people not in leadership view Christian leaders as really having it good. Enjoyable, fulfilling stuff, with lots of perks and prestige. But in fact, soon after one begins a ministry of leading, he or she discovers that it can be a real drag. It's a burden. The hassles, stresses, and aggravations can be overwhelming. Basically it isn't worth it—at least from the standpoint of some earthly 'payback.' Just read 2 Corinthians 11:23–29 for a reality check! There's only one worthwhile reason for accepting leadership: the privilege of serving Christ, knowing of His reward in the next life."

As those whom God has raised up to give leadership in His global harvest among the least evangelized peoples, let us constantly keep this promise in front of us. Pray today about your team leadership role and how you are fulfilling it. And let us remain teachable and accountable to one another, that we might grow to become the leaders God intends us to be.

11

The Role of the Church
Planters in Church Planting

What exactly is the role of church planters in church planting? At first this question may seem a bit odd. "To plant the church, of course!" might be your first thought. Or you might reply, "That's easy. We learned in seminary that our part is to stay on the sidelines and just encourage the nationals." In reality, those who have been involved in pioneer church planting for very long immediately recognize that this question is not simple. Do the church planters, especially expatriate ones, get real involved in the believers' meetings or remain outside of them? Do they do much Bible teaching? What if local believers will be persecuted if they have much contact with the expatriates? Do the workers help set up or influence the new church and its structure, or do they leave all the key foundational issues to the local people to sort out for themselves? Do the workers live on-site or elsewhere? As it turns out, the question of the role of the church planters is one of the most determinative factors for how the church gets planted. The question is not a simple one, but it is a vital one.

There is a wide spectrum of views on these issues among church planters working with unreached peoples, and that kind of diversity in the apostolic community is a good thing. I personally do have some views on these matters, which I will share. However, it is important that we unpack the issues for church planting teams to answer for themselves. Likewise, I genuinely esteem my fellow workers who would approach these matters differently than I; and I don't mean the slightest disrespect toward those of other philosophies. The importance of this topic should drive us to the Lord for direction and send us to His Word to discover answers and examples.

A typical scenario may look something like this: The team is resident in a city for some time, learning the language, getting involved in the community, making friendships, and seeking to win people to Christ. At some point they lead one or two to faith, and also "discover" another one or two already existing believers—in this case, Hindu-background believers (HBBs). These HBBs are looking to them for friendship, spiritual support, teaching, and an example to follow. The team may have already succeeded in pulling these believers together into a fellowship group, or maybe they are just on the verge of doing so. The questions the team begins to ask themselves—and upon which many pioneer workers differ from each other—become:

- Do we now pull this fellowship group together, leading and teaching the people? Or do we somehow stay in the background and have local believers do all the leading and teaching from the beginning—even if the group consists only of new, immature believers?

- How do we follow up on each individual to get back to their social networks and try to win others to Christ? What do we do with those individuals who either don't have a social network or who get ostracized from their social network?

- Who should do the shepherding and pastoral care?

- How are decisions that affect the group going to be made?

- If we do lead the group and teach the Bible at first, at what point do we encourage HBBs to assume these responsibilities? If they are new believers now, when *will* they be ready? Pretty much all would agree that once some HBBs are appointed as elders, then they are responsible before God for the leading, teaching, and decision-making. But what about during the period of incubation before that point?

There are various analogies for this crucial period at the start of a new church or network of churches:

a. Think of someone *trying to start a bonfire*. He gathers the kindling and bigger pieces of wood. Somehow he gets a spark and a little flame going. He knows it could easily go out, but hopes it will grow. So he shields it with his hands and blows on it—not too much and not too little. He slowly adds more twigs, then sticks, then branches or logs. If the ingredients are good and dry, the fire will grow well. It they are wet, it will take much longer, and may go out altogether.

b. The *midwife* is there for the delivery of a baby. She is neither the mother nor the baby, but only a temporary party to help ensure a safe and healthy delivery. She can't do everything. But if she doesn't play her role, the baby may die.

c. For buildings to be built, *scaffolding* is used. It is not the building, but a temporary necessity for the building to be built well. Then it is taken down and used elsewhere to start another building.

Once you have one or more believers who are committed to Christ and willing to serve, the questions become real and must be answered. It is between this point and the later appointing of elders that church planting teams will differ on their approach to the role of the church planters. For the vast majority of apostolic church planters the end goal is the same, namely to end up with a church (or churches) where the local leaders are fully responsible and in control. A few expatriate church planters retain control even after elders are appointed, but I do not advocate that at all. We might still influence things later on—even as Paul did with the churches he founded—but it is the local elders who have the responsibility and authority before God for the new church. That is the direction we want to go.

Here are the ministry components that need to be carried out by *somebody* during the early days of a new fellowship group:

1. Discipling younger believers (whether one-on-one or in group settings—actually both are very important). Loving care as well as exhortations. Ministering through relationship. Training (e.g., how to share your testimony, pray for the sick, study the Bible).

2. Gathering believers. Initiating the group getting together and persuading believers of the importance of this and how it is

part of following Jesus. Planning one-time events (e.g., retreats, parties, special fellowships) as well as ongoing meetings.

3. Cultivating body life in the group in all aspects, including mutual care for one another, being involved in each others' lives, prayer, worship, sharing, the Lord's Supper, etc.

4. Teaching the Word, leading in group study. Building them up in "sound doctrine," to use the apostle Paul's phrase.

5. Problem-solving.

6. Pastoring: giving care and support to individuals and couples in their personal needs.

7. Developing leaders.

And here are some of the variables that will frame the question of the role of church planters for you:

1. *The nature of the believers that God brings into the picture.* If your team has led them all to faith, or they are otherwise all young believers, this will probably influence you to do most or all of the leading and teaching until you see the believers at a place where giving them the responsibility of group Bible teaching won't cause harm. As James 3:1 says, "Let not many of you become teachers, my brethren, knowing that as such we will incur a stricter judgment." However, even brand-new believers—and indeed pre-believers—should be urged to share what they know about Christ and what they have experienced from Him to others.

   If, on the other hand, you are linked with one or more mature and ministry-oriented believers early on, then of course they are going to be undertaking much of the shepherding and feeding of the flock from day one. Similarly, their age and life experience is a big factor. Elders are usually not going to be twenty-five-year-olds. If everyone in your group is young, that will affect your approach.

2. *Your philosophy of ministry.* If your highest priority is maintaining cultural purity and 100 percent indigenousness in how the believers fellowship and identify themselves, without

the slightest possibility of foreign influence, then that will probably trump all other considerations. Some church planters have even told me that they would not meet with a group of brand-new believers or teach them anything from the Word, nor instruct them on how to be the body of Christ, because it would be impossible not to taint their indigenous forms of body life if they did. Other philosophy of ministry issues would include how you see the local church; the role of Scripture; whether you envision planting a cell church, house churches, or large church; and your model of discipling.

3. *The vulnerability of local believers to persecution specifically because of contact with you.* In some pioneer church plants this is a major factor and greatly influences how the team seeks to be a catalyst for the church to develop. But I would say that in most of our contexts this is not an overwhelming issue.

4. *The value you place on incarnational issues, such as language fluency, lifestyle and cultural adaptation, and belonging.* An active role for church planters presupposes a good measure of language fluency and probably also that they are not too geographically distant from the believers, either in terms of physical distance or lifestyle.

Again, your approach in these four areas will steer what you do as church planters.

Finally, one last introductory comment. Sometimes the Lord brings one or more national brothers or sisters who are keen to partner in your church planting work. For example, it is not uncommon on our fields to find a national from a Christian background who has a call on his or her life to reach people from the majority (or resistant) group with the gospel (e.g., Buddhists). Even when they are not from the people group you are focused on, they have the language and, perhaps to a lesser degree, the culture, and probably many excellent relationship inroads with the Buddhists you're seeking to reach. Some teams have sought to build their CP team with mostly local CBBs (Christian-background believers) like this. This can be a tremendous boost to the church planting effort. But I don't think this greatly influences the question at hand (the role of the church planters in CP), as these coworkers are in a very real sense *outside* church planters too, and the issues pertain to them as they do to the expatriate workers.

SOME HELPFUL PASSAGES

The following passages (all in NIV) provide some excellent insights into how new churches were planted in the pioneer contexts of Crete, southern Galatia, Thessalonica, and Ephesus, and what the role of the apostolic church planters was in each case.

> Titus 1:5: "The reason I left you in Crete was that you might straighten out what was left unfinished and appoint elders in every town, as I directed you."

> Titus 2:15: "These, then, are the things you should teach. Encourage and rebuke with all authority. Do not let anyone despise you."

> Acts 14:23: "Paul and Barnabas appointed elders for them in each church and, with prayer and fasting, committed them to the Lord, in whom they had put their trust."

Observations . . .

1. Paul urged Titus, who was doing the nearly identical task that our teams are doing, to lead and to teach authoritatively. Titus was an outsider to Crete and a pioneer church planter.

2. Until indigenous leaders who have the spiritual and character qualifications to become elders are appointed, the work is not done. The church planters cannot simply walk away and say "We planted a church there," as the foundation is not yet complete. It would seem that appointing the initial elders is something for

the church planters to do, implying that their authoritative role is recognized and that they function out of that role.

3. The church planters' role was temporary, like that of scaffolding in the construction of a new building.

4. A clear distinction was made between the role of the church planters and that of the elders. The former came from the outside, and at some point left. The latter were local believers who stayed, and "eldered" indefinitely.

5. "Elders" (plural) were appointed in "every town"/"each church" (singular).

1 Thessalonians 2:7–13: "We were gentle among you, like a mother caring for her little children. We loved you so much that we were delighted to share with you not only the gospel of God but our lives as well, because you had become so dear to us. Surely you remember, brothers, our toil and hardship; we worked night and day in order not to be a burden to anyone while we preached the gospel of God to you.

"You are witnesses, and so is God, of how holy, righteous and blameless we were among you who believed. For you know that we dealt with each of you as a father deals with his own children, encouraging, comforting and urging you to live lives worthy of God, who calls you into his kingdom and glory.

"And we also thank God continually because, when you received the word of God, which you heard from us, you accepted it not as the word of men, but as it actually is, the word of God, which is at work in you who believe."

1 Thessalonians 4:2: "For you know what instructions we gave you by the authority of the Lord Jesus."

Titus 1:13: "This testimony is true. Therefore, rebuke them sharply, so that they will be sound in the faith."

Titus 2:1–2: "You must teach what is in accord with sound doctrine. Teach the older men to be temperate, worthy of respect, self-controlled, and sound in faith, in love and in endurance."

Acts 20:20–21, 27, 31, 34–35: "You [elders of the church in Ephesus] know that I have not hesitated to preach anything that would be helpful to you but have taught you publicly and from house to house. I have declared to both Jews and Greeks that they must turn to God in repentance and have faith in our Lord Jesus. . . . For I have not hesitated to proclaim to you the whole will of God. . . . So be on your guard! Remember that for three years I never stopped warning each of you night and day with tears. . . . You yourselves know that these hands of mine have supplied my own needs and the needs of my companions. In everything I did, I showed you that by this kind of hard work we must help the weak, remembering the words the Lord Jesus himself said: 'It is more blessed to give than to receive.'"

Observations . . .

1. At the core of the church planters' task is teaching sound doctrine, teaching how God wants us to live, exhorting, and even rebuking where necessary. It is also vital that we pour our lives out among the believers, and nurture them with love and care. Paul says that he and his team related to the Thessalonian believers like a mother. Then he says they dealt with them like a father.

2. Another dynamic that really becomes apparent in these passages is the importance of the modeling done by the apostolic starters of new churches, not only in giving visible examples of how to live the Christian life but also in modeling ministry. Let me insert here that *how* we model is also very important. For example, if I give a Bible study using PowerPoint and reference nuances in the Greek as well as theological developments over the centuries, I'm communicating that Bible teaching is something done only

by highly trained people. We need to model that which local believers can do. We must model in a way that is maximally *reproducible*.

3. Apostolic church planters are significantly involved in the lives of new believers. This implies a time investment, as well as living around each other—them being in your home and vice versa.

To Illustrate . . .

Hassan was a young, single Muslim man when we first met, and we hung out together a lot back in Egypt. He has since come to faith and has now been in the Lord for many years. In his testimony he describes how our family life had a real influence on him. One day, in particular, my wife, Liz, said she wanted to go to this health club where she could work out and relax. And she often met Egyptian women there and got to know them and practice her Arabic. I urged her to go, saying that I would watch our daughter, who was three years old at the time. Hassan was shocked, as that would be pretty unusual for a husband to do in his culture. Of course, not all he saw in me or in our home life was positive—but it was *real*. And the close friendship of being with us a lot at that level continued to build the witness. (One little postscript: Our marriage that year was at a real low point. All the stresses of life on the field in that first year, compounded by our flesh, took their toll on us. Isn't it wonderful how the Lord can still use us despite our immaturity?!)

A friend of mine who is a team leader in Asia told me how one day he came in to his apartment along with three friends, who were young believers. For some reason he and his wife wound up getting in a big fight—a loud and emotional argument—right in front of the believers. Later on, fearing he had just set back discipleship with them five years, he apologized to them. He was stunned as each one shared how honored they felt to witness such transparency before their eyes. They were so grateful that this man and his wife did not do what most of us would have done: mutter a few grunts under our breath and save the confrontation for later. These believers had no examples in their backgrounds of how a husband and wife can differ very strongly and emotionally and verbally over something, and yet maintain love and respect.

All of the above passages pertain to that initial incubation period for the nascent church. It would seem from these New Testament examples that for a group of new believers in a harsh environment to progress to a strong and mature point on their own, without the help and teaching of apostolic workers, would be pretty unlikely, and is not encouraged. Indeed, in our experience, most such situations without careful apostolic nurturing result in disintegrated or "stillborn" churches. This makes sense in light of these New Testament examples where the outside church planters played an absolutely vital role in getting the new church to the place where it could survive and thrive on its own—not just for a year or two, but hopefully for generations.

All pioneer apostolic workers want to plant churches that reproduce, even becoming a *movement* of rapid multiplication, if God so allows. It's like an apple: We can ask, "How many seeds are in this apple?" Or we can ask, "How many apples are in this seed?" Every new church has the potential to reproduce itself many times over. So should the expatriate church planters stay *outside* the fellowship in order to maximize the hands-on work of local believers, which is inherently more reproducible? Or should they work closely *inside* the fellowship to ensure a healthy first church in the chain, as it were?

Arguments for Minimal Foreigner Involvement

- Indigenousness and contextualization.
- The more that local believers are responsible for ministries early on, the more they are likely to take ownership for the work of God among their people. This will also force them to trust God.
- Better chance for a movement if locals have the reins as early as possible.

Arguments for a Greater Foreigner Role

- The New Testament examples.

- The risk of young believers having too heavy of a spiritual leadership or teaching responsibility before they are ready, causing danger both to themselves and to the embryonic church (cf. 1 Timothy 3:6; James 3:1). This threat is more acute when the group itself is mostly younger believers who are not mature in life, much less in faith.

- The concept of a temporary incubation period: that is, in order for the church to truly stand on its own feet it must first be dependent *for a while* on those God provides who better know the Lord and His Word and who are called to get the new church established.

- Better chance for a movement if what you birth is healthy (for example, in biology a new virus can have explosive reproduction only if it is strong and viable).

My own view, shaped by personal experience on the field as well as by serving in the role of field director for eleven years, is that concerns over foreign influence are important but secondary, by comparison, to laying solid biblical and spiritual foundations.

To Illustrate . . .

A recent report from one of our Middle East teams illustrates their view on this:

> Farid stood up, saying enthusiastically, "Today God has spoken to us. I can see what He wants to do through us." I [the team leader] was really happy at his positive response, as I had just spent the whole day presenting a teaching based on the Acts of the Apostles on how to plant and consolidate the church. Farid has become one of the most active leaders in the church. He is about fifty years old. His children, who range in age from primary school to college, are also following Jesus. Now he has been used by God to consolidate the evangelistic work of Boulos and establish eight churches in the areas outlying our city. He and the other church leaders are serving the Lord with dedication and enthusiasm, without regard for

the danger they may have to face. Five brothers and several sisters are also now in training.

In this case, it is precisely the active ministering of the foreign apostolic workers that is catalyzing this swift church reproduction.

BUT WHAT ABOUT HIGH-PERSECUTION ENVIRONMENTS?

The term "shadow pastoring" was coined by Nik Ripken, a highly experienced fellow worker from another agency who has been extremely helpful to many teams around the world. It arises from Nik's extensive interviews with over 500 individuals, around 40 percent of whom were MBBs in high persecution environments.

The basic idea is that expatriate gospel workers have to really limit their presence around groups of believers, as not doing so might severely endanger them. Therefore, evangelism, discipling, and teaching is done more in the background by working closely with "Timothys" and "Lydias," enabling them to effectively build up the emerging church. Attendance at believers' meetings by the foreigners would seldom or never occur. The hope is also that this reduction in direct involvement will lead to greater contextualization as well as to less dependence on Westerners. Here is an illustration from one of Nik's interviews:

> "Peter" and his family have lived for a number of years within environments of persecution. This family has paid the price in language and culture learning. Peter especially is fluent enough in the local language and culture to not only share the good news, but disciple a national to maturity.
>
> Peter's entire family has been a witness to "Mustafa" and his family. They share meals, visit and attend social functions together. Witness takes place over many months and in hours of discussing the merits of Islam and Christianity. Christian family is modeled. The time arrives when Mustafa quietly seeks Peter and states that he wants to seriously dialogue concerning the Person of Jesus.

Peter sends Mustafa home with the encouragement that God will send him the answer he seeks. Peter has meanwhile discipled and cultivated a relationship with a number of more mature MBBs. He makes an appointment to see "Hussein" and tells this brother about Mustafa. By this time Peter knows where Mustafa lives, the name of his wife, the number of children they have and where Mustafa goes to drink tea.

Hussein begins to follow Mustafa. He watches Mustafa in the community. He listens to Mustafa in the marketplace. He begins a casual conversation with Mustafa. If Mustafa is a serious seeker, Hussein will lead him and his family to Jesus. Peter has enabled Mustafa to hear the gospel from someone within his own culture, clearly in his own language. Many of the agendas of coming to the missionary for a job, education, extraction, a wife, etc. are short-circuited. Also the missionary has empowered Hussein to lead someone from within his people group to Christ with the joy that brings. Peter has modeled evangelism and servanthood.[1]

Ripken's own field experience includes an MBB church plant where the believers were literally wiped out through martyrdom, thus bringing the new church to an end. It was later determined that one of the factors in what occurred was the frequent and in-depth contact the new believers had with the foreign gospel workers. Obviously, none of us would want to see that happen nor in any way bring serious danger to the precious believers we work with through an unwise approach in ministry.

On the other hand, sometimes the connection local believers have with expatriates can in fact protect them. I've seen more than once how a local police official wants to oppress or arrest local believers, but has to back off when he considers that the news of this will travel internationally and that his higher-ups will quite possibly receive calls from the Foreign Ministry. Discernment is called for based on the kind of situation you may be in. No two field situations are the same, and we really need to be led by the Spirit of God into the right approach for our own context.

To Illustrate . . .

Here's a report we got from a team in Central Asia:

Responding to a neighbor's phone call the police arrived at the house of Ahmed, where they found Richard, a foreign worker, and the five key leaders of a network of house churches. They were immediately taken to the security service and made to give written statements about their activities. As all were a bit nervous, they wound up writing not the wisest of reports. This whole situation set off prayer throughout the region, both by expatriates and local believers. The following evening, with all the detainees released until Friday, we were at Steve's house praying with Richard who had been at the house the previous night. We prayed specifically that the reports from the previous night would not be found the next morning and that the next day God would show His power, pour out His grace and favor on the believers, and that the judge, even in her dreams, would hear from God.

The following morning while waiting with the police for a hearing with the judge, the papers did not arrive. So [the believers] were forced to rewrite the information. This time they wrote what they had already agreed among themselves would be the best way to express what had happened.

The two police officers also had to wait with the others five hours for the judge to receive them. During this delay, the tensions were decreased between the believers and the officers to the point that one of the security agents invited Richard and his family to a meal at his house! This man was just named the provincial head of anti-terrorism.

Finally, when they had the hearing with the judge, it was very short. She said that according to penal code she could pronounce one of three options: 1) Send all to the jail; 2) Apply a fine to all; or 3) Scold them for what they had done. Then she asked Richard what he wanted her to do. He responded that he would prefer the third option. Then she asked each one of the nationals the same question and each one responded in the same way. And that was what she did in the end.

The following day one of the leaders said that that judge had said to him that the New Testament was a good book and they should not give up studying it. She just suggested that studying in smaller groups was better! We had much to thank God for.

There is no question that the principles and methods of "shadow pastoring" are best for certain high-persecution environments. And workers in less severe environments can also use some of these principles to good effect. But I also believe that in many contexts the church planters still need to exercise substantial apostolic ministry directly, in order not to weaken the believers. For example, where church planters are forced to remain at a distance from the embryonic church, working only with one local leader, this imposes serious limitations to the apostolic ministry the church planters can have. Their eyes and ears are not in the fellowship group, but rather they have to rely 100 percent on the accounts given to them by the leader. They cannot teach and minister the Word. They cannot develop other leaders. They cannot model, exhort, encourage, train, or directly help the young fellowship on how to overcome pitfalls, sin, and division in the group. Their only input *from* the group, or contribution *to* the group, is via one leader—which is sort of like planting a church through a straw.

Of course, the bottom line is what is best for the emerging church, both in terms of spiritual growth and their not incurring more persecution than is necessary. Staying in the background and shadow pastoring are absolutely necessary at times, and perhaps strategic at other times. There are principles here that apply in all contexts. But when we're not dealing with a high-persecution environment, I believe the emerging church truly needs the apostolic church planters to teach and minister for a while.

SOME CONCLUSIONS

It should be fairly obvious now to the reader that I personally lean toward a more active involvement of at least one apostolic church planter from the team, for a season of time, and especially in spiritual leadership and Bible teaching. But I recognize the reality of situations where that cannot happen, and I respect those who don't necessarily agree with me.

Am I advocating that all the leading and teaching are done by the foreign church planter until, one day, elders are appointed? Certainly not. Part of helping younger believers grow is to urge them to be sharing what Christ has done for them with others—both believers and unbelievers. They should likewise be taught from day one that Jesus wants them to serve fellow believers in all sorts of ways, including sharing what they have learned. At the earliest possible point, believers should be given responsibilities in the body. For some this will include leadership and pastoral care. For others it will include teaching God's Word.

I remember one day when I was invited by a friend from a sister agency to participate in a fellowship meeting of new believers. I knew some of the believers; I didn't know others. We fellowshipped together and prayed for each other. Then it was announced that Brother Ravi was going to lead us in a study in Galatians. Ravi, who had come to faith only about three months earlier, did a fantastic job! It was such a clear example to me of how Christ gives gifts to His new churches, as we are promised in Ephesians 4:11–12, and how this brother's gift of teaching—though not yet refined—was unmistakable. It is such an encouragement when you see plainly that the new church isn't going to need you for very long, as Christ through His Spirit is going to take care of them and make them what He wants them to be.

The James 3:1 instruction about not many becoming teachers does not mean that young believers should never open their mouths to lead a study until they're fully mature (whatever that means). This is a *process*. And for the protection of the embryonic church there needs to be freedom for younger teachers to try ministering the Word in an environment of apostolic oversight for a period of time. Indeed, one of the responsibilities of the church planter is to recognize those who have giftings in this area and make sure these gifts are developed and that opportunities to teach are given.

In most cases, good church planters will want to exit as soon as it is feasible. That means that as early as possible they want to put responsibilities into the hands of the local believers. This requires a process of training, delegation, review, and further equipping. And throughout that process the local believers will both fail and succeed—with ups and downs, with good motives and bad—and through all this they will grow up in Christ and develop their gifts.

We have called the period between the time when you first have one or more believers willing to serve and the eventual appointment of elders an *incubation period*. How long should that last? I am personally in favor of it being as short as possible. It may take longer in some of our contexts, if persecution prevents the believers from getting to where they need to be in the Lord to assume full shepherding responsibilities. A close friend, who has thirty years of church planting experience, tells me that more often they waited too long to appoint elders rather than doing it too quickly.

Christ is calling forth His bride from Buddhist, Muslim, and Hindu peoples across the 10/40 Window. What a wonderful privilege it is to be a part of this enterprise . . . and to have to wrestle with these difficult issues. May the Lord grant you His wisdom and guidance!

12

What about Church Planting Movements in Highly Resistant Cultures?

As pioneer church planters we all long for the same thing: to see the gospel of Jesus Christ enter our chosen people group, and then not only see churches established but also see those churches plant other churches far and wide, resulting in a massive spread of the gospel. We yearn for the gospel to become the topic of conversation from family to family, street to street, town to town. A wildfire is the picture that comes to mind—though in the most positive sense. Using another metaphor, the gospel leavens not just a piece of the lump, but the whole lump.

Among today's least responsive peoples this seems like an utter impossibility. However, throughout the centuries apostolic teams have taken the gospel to people groups that at first were completely resistant, hostile, and impenetrable. Then came a period in which a few embraced Christ, faced persecution, and then struggled for a while with unity and growth in small fellowship groups. But at some point the power of the gospel can break out in a way that results in rapid church reproduction and irrepressible growth. For those working in the most resistant cultures today, it is encouraging to remember that at the beginning of the twentieth century there were only a handful of struggling believers in Korea.

Those who are working today in unreached people groups realize that nothing less than *church planting movements* (CPMs) are going to bring the kind of change in the country's spiritual landscape that is so absolutely necessary. Without a significant spread of the gospel brought about by rapid church multiplication, most men, women, and children among the people will never truly hear the good news of God's forgiveness in Christ in their lifetimes. The compassion of God compels us to aim at nothing less (1 Timothy 2:4; 2 Peter 3:9).

Gospel workers in Japan struggle with the culture's powerful group orientation, which works to prevent individuals from embracing Christ. And yet there is hope that the way society can suddenly and pervasively accept new things (what are called "booms" there) can one day be true of the gospel message.[1]

But how realistic is it for a CP team among a very resistant people group, such as are many Buddhist or Muslim people groups, to aim for a CPM? Is it possible that such an ambitious goal might even be counterproductive if the environment is highly unresponsive to the gospel? Or will aiming at a goal that is lower than a church planting movement permanently build in a limit to how much that ministry can attain? Should workers invest the time it takes to become true belongers in a culture and fluent speakers of the language, or should they more quickly seek to simply nurture a CPM from outside the locale?

This chapter will seek to address some of these issues, though *fully* answering them isn't possible. In fact, because these are days of harvest and the spiritual landscape of the unreached world is changing rapidly, it would even be good if this treatment is somewhat outdated by the time you read this!

What Is Happening Today?

All of us working among unreached people groups are deeply indebted to David Garrison for his recent book, *Church Planting Movements*, which has already served as an outstanding introduction and catalyst for discussions of CPMs among Hindus, Muslims, Buddhists, and animists. Garrison's definition of a CPM is "a rapid multiplication of indigenous churches planting churches that sweeps through a people group or population segment."[2] Garrison outlines a wide array of truly thrilling testimonies of CPMs, with numbers that remind us of the extraordinary harvest our heavenly Father is producing all around the world. For example, the claim is made that 30,000 people are being baptized in China every day!

However, the various examples Garrison provides do not come from highly resistant peoples, and few examples come from the Muslim world. What is happening there?

We rejoice that the Muslim world *has* witnessed some CPMs: Indonesia in the 1960s, the Kabil Berbers of Algeria, Bangladesh, Berkina Faso, etc. And I am aware of various places around the Muslim world that currently are seeing sort of "mini-CPMs," or at least MBB churches reproducing with the ingredients for something even faster and bigger. For example, at the breakup of the Soviet Union in 1991 there were no known MBBs in Kazakhstan. Today there are reported to be over 13,000, with the number of churches increasing daily. Political turmoil or rapid cultural change is creating an openness to new ideas in some places. On the streets of Dakar, for example, you can see minibuses with a picture on each of the two back doors: one of Osama bin Laden (no surprise there); the other sometimes of Madonna! Islamic fundamentalism and the allure of Western culture, somehow existing side by side.

Nonetheless, the vast majority of Muslim people groups are not yet responding abundantly to the gospel, and most are not yet even engaged by pioneer church planters. The biggest factor in this lack of responsiveness, of course, is that of "little sowing, little reaping." According to Greg Livingstone, church planting among Muslims—especially the concept of establishing MBB churches with their own leadership—has only been in practice since the 1960s, and in earnest since the 1980s. "Until the '80s, missionaries actually 'planning' on establishing an MBB church (never mind one that would reproduce) were almost unknown."[3]

Most Muslim-majority cities in the world today are like Tripoli, Cairo, Damascus, Ankara, Ashkabad, Kabul, Karachi, Kuala Lumpur, and Jakarta: there are very few MBBs; only a handful of MBB fellowships, if any; and the MBB church is far from flourishing, much less reproducing. This raises the question: How can the lessons learned from CPMs in South America or Africa apply to today's highly resistant contexts where there is as yet little or no harvest, where a variety of factors continue to keep the church small, and where severe persecution of believers is an ever-present reality? A reality check calls to mind numerous obstacles to any rapid expansion of the gospel in such contexts: believers facing ostracism, job loss, arrest, torture, imprisonment, and martyrdom. These believers face opposition from the government and secret police, from family, and from the surrounding neighborhoods. Add to this that many Islamic cultures create a climate where trust and unity between MBBs is nearly impossible to create. Also "abundant evangelism"—a requisite for CPMs according to Garrison—seems beyond possibility in places like Morocco, Saudi Arabia, Pakistan, or Malaysia.

In 1982 our church planting agency was launched with a seemingly audacious claim: we believed the Lord was raising up this new movement to plant churches among the world's most resistant peoples. People called us naive, presumptuous, even arrogant—and we were certainly guilty of all that. One leader from an organization that had courageously ministered in the Arab Gulf for decades, who was near retirement, told our team in Egypt to forget about church planting and just be content with "sowing seeds." Brother Andrew of Open Doors met with our leaders in 1984 and counseled us to "tone down our rhetoric" and take a lower profile until we had actually seen God bring fruit in our ministries—wise counsel indeed. So for a number of years our workers focused mainly on language learning and residency; but eventually the fruit came. Today over 160 fellowships and churches have been planted by teams in the organization. To God be the glory! Here's the point: for years we felt that God had spoken to us about church planting among the most needy, but at the same time it seemed so fanciful.

Today many of us believe that CPMs are in our future, and must be in our future, for the sake of seeing the vision God has given to us and to others becoming a reality. How can we talk about CPMs among Muslims and other resistant peoples? We must discuss these dreams humbly, and by faith, acknowledging that there is so much we don't yet know about how it is going to happen. But just as God previously gave us a sense about what He was about to do back in the '80s and '90s, so His leading seems to us today regarding CPMs. How do we reconcile the seeming impossibility of CPMs among resistant peoples with the anticipation of them and urgent need for them? I'm not sure. But isn't it exciting to be part of such an adventure by faith, as a fellow worker with the Lord Himself?

EINDHOVEN CONSULTATION

In 2003 dozens of field leaders met together in the Netherlands to grapple with CPMs and church reproduction, particularly engaging four case studies: three from within our work (West Africa, the Middle East, and Central Asia) and one from another agency's work in South Asia. Four presenters shared, followed by lively questions and interaction from those working across the 10/40 Window.

Of course, these case studies were just glimpses. We do not claim to have authoritative experience in CPMs or even in widespread church multiplication, though our faith was strengthened by the fact that in 2002 the Lord let us see churches reproduce daughter churches in seven of our eight regions, all of them difficult fields. Here are some common factors we discovered from these four case studies:

1. All the believers were taught that they were saved for a purpose beyond themselves—that is, for the building up of the church.

2. The most crucial point is when certain believers "own" the vision, coming to understand and accept that God is calling them to the work of spreading the gospel and planting new churches among their people. This burden will be very costly. But it comes not from the expatriates, but rather from the Lord, who will be with them throughout. God raises up local evangelists and apostles.

3. Worship occurs in the ethnic language. And there is a measure of *contextualization*, as the new body of believers learns to fit well in the local culture, retaining and adapting existing forms as they are able to biblically.

4. There was a struggle to overcome fear, and in each case they successfully did so.

5. In all four cases, persecution caused growth.

6. A deliberate structure was in place. Structure in both the local church and in expansion work is an essential element.

7. There was a quickly developed national leadership.

8. There was a deliberate holding off of outside groups that were bringing in unhealthy church influences.

9. It is extremely common to experience "three steps forward, two steps back" in this sort of CP.

10. Expatriate CPers played a vital and active role early on, but then, when it was strategic to do so, withdrew to allow local leaders to blossom in their ministries.

11. Deeply imparting the Word of God was an essential component in each case, and its authority was foundational to the new church.

12. The CP team was able at times to make key adjustments in strategy and tactics.

13. The team intentionally worked with local believing women to help them grow and join in the work.

14. In each case small house groups (cells, house churches, etc.) played a key role.

15. In each case there was some form of enabling key believers to spend more time in ministry (through support, flexible employment, etc.).

The Role of the Expatriate Church Planter

As mentioned in the previous chapter, there is currently a growing spectrum of views on the question of the apostolic worker's role. The debate is a healthy one, though we need to avoid polarization. Some in the "CPM camp" suggest that traditional activities such as becoming fluent in the language, teaching the Bible to the emerging church, and being active in the formation of initial body life can get in the way of realizing a CPM. It is felt that these activities might delay catalyzing a movement, or even that the expatriate's ministry will undermine nationals grabbing the baton.

On the other side, some church planters in particularly hard fields bristle at the notion of workers living in another city apart from the local believers (often at a lifestyle level many times higher than them), not learning the language, somehow being a catalyst by directing activities from afar, and not going through the painful labor that Paul did for a season to see his churches birthed (à la Acts 20:17–38; Galatians 4:12–20; 1 Thessalonians 2:1–12). One team leader recently shared his heart: "I fear that the classical, biblical, historic, self-emptying means of planting churches is falling into disgraceful disrepute among us. Teaching the whole counsel of God patiently for years to a few quality elder candidates seems like an incredible waste of time to some . . . even though after we leave, the blood of any straying sheep is on their neck before God!"

Can these views be reconciled? How can we ease the tension between "CP" and "M"? Surely an important factor in approach is this: At what point does the church planter enter the process?

a) Is it from the beginning—starting with no believers, and leading people to Christ?

b) Or sort of "in the middle"—meeting existing believers and helping them come together?

c) Or arriving "late"—where a fellowship already exists, and the expatriate comes alongside to help only as a coach, catalyst, or networker (perhaps similar to Paul's relationship with the church at Colosse)?

No doubt scenarios a and b require a higher degree of incarnational ministry. Scenario c may not require language fluency, for example, though there is the challenge of somehow earning credibility and a role, convincing the local leaders that he or she has a significant ministry contribution to make.

Regardless of where one is on this spectrum, all would agree that new churches should be formed in such a way as to lead quickly to them planting daughter churches, which will themselves reproduce, and so on. This involves imparting a vision that becomes part of the new church's "DNA" toward reproduction at every level.

Many believe, as I do, that the expatriate church planter must play an active leadership and teaching role at the beginning, in the incubation period. But they also believe that leadership and Bible teaching roles must be given to the local disciples themselves as early as possible. As soon as individual believers are ready—and often even before they *feel* ready—they should be the ones leading meetings, solving pastoral problems, organizing events, leading worship, and ministering the Word of God. What ultimately drives this is the push toward appointing elders—a crucial element in the expansion of the New Testament church.

INDIGENOUS CHURCH PLANTERS AND APOSTLES

As followers of Christ from the majority religion mature, many will develop into gifted elders and teachers. But a delightful surprise in my brief twenty years of experience is that in many cases God was raising up believers with strong gifts who drove growth and expansion. Some were not called to be local elders but were in fact called to be *apostles* with a broader, expansive ministry. Though I'm not able to provide details because of security concerns, I can easily think of examples in North Africa, the Middle East, the Balkans, Central Asia, South Asia, and Southeast Asia. We are told in Ephesians 4:11–12 that Christ gives special leaders, including apostles, to the church as gifts; and He is doing that in our day as He raises up indigenous apostles—even from the world's most resistant peoples! In hindsight, this shouldn't have been a surprise, but I'm just being honest that it was.

Much could be said on this whole subject of indigenous pioneer church planters. No one will disagree that a CPM cannot emerge where all the church planting is done by expatriates. But as more and more local believers own the burden of spreading the gospel throughout their country and people group through multiplicative church planting, the possibilities for explosive growth are limitless. This is, in fact, the only way most resistant unreached people groups are going to be truly evangelized.

In CPM theory, the emphasis is on a church planting another church. However, the dynamic with most emerging CPMs in today's most resistant fields is that key individual disciples are uniquely called, gifted, and effective in starting new fellowships. They may operate out of a particular church, or they may have a broader territory in view—perhaps the whole country. Also, there is often a difference between local evangelists and local apostles. The former are driven by an evangelistic zeal to go to new towns and stir things up for Christ. They may or may not yet possess a lot of depth and maturity. But it is not uncommon for these individuals to lead several to Christ in one trip. Indigenous apostles, on the other hand, are those with strong biblical gifts who are able to follow up and consolidate the body of Christ in a new place. This seems similar to the Acts 8 pattern, where Philip the evangelist saw a breakthrough among the unevangelized Samaritans and then the apostles Peter and John needed to come and solidify the fruit, teach God's Word more thoroughly, and establish the believers as an *ekklesia*.

When these vital, expansion-gifted HBBs, BBBs, or MBBs emerge, a tension quickly develops between their gifts and calling and their time available for ministry. Workers or local believers begin to ask if there is any way to enable these key believers somehow to have more time for the work of the gospel. The International Mission Board of the Southern Baptist Convention has developed an approach to church planting known as "POUCH," which stands for "*p*articipative Bible study and worship groups, *o*bedience to God's word, development of *u*npaid and multiple lay or bivocational *c*hurch leaders and meetings in *c*ell or *h*ouse churches."[4] Likewise, speaking in the Hindu context, Subbamma writes, "It is a glaring fact that paid workers are the chief ones to carry on the main task of the Church, hence, professionalism is predominant in the Church. A new type of non-professional work is needed for effective Christian witness."[5]

While I genuinely respect the wisdom of the "U" element ("unpaid workers"), *unpaid* in the developing world often means *unable* to be much involved in concerted expansion work. In the majority of these countries the economy is so weak that people either are not working at all or else they have to work sixty hours a week. The mature and gifted layman[6] who has a good job and a fair amount of discretionary time is very rare indeed.

So we have this three-way tension:

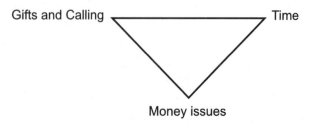

Gifts and Calling — Time

Money issues

Am I saying that the solution is always for the indigenous worker to enter some mode of vocational ministry? Certainly not. Throughout history, the spread of the gospel and the reproduction of churches has been driven to a good extent by those *not* in vocational ministry (i.e., laymen). But it does seem that a vocational mode of ministry for *some* local workers is both biblical and strategic in many of our fields. If a local disciple has a vision from God for evangelism and church planting, is mature, gifted, proven, not drawn into ministry for financial gain, and willing to accept the risks of Christ's work, can these brothers and sisters somehow be enabled time-wise? Are creative solutions of support, flexible employment, or bivocationalism the answer? Or is there simply too much of a risk that any involvement of finances to accelerate the spread of the gospel will actually result in ruining the work later on? I am convinced that this question is a pivotal one for CPMs in today's most challenging fields. We need wisdom from God!

Simply looking at what is occurring presently across various unreached fields, here are the six main models regarding finances for local workers being especially active in expansion ministries:

1. The worker is on some sort of salary or regular stipend.

2. The worker raises ministry financial support (i.e., from local and/or nonlocal sources).

3. The worker is employed by the expatriate's secular project or business, with flexibility in working hours.

4. The worker is bivocational: involved in supported ministry part of the time and in an income-generating project part of the time.

5. No ongoing support, but assets are loaned to the worker to set up some income-generating business (e.g., a car is purchased and is loaned to the worker for taxi income; a shop and some minimal equipment is purchased and loaned to the worker for sewing work).

6. No material help. The worker is completely self-supporting, but is able to give himself to the work to a good extent.

Where money or help is involved, there are the usual suspects of potential problems: Motives can be mixed. The worker might be benefiting in lifestyle by going into vocational ministry. Whereas going into ministry in the West usually means a drop in lifestyle, the opposite is often true in developing countries. If not handled well, it can cause envy or strife in the churches. The expatriate CPer can be put in the unenviable position of "paymaster." To the extent indigenous workers are enabled by outside funds, it usually limits reproducibility. I say *usually* because I can think of a major CPM among Muslims in South Asia that seems to continue to enjoy high reproducibility despite the role of outside funding; in that case the workers are bivocational, as in the fourth option above—about half-time in ministry and half-time in a large income-producing project. Finally, if many are in some form of vocational ministry, it shrinks the ranks of committed laymen, which is not a good development.

So are there any points left in favor of helping certain local believers into vocational ministry? Yes. When the right people are freed up in their time, it can really jumpstart and accelerate progress. It also follows a New Testament model. It seems from the beginning that certain key workers were permitted to raise support or receive financial enablement for the task of spreading the gospel. And while the money to help certain local elders was evidently local money (1 Timothy 5:17–18), there doesn't seem to be any such limitation with regard to pioneer church planters or apostles (1 Corinthians 9:1–18). This phenomenon of ministry support for apostolic workers seems to have begun fairly early in the first-century church. And while we can react with fear concerning local believers in vocational ministry, there are always "money issues" with expatriate workers too.

And so it seems that perhaps the criteria for selection of workers and administration of funding can be the same for workers from the West as for local workers, such as:

1. proven commitment to Christ and the work of the gospel;

2. proven character;

3. purity of motives (not for financial gain);

4. not actually gaining (some ministries will not allow local workers to receive more in full-time ministry than what they had earned previously in secular work, or perhaps the income level of a teacher);

5. at the end of the day, having to trust God for provision.

I am placing this section on indigenous church planters and possible financial help for them in this chapter on CPMs only very reluctantly. I do not believe that having certain believers in vocational or bivocational ministry is essential to having a church planting movement. I don't even think this issue is central. But I do believe that this can be a strategic part of some emerging CPM ministries. And besides, the subject always comes up. We have to grapple with these questions, both now and in the future. I personally look forward to seeing more and more creative and fruitful models emerge in the years ahead.

13
Three Models of Church Planting

Most Christians sort of develop a common picture of "church" that is pretty simple: a group of people, oftentimes connected to a larger denomination, that meets every Sunday morning for a worship service, and then for other activities during the week, usually in a church building they own. Because this is the most conventional view of church among Westerners, and indeed very common around the world, I am calling this the *prevalent church model*. By giving it that name, however, I don't mean to imply that it is the most biblical or even necessarily the most common historically.

It's exciting to realize that this isn't the only model of church. Though most Westerners were unaware of it, other models were gaining prominence in Africa, Latin America, and Asia in the latter half of the twentieth century. These other models are now gaining in popularity even in the West. But more importantly, they offer huge advantages today in church planting among unreached people groups in hostile or resistant contexts. The two primary alternative models are the *cell church model* and the *house church model*. It almost goes without saying that today's apostolic church planters need to be conversant with these three models, and able to discern which one fits best with their own pioneer context.

Many books have been written about both cell churches and house churches, and books about the prevalent model fill libraries. The aim in this chapter is to present a thumbnail sketch of the three models. Let me state here that because this is brief some of the generalizations below don't hold true all the time. My intent is to observe the key differences between them and the relative advantages and disadvantages on the field.

THE PREVALENT CHURCH MODEL

There isn't a need to say much about this model, since most of us are very familiar with it. Most of these churches are forty people or more in size; and it's not uncommon for their active membership to be in the thousands. Smaller churches typically have the advantages of closer relationships, getting a higher percentage of people involved in service, and the blessing of knowing pretty much everyone in the body. Larger churches generally enjoy benefits such as high-caliber Bible teaching, impacting a city for Christ, launching many kinds of ministries, having well-developed children's and youth programs, and being able to contribute significantly to ministries overseas. Large churches can also have a significant impact on social problems such as alcoholism, drug addiction, poverty, and joblessness. This has sometimes given them much favor with local mayors and government officials, and has allowed them to continue in countries that are not "open" to the gospel.

Generally there is no intrinsic limit on size in this model. Indeed, probably most churches of this kind feel that *the bigger the better*. The nature of evangelism and numerical growth is usually simply to grow larger in the mother church, though many prevalent-type churches do have a vision for planting daughter churches.

Leadership is either through a group of elders, oftentimes including at least one pastor, or through a senior pastor along with subordinate pastors. In both cases, they lead a single congregation. Alternatively, some churches are under a board of trustees or other forms of a non-elder board. Most have at least one paid pastor; and many have a large staff of salaried pastors and support staff.

The essence of church life is mostly centralized. However, many medium and large churches emphasize active involvement in smaller home groups, and this really becomes the lifeblood of the congregation.

The stereotype of prevalent-type churches around the world is that they are institutional, denominational, stuffy, formalistic, comfortable, and mostly concerned with ministering to their own needs through programs rather than boldly reaching out with the gospel locally and beyond. This is an unfortunate caricature, as many times the picture is much different. Oftentimes life in the church is biblical and healthy, especially when there is a good emphasis on *koinonia* and on being spiritual revolutionaries in obeying Christ's commands whatever the cost.

Pioneering church planters tend to be iconoclastic or nontraditional by nature, so for their church planting effort in their field of ministry there is a danger of rejecting this model of church out of hand, sort of throwing the baby out with the bath water. I urge my fellow workers: the cell model or house church model might be best for your people group, or they might not. Examine all three. Teams from our agency have planted a handful of larger, prevalent-type churches, which mostly continue to do well. As one might imagine, none are in high persecution environments.

THE CELL CHURCH MODEL

The Yoido Full Gospel Church of Korea, under the leadership of its founder and senior pastor, Paul Yonggi Cho, is the largest church in the world. From its humble beginnings with a small number of believers meeting in an army tent in 1958, to claiming a membership today of around 700,000 and an annual budget over $100 million, it has made famous the cell church model. This model has become increasingly well-known by books such as Ralph Neighbour's *Where Do We Go from Here?*[1] and Cho's *Successful Home Cell Groups.*[2]

The basics of this model are as follows: The entire church is made up of small cells. If you are a member, you are in a cell group. Cells meet at least once a week, and there is a strong emphasis on each believer, no matter how spiritually young, sharing Christ with friends and family. The two essential functions of cell groups are ministering to one another and reaching out to nonbelievers. As cells grow, there is an implicit plan to subdivide or multiply when a certain size is reached, such as twenty people. Each cell is led by a cell leader; and there is also a leader-in-training, who will lead the new subdivided cell. Cell leaders can be young believers, and are not expected to be Bible teachers or elder-level in maturity.

Overarching all of the cells is a leadership structure that is elaborate and hierarchical (with levels of cell leaders, zone leaders, congregation leaders, and the senior pastor). Usually there are no elders, but one leader at the top having vast executive authority. All cells gather together in a larger "celebration" weekly or monthly. Cells are not autonomous, but very much part of the greater congregation and under the broader chain-of-command structure. To keep the cell groups closely tied to the central leadership, the cell leaders, in many cases, are given a program each week to carry out in their cell group. There is a strong emphasis on numerical growth and measurement, and detailed reporting mechanisms are in place. You could say that the spiritual life and activities of the church are decentralized, while being under a very centralized leadership. Because of the centralized leadership and the larger gatherings, the cell model has not proved as successful in high-persecution environments.

I was fortunate to visit an MBB cell church that has been quite fruitful in Central Asia, growing to about 700 members. It has ministered among two or three different people groups.

As we will see in the next chapter, the appointing of elders is an extremely important factor in the establishing of new churches in pioneer contexts. While the normal cell church model does not provide for elders, the model can be modified to allow for such. There are a number of cell churches in the United States that are led by elders rather than a senior pastor.

HOUSE CHURCH MODEL

A major leader in the revitalized house church movement in the West is Dick Scoggins, who has led a team of house church planters in New England. Many field agencies are deeply indebted to Dick for his championing of house churches in pioneering fields. His books *Planting House Churches in Networks—A Manual*[3] and *Church Multiplication Guide*[4] (coauthored with George Patterson) have proved invaluable to our teams. Most teams in our agency are pursuing the house church model in their CP work.

Of course, the most prolific example of the house church movement in recent times has been in mainland China, where the number of Bible-believing Christians is said to have grown to around 90 million. This makes it the largest church growth phenomenon in history. While the visible Three-Self Church is along the prevalent model, the vast majority of Chinese Christians are in persecution environments in underground or semi-underground house churches.

House churches are best known for their smallness and their autonomy. Because house churches thrive in persecution environments, some say they were the most common form of church in New Testament times, as evidenced by phrases such as "the church that is in their house" and "*so-and-so* and all the saints who are with them," and the fact that purposely built church buildings were unknown before Constantine. Many believe this is the model best suited for most hostile contexts, in view of the pervasive reality of persecution.

Unfortunately, when believers from non-Christian cultures first begin to gather together as the body of Christ, oftentimes the only model for church they have ever seen is the prevalent model—for example, CBB (Christian-background believers) churches that are large and public. This becomes their default model, and to direct them toward house churches can take a lot of effort and persuasion.

House churches don't have church buildings or paid pastors. Subbamma writes of India, "Since we cannot expect Hindus to build large churches before they know the Lord or experience the Gospel, the house church which they can patronize before baptism seems a reasonable procedure."[5] Like cells, house church members are encouraged to evangelize friends and family; and house churches hope to grow and subdivide or reproduce. This normally is to occur when the size of the group reaches twelve to fifteen adult members. There are the twin emphases of every person being involved and of the group *covenanting* to be Christ's body together. No wallflowers! Leaders of house churches are expected to be at a certain level of character maturity, being either an elder or a candidate in training to be appointed an elder.

Because most house churches will have no elder or only one elder, the plurality of elders is formed by all the elders in a network or cluster of house churches. Indeed, this informal networking or clustering of a few house churches is critical for synergy and wider fellowship. Groups of house churches sometimes get together as a larger group, if the security situation permits. There is also a high value placed on starting new house churches from scratch, around one or two key individuals, and then pursuing relationships in their natural social networks—even if the person is not yet in Christ, but is at least an avid seeker. As the house church model is the most decentralized of the three, it isn't hard to see why it has been so successful in China, and why it has gained such attention among church planters in persecution environments today.

Here is a recap of what we have just discussed:

	Prevalent Model	Cell Church Model	House Church Model
Leadership	One board (of elders) over one congregation. Professional pastor(s).	Hierarchical structure, with senior pastor at the top. Usually no elders. Lots of cell leaders.	One or two leaders in each HC; in some cases they are elders. Plurality of elders jointly over cluster of HCs.
Centrality	Centralized spiritual life and leadership. But closer fellowship can be developed well in home groups and special groupings.	Decentralized spiritual life. Centralized leadership.	Decentralized.
Growth Strategy	Just grow into larger congregation. Get a bigger building. Sometimes plant daughter churches.	Cells are supposed to continually grow and subdivide.	HCs are supposed to grow and then reproduce. Also start new HCs from scratch.

SOME DISTINCTIVES, ADVANTAGES, AND DISADVANTAGES

It is common for cell churches not to own a building. They rent facilities, such as schools, for their occasional large group functions. House churches never own buildings. This can free up funds for other ministry. And when a church—as a group of believers committed to one another—isn't tied to a building, that church will inevitably have a less "institutional" feel. Indeed, in the United States these days even many prevalent model churches, for example in the Presbyterian Church of America denomination, are letting go of their buildings and meeting in rented facilities (e.g., on college campuses).

Having a building is normally a moot point in hostile, resistant fields. And because house churches seem to be the most flexible and persecution-resistant, this model is pervasive in works among resistant populations.

A key challenge for pioneer house churches will be to find ways to minister to the children. These kids are often both precious, in that they are the next generation of the church on the frontlines, and under fire. Many of them face serious pressure from their grandparents and aunts and uncles. At school they can be the objects of ridicule or worse. New churches, of whatever model, need to seize the opportunity to make sure that the children hear the gospel, are taught the Scripture, and are equipped to deal with the special challenges that lay before them.

The cell church combines the advantages of small church life with the synergy of something larger. For example, such churches may have more clout with the government. Because of their overall size, larger churches (whether prevalent model or cell model) are more likely to have excellent teachers that can teach in the large celebration meetings or in the cells. They can mobilize special outreaches. House churches, on the other hand, can often develop deeper *koinonia*, and are safer in terms of security.

Historically, larger (prevalent model) churches make the biggest impact for global evangelization, at least in terms of larger, joint efforts at sending and funding.

Conclusion

It is impossible to say that one of these three models is *the* best model for church planting among various unreached people groups. Every situation is different, and each team must wait on the Holy Spirit to reveal the key for their particular city and context.

I'll close by sharing a bit about a particular work in the Arab world with which I have been associated. The ministry started out with a vague, undefined house church model. In hindsight, this is probably because we couldn't dream it would ever be larger than twelve adults, and we figured the believers would need to meet mostly in secret. When it grew well beyond that, the government security services persecuted the believers by bringing in almost everyone for questioning and serious threats, ordering them to no longer participate in the group. So our house church became a nonchurch.

As things began to rebuild over the coming months, there were two developments. First of all, the believers began a strategy of meeting together at a registered CBB church building. Secondly, the main leader received training in the cell church model.

The group never really implemented the cell model, though the ministry benefited by some of the principles. However, the group grew and moved out of the CBB church meetings, and became a medium size church themselves, meeting somewhat openly in other facilities. Eventually the group once again sort of broke apart, but this time it was due more to internal tensions rather than to police persecution. As of this writing, they are more or less pursuing a house church model, with mixed results so far.

What lessons have we learned from these attempts at different models? First, choosing the right model doesn't guarantee success, as we have tried all three and growth is still limited. This shouldn't surprise us, as having the right strategy is never a guarantee of fruitfulness. Second, church planters must seek the Lord constantly for guidance about what models or strategies will be fruitful. Over time, you must be open to experimentation and even to trying things that may seem counterintuitive.

14
The Crucial First Group of Elders

As human beings, when faced with challenging and lengthy tasks, we have a need to visualize the end from the beginning. If we don't, our vision and energy will fail. The runner has to be able to see herself in her mind's eye crossing that finishing line and breaking the tape. The shipbuilder imagines the ship completed and those champagne bottles breaking against the sides of the hull, christening the vessel for service. And in the early days of church planting, God's worker must have a picture within himself or herself of the apostolic task being completed and of being able to move on with a great sense of accomplishment and with confidence in the new body of Christ.

In church planting, what does the "finish line" look like? There are perhaps as many answers to that question as there are church plants. However, in the New Testament there is one consistent ending point: the appointing of the first group of local elders for the new church by the apostolic church planters. For example, at the end of Paul and Barnabas' first apostolic journey we see: "After they had preached the gospel to that city and had made many disciples, they returned to Lystra and to Iconium and to Antioch, strengthening the souls of the disciples, encouraging them to continue in the faith, and saying, 'Through many tribulations we must enter the kingdom of God.' When they had appointed elders for them in every church, having prayed with fasting, they commended them to the Lord in whom they had believed" (Acts 14:21–23).

The apostles felt they could not return home with a sense of "mission accomplished" until they had established indigenous leaders, called elders, in the churches they had started. Of course, church planters may sometimes stay on after this point for various ministry purposes. But it would seem that the primary objective of planting a church or churches has not been accomplished until that crucial first group of local elders is appointed and installed in shepherding ministry.

I've been involved with a particular church planting ministry in Central Asia for a number of years. The ministry progressed well over the years, as many came to faith and groups multiplied. But matters became particularly interesting a couple of years ago when it was decided that the time had come to train elder candidates and then appoint the first group of elders. Knowing how easily things can go awry, I breathed a great sigh of relief when the appointing and laying on of hands actually took place after a four-month process. It was a historic day for that people group. I was reminded of this group of house churches today when I received an e-mail from one of those elders, who shared with me how he and his wife were commissioned by the church over the weekend as their first *sent ones* to go out and plant churches further afield.

It is ironic that the subject of elders in pioneer church planting might seem a bit boring to some when, in fact, the appointing of that first group of elders in an unreached people group can ultimately change a country. It is a watershed moment, a pivotal event. In my observations of pioneering ministry over the years, by far most new fellowships that don't reach the point where a plurality of elders are appointed eventually fall apart. By the same token, the vast majority of such fellowships that do have elders established not only survive but grow and even reproduce. I would assert that once a resistant people group has a church under the leadership of indigenous elders, in most cases that people group will never be the same. It will represent an irreversible foothold for the gospel and for the body of Christ, a seed that will become a field.[1] The church has been termed a "community of love, truth, and mission."[2] When that community has leadership that is indigenous, biblical, and responsive to Christ, who is the Head, it has become a strong organism that will last, grow, reproduce, and impact the country for generations. Can you think of a more exciting subject?!

We must beware of faulty thinking. Some see structural issues such as the nature of leadership in a fellowship as unimportant. But when the storms come, whether from within or from without, experience shows how crucial the local leadership is—not just their character, but also how they have been formed and how they relate to the body. Some imagine that the New Testament doesn't say much about church leadership (or "governance" or decision-making); but there is actually quite a bit of material. In order to avoid polluting the new church with outside cultural influences, I've heard some advocate that the church planters must not form anything in regard to the church's leadership, but rather leave it entirely in the hands of the new local believers to figure out on their own. But is that the biblical model? It wouldn't seem so. Others might say the opposite: that the Bible teaches a very specific model of church polity, almost down to the bylaws. Instead, a look at the biblical data shows us a few broad principles or norms and that the actual forms of how elders operate can vary greatly from one place to another.

If you are in the early days of ministry on the field, you might be tempted to skip this chapter—assuming it is too advanced or not relevant for a few years in your setting. But I would encourage you to read on. First, things can happen fast. You might find yourself in the work of elder preparation a lot faster than you think. Second, imagining that finish line and grappling with elder issues even now can energize and inspire you, as you see the end from the beginning. This subject is a vision-builder for your team.

A Few Key Passages

After they had preached the gospel to that city and had made many disciples, they returned to Lystra and to Iconium and to Antioch, strengthening the souls of the disciples, encouraging them to continue in the faith, and saying, 'Through many tribulations we must enter the kingdom of God.' When they had appointed elders for them in every church, having prayed with fasting, they commended them to the Lord in whom they had believed. (Acts 14:21–23)

Taking another look at this thrilling example, it is very noteworthy that *elders* is in the plural while *church* is in the singular. *Every church* (singular) had *elders* (plural) who were appointed by the apostles. This is a consistent pattern in the biblical record. Of the nineteen occurrences of the word *elder* in the New Testament (not including those references to the heavenly elders in Revelation), thirteen specifically refer to *elders* in the plural in the context of *church* in the singular. And the other six instances are not contrary to this; they are just more general.

> From Paul's final address to the elders in Ephesus: "Be on guard for yourselves and for all the flock, among which the Holy Spirit has made you overseers, to shepherd the church of God which He purchased with His own blood. I know that after my departure savage wolves will come in among you, not sparing the flock; and from among your own selves men will arise, speaking perverse things, to draw away the disciples after them." (Acts 20:28–30)

When Paul "sent to Ephesus and called to him the elders of the church" (20:17) and gave his parting words to them, what a wonderful legacy he was leaving us about what a church planter does and the kind of ministry responsibility the local elders take on. We again note *elders* in the plural and *church* in the singular. Paul recounts to them the very extensive ministry he had among them in getting them started in the faith and forming them as a church. He goes on to warn them of the inevitable troubles ahead. It is interesting that the biggest dangers will come from within—one reason why it is vital that a church not have just one elder. This is also one of a handful of passages where *elder*, *overseer* (or bishop), and *pastor* (or shepherd) are used concerning the same role (see vv. 17, 28). Finally, we note that the elders have a threefold responsibility, according to verse 28, for being "on guard" 1) for themselves in the sense of each elder watching out for his own spiritual condition; 2) for themselves in the sense of watching out for their fellow elders; and 3) for all the flock (i.e., the rest of the church). Doing this well will help insure that this flock carries on to the next generation.

> For this reason I left you in Crete, that you would set
> in order what remains and appoint elders in every city
> as I directed you. (Titus 1:5)

Paul again uses the terms *elder* and *overseer* interchangeably (see Titus 1:7). Evidently Paul and a team with him began this evangelistic effort on the large island of Crete. In many towns and villages people responded and were formed into fellowships. As the work was progressing well, Paul felt he could leave the island, placing Titus in charge of completing the church planting work. Paul reminds Titus here that he needed to finish up the things that remained to be done (probably a reference to the doctrinal and practical teaching emphases in the book), and to appoint elders (plural) in every city (singular). At that point the teaching, shepherding, and leadership responsibility would rest fully on the shoulders of local elders. And then Titus was to leave (3:12).

In every New Testament account where it is specified, the first group of elders is appointed by the apostolic team. Does it always have to be that way? It's hard to say, because there isn't more biblical data. If the new group of believers makes the selection of elders, there might be relational tensions or harm—men becoming elders who aren't ready but who have personal sway, and maybe others who aren't chosen due to being opposed by one person but who are qualified—whereas the expatriate church planters would hopefully be able to be more objective and make choices based on character rather than personal politics.

> The elders who rule well are to be considered worthy
> of double honor, especially those who work hard at
> preaching and teaching. For the Scripture says, "YOU
> SHALL NOT MUZZLE THE OX WHILE HE IS THRESHING," and
> "The laborer is worthy of his wages." (1 Timothy
> 5:17–18)

I see two points here. There does not seem to be an absolute equality of elders, as Paul alludes to three categories: 1) elders in general; 2) those who rule well, but aren't especially active in preaching and teaching; and 3) those who rule well *and* work hard at preaching and teaching. Secondly, this seems to form the basis for certain elders receiving payment. The source of this possible "double honor" (financial remuneration) would be the local congregation.

People often wonder what the specific responsibilities of elders are, according to the New Testament. What are they supposed to do? For this question please see "What Elders Do" at www.churchplantingphases.com under "Related Papers."

One parenthetical note before we move on. I've been referring to elders in the masculine. That's intentional. As I understand the New Testament record, while both men and women can fill various kinds of key leadership roles in the church, the role of elder is for men. However, I have dear friends who would differ with me on that, seeing women elders as valid, and I respect their handling of Scripture. We just interpret some of the texts differently. The point is, while I refer to elders as men, I hope this chapter can be of help to you if women elders is part of your understanding, and that my referring to elders as men will not be a stumbling block as you read on.

Is It Really Necessary to Have Multiple Elders?

Most would agree that the New Testament data is pretty unmistakable in teaching that each local church should have a plurality of elders who together shoulder the responsibilities of leadership, teaching, and shepherding. And, as I argue below, while two would technically meet that requirement, three elders results in a more practical, functional eldership.

Various fellow workers have shared with me something like, "Dan, I see how the New Testament indicates a plurality of elders, and how this is important for the first group of elders. But this really doesn't fit the culture—with its strong single-leader model—where we are ministering." Indeed, whether in the Arab world, most of Asia, or other regions in the 10/40 Window, there is often not much precedent for collective or shared leadership. Most such countries are under a strongman leader, and this leadership model permeates the whole of the culture, including the religious sphere. Many MBB fellowship groups, for example, begin under the leadership of a single person, usually a man. This is good, and almost always these are godly leaders who are eager to minister in a way pleasing to God. The problem is that they're usually quite a bit more qualified than others at the beginning—in terms of education, Bible background, and years in Christ—and that can tend to close the door on others coming behind them. In some cultures, that by itself stifles others from developing further or taking leadership responsibilities. Doing so might even communicate disrespect for *the* leader.

I point out to my fellow church planters that according to the New Testament a plurality of elders does not necessarily mean an equality of elders. We just saw that illustrated in the 1 Timothy 5 passage. There were differing roles and differing levels of respect or influence. We also have the example of James in Jerusalem, who was not one of the Twelve but probably the brother of Jesus. He was clearly very prominent in that group of elders, even in the midst of the apostles. In the New Testament, a plurality of elders does not necessarily imply a one-man one-vote system—that is, a complete equality of influence. In fact, how decisions are made by the elders seems to be left up to churches to figure out for themselves what best fits in their situation. And one man being prominent in a group of elders has a precedent, and may even reflect what happens most of the time. I cannot remember a single resistant-context church that I have seen where there is not one or two key individuals who exert lots of influence—more than other leaders or elders. In such a case, a prominent leader all the more needs other leaders/elders around him.

Here are some reasons why I believe having only one elder/overseer/pastor is not good:

1. The strong single leader is very susceptible to pride and from falling into a heavy-handed style of leadership. Call it the Diotrephes Syndrome, from 3 John 9: "I wrote something to the

church; but Diotrephes, who loves to be first among them, does not accept what we say."

2. Even if the leader is very godly and gifted, one person cannot have all the gifts nor the fuller cluster of ministry abilities that a group of elders brings.

3. One person cannot see situations in the church from all the necessary perspectives. For example, my wife and I are very different in personality and outlook. On a particular personality test, we came out as polar opposites on each of the four couplets. On one scale we are extreme opposites! How much more harmonious and serene our marriage would have been over the years if we had the same personality type. But this difference brings a powerful asset. Whenever we face any situation—whether in ministry, with the kids, or whatever—we are almost certain to see things from all angles. If an elder board has men who are very different from each other, it will cause clashes. But over the long run it will be a tremendous benefit to the body.

4. No one person can relate well with all personality types, age groups, etc.

5. As you look over the New Testament's descriptions of the responsibilities of church leaders, it becomes apparent how much work there is to do, especially as the local church or churches grow. It's just too much for one person. The single leader will become weary oh so easily! Discouragement and loneliness are bound to set in because of this heavy burden. It's not part of God's good plan that one man should have to shoulder all of that, even if he could (which he can't).

6. A solo leader is vulnerable. Not just in regard to emotional and physical strain. He's also vulnerable to being taken out by the Enemy (Satan), or by enemies of the gospel. How many underground churches have been scattered because the authorities simply put one man in prison? Likewise, if the single elder falls morally or spiritually, that's it. For a church to stand or fall depending on one man's resistance to temptation is foolishness and poor stewardship of that precious church.

Demonic forces will jump at the chance of using character flaws or damage from the past to find an opening in these leaders' lives. That's why it is essential that areas of weakness are acknowledged and are being dealt with. And there is mutual accountability in a team.

7. Having one strong single leader keeps other potential leaders from being developed, and it ensures that others in the body will be tragically underutilized.

8. If the church planters appoint only one elder, chances are they will stay around and continue having strong influence in the new church. This will create an ambiguity and confusion of roles. It will probably actually *delay* the appointment of Elder #2 and Elder #3.

9. The strong single leader will create a bottleneck. The church can only move forward per the leader's capacity, which is limited.

I can certainly sympathize with how building a plurality of elders—that first crucial group—is going to be difficult in many of our cultures, and maybe even countercultural. But at the end of the day, it is a biblical mandate and a strategic necessity.

Finally, I would just like to say that I believe establishing a plurality of elders is strategic and possible regardless of what church model you are using (see chapter 13, "Three Models of Church Planting"). Doing so with the cell church model might require more creativity. But it is doable, along with the house church model and the prevalent church model.

SOME PRACTICAL ISSUES

To remind the reader, this is not a chapter about biblical eldership in general, but about developing and appointing that first group of elders from an unreached people group in a hostile environment (e.g., HBB elders in an HBB church). One of the richest blessings the Lord has given me is to be able to meet with local elders in a variety of cultures around the world. Here are some issues that arise:

How mature does someone have to be to be appointable to eldership?

We all know how lists and schemes abound merging and expounding the qualities of 1 Timothy 3 and Titus 1 for eldership. The problem arises when we take the various qualities as *qualifications*—a word that is not in either text. When we do that, the list immediately becomes a checklist and a candidate fails if even one box can't be checked. Is that what the Spirit intended? Is that what Paul meant for Timothy and Titus to do? That interpretation is understandable, given that in both passages Paul wrote "an overseer must be above reproach" and so on. But is that the right interpretation?

Help comes when we realize that most of these facets are qualities; they are traits that are relative in a person's life. For instance, an elder should be gentle (1 Timothy 3:3). But no one is perfectly gentle—certainly not myself, nor many elders I know. It's not hard to see why gentleness is a valuable quality for an elder, and how an elder who is too *ungentle* may do more harm than good. Paul was a practical apostle, and he was dealing with the question of who should be an elder in a practical way. These are qualities to be assessed in a relative manner.

As these are relative qualities, they no doubt varied from church to church. The new elders in the Antioch church were probably not quite as mature as their Jerusalem counterparts. And the new elders in Paul and Barnabas' brand-new pioneer churches in Acts 14 were certainly even less mature, in terms of years in the Lord, spiritual depth, and elder character. But they were mature enough. How is it that some of those churches could have been planted, and elders appointed, in a matter of weeks or a few months?

Many have pointed out that most of the qualities are social traits rather than spiritual ones, though within the context of commitment to Christ. In other words, a person may have strength in that area even before he came to faith. This would explain how Paul could appoint elders among new believers after only a few months, or even weeks. On the other hand, the calling of eldership is one of leadership, shepherding, and teaching. Not everyone—no matter how mature—is going to have that calling and those gifts. I do not believe that eldership should be the aim for every man.

Finally, at the risk of beating my drum again, this understanding of eldership qualities underscores the necessity of having more than one elder. The elders can be mature *collectively*, even though individuals will have gaps. They can complement each other. And they can corporately spur each other on to growth in areas of weakness. Surely that's how it was in those first churches Paul and Barnabas planted among the Gentiles. And when we look today at Buddhist contexts, or Hindu, or Taoist, or whatever, we must treat the question in the same way. The alternative is to wait for *fully qualified* men to be formed. You may be waiting an awfully long time, while the fruit goes sour on the branch and the opportunity passes.

Should you work toward appointing elders early on in the process of church planting or do it later?

Those who argue for later will cite 1 Timothy 3:6—". . . and not a new convert, so that he will not become conceited and fall into the condemnation incurred by the devil"—and 1 Timothy 5:22—"Do not lay hands upon anyone too hastily and thereby share responsibility for the sins of others; keep yourself free from sin." But how "new" is *too* new, and how "hastily" is *too* hastily? Again, these are relative matters that require practical judgment. In the first case the danger Paul points to is the onset of pride. That won't be a danger for all elder candidates, especially for older men who are already respected in other capacities, even if they're new in Christ. Look for where a person's motives are pointing and how they respond in situations where egos are involved. Regarding 1 Timothy 5:22, scholars differ on whether or not the verse even applies to the appointment of new elders. But even if it does, Paul is again just urging good judgment rather than advising excessive caution or procrastination on elder appointment in general.

Dick Scoggins, who planted many house churches in New England (sort of a hostile and resistant field!), told me after his decades of church planting that when he erred on the question of timing it was usually on the side of waiting too long rather than appointing too early. "First Timothy 5:22 is not a stop sign," he's been known to say.

As you begin moving toward preparation of elders, guess what? Don't expect things to go smoothly. I've heard of a few cases where everything went smoothly (or maybe I just read the glossy version), but most of the time they do not. This makes sense. Among your people group, the appointment of the first group of elders in the new pioneer church may be an utterly critical landmark in taking territory back from Satan. Do you think he's simply going to fold his arms and walk away?

Several years ago church planters were about to lay hands on four men to be elders among the Kurds in northern Iraq—a first in history. One day an extremist walked into the workplace of Mahmoud, one of the key proto-elders, and shot him in the head. He became the church's first martyr, leaving behind a pregnant wife and a child. Actual elder appointments were not able to take place until a few years later.

In another Middle East city, workers were about to appoint three men to be elders. This might have become the first MBB church in the Arab world under the leadership of MBB elders. But it was not to be. During a fellowship meeting the wives of two of the elder candidates got into a quarrel regarding one of the kids, and their emotional and hurtful argument led to the breaking of fellowship between the two families for an extended period. When they were reconciled, no one felt that the group was ready to move ahead with eldership. Now, years later, elders still haven't been appointed, and there is a serious fragmentation among the MBBs in the country.

In a large Southeast Asian country, the workers successfully appointed three elders, a near-first in this strategic people group. When one of the workers asked the wife of one of these men that day why she didn't seem happy about this joyous occasion, she explained, "My husband and I had a bad argument this morning, and he punched me in the face. I hate ministry."

This is real life. The absolutely wonderful assurance is that it has always been this way. Throughout the centuries God has expanded the boundaries of the church through extraordinarily deficient church planters and imperfect local believers. We are all damaged goods that God is in the process of healing and restoring. That's encouraging to me.

What if I only have two potential elders? Should I go ahead and appoint them?

I don't think there's an automatic answer to that. Three is better for a myriad of reasons. But I have seen two work in at least a couple of churches. I also know of a situation in Central Asia where the church has done well under two elders, but recently one of them had to move away. That has caused some real difficulty, and the expatriate church planter has had no choice but to jump back in again and provide leadership. In general, I would say that if you appoint only two elders then you need to make sure that developing a third elder is an objective earnestly shared by those two elders and the church.

Should expatriate or apostolic workers become elders in the new church for a while?

I would personally discourage this. In the New Testament there is never any confusion of roles. The apostle is there temporarily to plant the church and move on; the elders are local believers who remain and shepherd the church. To confuse the two roles leads to . . . well, confusion. And while having the church planters serve as elders might help in the short term, it might also actually delay indigenization and the church getting established on its own feet.

Likewise, what about local leaders who are both elders (or elder candidates) and gifted church planters?

This situation comes up a lot in pioneering work today, which is a magnificent reality. It shouldn't surprise us that God raises up key persons, since we know His promise to give specially gifted individuals to churches in Ephesians 4:11–12. But, as we have seen, the roles of elder and apostolic church planter (who is focused primarily on planting new churches further afield) are biblically and practically two very distinct roles. The church planter often has some sort of vocational ministry role, which is usually not true of an elder. My advice is that an individual not wear both hats for long, but rather tries to discern the Lord's long-term calling on his life and goes in that direction. The itinerant church planting calling and life is different from that of the local elder. The former is concerned with pioneering, breakthroughs, and expansion. The latter is primarily focused on the shepherding well-being of one church (or a cluster of local churches).

Should church planters try to establish deacons before elders?

This is not an easy question, and I've seen both scenarios work. Some would point out that deacons are not just to set up chairs, hand out bulletins, or wait on tables. The requisite qualities listed for them in the New Testament are very similar to those of elders. Paul addresses *both* at the beginning of his letter to the Philippians. And I believe he explicitly says that women can be deacons in 1 Timothy 3:11. So, in view of the fact that deaconship is a responsible position, some church planters prefer to first appoint a group of deacons and then later, from that group, appoint some to be elders.

While I personally believe that to be a valid approach, it is not what I advise. Why not? First of all, we don't see this in the new church plants of the New Testament. They always went straight to elders. Secondly, even though eldership and deaconship are two distinct ministries or offices in the New Testament, if you start out this way you will be enshrining the notion that deaconship is a stepping stone to eldership, which isn't necessarily what it was intended. Some believe that in New Testament times only the more developed churches launched deaconship, probably as a way to take some of the serving burden off the elders. And thirdly, it seems to me that the approach of starting with deacons and then establishing elders is likely to prolong the new church's dependence on the church planters.

Should eldership be a full-time, paid position?

Again, quoting 1 Timothy 5:17–18: "The elders who rule well are to be considered worthy of double honor, especially those who work hard at preaching and teaching. For the Scripture says, 'YOU SHALL NOT MUZZLE THE OX WHILE HE IS THRESHING,' and 'The laborer is worthy of his wages.'" It seems we can infer three principles:

a. It is OK for a church to have no paid elders. That was probably the case in Ephesus when Paul wrote to Timothy there.

b. To have one elder (or a few elders, in a larger church or cluster) who are paid because of the high time commitments involved in "ruling well" and "working hard at preaching and teaching" seems to be what Paul is talking about. Even so, I would imagine this to be a small minority.

c. The focus of the paid elder's ministry is the local church. And the funds that Paul spoke of were from the local church. I personally do not see a biblical basis for outside funds paying local elders/pastors.

How are elders to make decisions—whether in the West, East, or South? Is there a prescribed way in the New Testament?

It is safe to say that elders should seek the Lord earnestly regarding issues before them, in worship, prayer, and perhaps fasting. They should discuss all matters among themselves with a keen listening ear, with respect, and with the putting away of personal agendas and questionable motives. Likewise, consulting the congregation is certainly precedented. How the apostles consulted the congregation in Acts 6 is a good example.

But how elders are to actually process decisions seems to be an open matter. How a group of African elders might make decisions could be very different from how the elders of an urban church in Chicago or a group of HBB elders in Tibet do so. Subbamma writes, "In Andhra, not only must we have Indian churches, but also churches which fit the main subcultures and main ethnic units of this great province."[3] It seems to me that there is lots of room for cultural factors.

You Can Get There from Here

Those are some practical issues that often arise when dealing with the appointment of elders in a pioneer setting. But how do you get there? Let's say you are working with a fellowship group of fifteen to twenty believers. How can you teach the concepts of biblical eldership and work with this group to develop, appoint, and install elders? It sounds a lot easier in a book than working it out in real life.

While there would be similarities, this is not like appointing elders in a new church in Los Angeles or London. We are talking about new believers who have come out of a very different approach to God, out of Hinduism, Buddhism, animistic beliefs, or whatever. Many are likely to be struggling still with their faith and with feelings of having betrayed their families and heritage, perhaps wondering if they really are apostates as their relatives bitterly accuse them daily to be. Some who were Muslims may still tend toward a legalistic mentality. Some may leave the faith.

There may be huge issues of trust, and even the possibility of informers lurking in the group. There is probably not a visible example of what they are to become. Or if there is a Bible-believing church locally, it is probably from a "Christian" cultural background, which is not profitable for the new body to emulate. And in a hostile environment it is normal for governments to target the leaders for arrest and possible torture or imprisonment. The potential elders will have to grapple with this reality and come to their own way of dealing with it. Church planting—including the appointing of elders—in such contexts is not just difficult; it's revolutionary.

While I cannot give you a recipe or a road map, here are five recommendations that should help move the work along in the right direction.

1. Teach the whole fellowship over time the New Testament concepts of what the local church is and how it is to function. Teach all the "one another" passages that describe how believers are to be closely linked with each other and how they are to serve and edify each other. "Church life" is not merely a set of meetings, but the day-to-day life of a healthy organism. What happens in their relationships *outside* of meetings is as important as what happens in meetings.

   Then teach about elders and their vital leadership, teaching, and shepherding role in the local church. Along with this, teach how your own role as God's apostolic messenger will be changing and no doubt shrinking. Share with the believers that they will begin to see you less and less, and at some point you will be leaving. (Or it may be that you are already not in a dominant role in the fellowship. That is good, as long as you have the position and influence to exercise your apostolic role in helping the church become what it needs to be.)

2. Begin to strategically pull back. This is to help the fellowship become less dependent on you in terms of teaching and leading and to free you up to focus on developing leaders. This mode is typical of latter Phase V and all of Phase VI (see chapter 5, "The Pioneer Church Planting Phases").

Focus most of your energies on mentoring and developing leaders and teachers, especially potential elders. As you discern who these individuals are, you also need to ask them, "Are you interested in growing spiritually, being mentored, and possibly moving into leadership more and more?" Isn't this what Paul was saying to Timothy when he wrote, "The things which you have heard from me in the presence of many witnesses, entrust these to faithful men who will be able to teach others also" (2 Timothy 2:2)? Some talk about finding those who are FAT: faithful, available, teachable.

This involves working on character, attitudes, recurring sin patterns, and motives. It means being involved in such matters as marriage and family life, employment, and other relationships. It also means looking for all kinds of ways to get these emerging leaders into all sorts of ministry. Delegate. Train. Review. Delegate again. Discern giftings. As they are stretched, good leaders will grow and learn to draw on the Spirit. Others may fall to the side, deciding that leadership is not for them.

3. When you think the believers are ready, establish the role of "elder candidate" and begin to discuss it in the fellowship group. As these are men whom you believe can become the first elders, you can go to them and challenge them to pray about accepting this role of elder candidate. This means that they will go through some teaching and orientation, most likely leading to elder appointment. This process sets the stage for the following:

   a. Helping them experience what a special commitment eldership requires.

b. Making the process very clear and intentional.

c. A period of special training (two to six months).

d. An opportunity for intense character work. For example: "Mahmoud, you have said that you aspire to the office of elder in this group, and I believe that would be a good step for you. I believe in you. But I have heard some things about your business dealings. Can we discuss and pray about that?"

e. Preparing the body for certain individuals eventually leading. It gets the fellowship involved. You can also choose to invite feedback on the candidates. If you learn about something serious that you were not aware of, it might be best to delay one's appointment.

f. As you are having multiple elder candidates, this avoids the strong single leader bottleneck.

4. In a variety of situations, I have seen how elder preparation and training affords a wonderful opportunity to teach on the particular subjects of the church, leadership, humility, heavenly wisdom, character, suffering, feeding Christ's sheep, etc. Don't be surprised if your elder candidates take a real leap forward in their walk with God.

This may be a perfect time to bring in a special Bible teacher for these sessions. In one Middle Eastern capital there was a Christian-background leader who was a very gifted teacher and who had a deep heart for majority ministry. It was a perfect match, as the church planters and elder candidates met weekly at his house.

You can also use specific tools on the church and eldership. One such work is John Piper's *Biblical Eldership: Shepherd the Flock of God Among You*.[4] In one Central Asia country this twenty-page tool was translated into the local language, and its use spread among a large number of church plants to great profit.

5. It is no accident that just prior to appointing elders Paul and Barnabas drove home the point: "Through many tribulations

we must enter the kingdom of God" (Acts 14:22). In pioneer and hostile environments, we must not pretend that persecution may be avoided. Instead we must talk candidly about suffering and persecution, and help fellow believers become equipped biblically and spiritually for what lies ahead. If, as an expatriate worker, I feel timid to make this point because I feel I am not as likely to suffer—an assumption that may or may not be true—this does not relieve me of this responsibility of teaching.

CONCLUSION

When you reach the momentous day when you appoint that crucial first group of elders in your unreached people group, don't expect CNN or local cameramen to show up. But that doesn't change the fact that this is likely to be a historic event, a pivotal moment in the destiny of your people group and country. It is a precious milestone for the kingdom of God that will echo in eternity. Join Paul as he dreamed about being in heaven with the precious brothers and sisters who had found eternal life through his church planting ministry: "For who is our hope or joy or crown of exultation? Is it not even you, in the presence of our Lord Jesus at His coming? For you are our glory and joy" (1 Thessalonians 2:19–20).

TEAM DISCUSSION QUESTIONS

1. Does our culture favor strong one-person rule, or are there examples in this society of collective leadership?

2. Do we accept the premise that the first group of elders must be at least two or three men, rather than establishing one person as lone elder?

3. What kind of problems can we expect as we near this process of elder appointment?

4. Are we, as a team, on the same page about the kind of leadership or eldership structure we think the new church should have?

5. Do passages such as Acts 14:21–23 and Titus 1:5, and the confidence that we will get there at some point, motivate and inspire us?

6. How mature do local believers have to be to be ready for eldership? Which is worse: appointing too early or waiting too long?

7. What do we think of the elder candidate process described in #3 above?

Epilogue
What Really Is Church Planting Ministry?

The limousine carefully made its way across a cold, dark, and rainy Washington DC. It was October 26, 1962, and the Cuban Missile Crisis had nearly reached a point where thermonuclear conflict was very possible. From released Soviet records we now know that Cuban president Fidel Castro had urged Nikita Khrushchev to carry out a nuclear first strike against the Atlantic seaboard. Soviet submarine commanders had been given authority to launch nuclear weapons in the event of confrontation at sea due to the American blockade. On this evening, American Attorney General Robert Kennedy was meeting with the Soviet ambassador, Anatoly Dobrynin. Fortunately, they were able to come to an agreement that night that spared the planet a World War III nightmare.

The primary reason they were effective is not that they were good negotiators. They were not merely exchanging ideas, but were acting with authority. Robert Kennedy was mandated to speak in the place of the president—who just happened to be his brother—with his authority and in his full stead and prestige. Likewise with Dobrynin.

Remarkably, our role as God's ambassadors is much the same. Consider:

> As each one has received a special gift, employ it in serving one another as good stewards of the manifold grace of God. *Whoever speaks, is to do so as one who is speaking the utterances of God*; whoever serves is to do so as one who is serving by the strength which God supplies. (1 Peter 4:10–11; emphasis added)

Peter divides up all ministry into two broad categories: speaking ministries and serving ministries. Of course, all ministry is serving, but there are types of service which are nonspeaking in nature (e.g., helps, logistics, administration, physical arrangements). What are speaking ministries? Teaching (large groups, small groups, one-on-one), leading, counseling, evangelizing, church planting, encouraging, and the list goes on and on. Peter's point is this: When you are in any speaking ministry situation, you are to speak the words of God in God's place. You are not simply relaying information or concepts, but you are actually speaking *for* God. You and I are going to be effective or ineffective in our ministries to the extent our efforts are actually ministering God's words. You are not just a team leader, or a Bible teacher, or one who shares the gospel, or the person leading a meeting. The bottom line is that *ministry is simple: it is speaking God's words, in God's place, with God's authority.*

Let's first see this borne out further in the New Testament, and then we will examine the crucial implications for our work of planting churches among unreached peoples.

Examples of New Testament Apostolic Work

> *"Pay close attention to yourself and to your teaching; persevere in these things, for as you do this you will ensure salvation both for yourself and for those who hear you."* (1 Timothy 4:16)

> *"You therefore, my son, be strong in the grace that is in Christ Jesus. The things which you have heard from me in the presence of many witnesses, entrust these to faithful men who will be able to teach others also."* (2 Timothy 2:1–2)

> *"You, however, continue in the things you have learned*

*and become convinced of, knowing from whom you
have learned them, and that from childhood you have
known the sacred writings which are able to give you
the wisdom that leads to salvation through faith which
is in Christ Jesus. All Scripture is inspired by God and
profitable for teaching, for reproof, for correction, for
training in righteousness; so that the man of God may
be adequate, equipped for every good work. I solemnly
charge you in the presence of God and of Christ Jesus,
who is to judge the living and the dead, and by His
appearing and His kingdom: preach the word; be ready
in season and out of season; reprove, rebuke, exhort,
with great patience and instruction. For the time will
come when they will not endure sound doctrine; but
wanting to have their ears tickled, they will accumulate
for themselves teachers in accordance to their own
desires, and will turn away their ears from the truth
and will turn aside to myths."* (2 Timothy 3:14–4:4)

*"[The overseer must be] holding fast the faithful word
which is in accordance with the teaching, so that he
will be able both to exhort in sound doctrine and to
refute those who contradict."* (Titus 1:9)

*"[Paul said to the elders of the church at Ephesus:] 'I
did not shrink from declaring to you anything that was
profitable, and teaching you publicly and from house
to house . . . I did not shrink from declaring to you the
whole purpose of God.'"* (Acts 20:20, 27)

*"We proclaim Him, admonishing every man and
teaching every man with all wisdom, so that we may
present every man complete in Christ."* (Colossians
1:28) It is encouraging to observe how Paul's teaching
here was oriented to every individual: "every man." In

pioneering work, especially, so much of ministering the Word is one-on-one.

Luke summarizes a year and a half of Paul's ministry at Corinth in this way: *"He settled there a year and six months, teaching the word of God among them."* (Acts 18:11) Wow! A whole year and a half of Paul's work summed up that way.

And what should perhaps be the life verse for all pioneer church planters: *"Be diligent to present yourself approved to God as a workman who does not need to be ashamed, accurately handling the word of truth"* (2 Timothy 2:15). Please note how in this brief sentence Paul points to Timothy being a "workman" with skills that require developing, who operates with creativity and the urgency of diligence, and who recognizes the bedrock objective of going for the approval of God rather than other people. There is the possibility of falling short or of being effective. And our aim is to speak *accurately*—that is, we work hard over time to correctly understand what God is saying and to convey that properly. We teach *His* words rather than merely using the Bible as a source of illustrations for teaching our personal ideas.

My dear fellow apostolic workers, let me encourage you with a very powerful truth that arises from these verses. Our work can seem so very, very complicated. The field team leader can especially feel absolutely overwhelmed and incredibly inadequate. You might feel you have to be a top leader of people, an expert in your tentmaking area, a skillful evangelist, one who learns the language flawlessly, an insightful cross-culturalist, and on and on. It's good to know we are inadequate in ourselves and derive our adequacy from God (2 Corinthians 3:5). But to place ourselves under crushing expectations is not good. Let the verses above greatly lighten the burden from your shoulders: *Your main job is to speak God's Word in God's place.* The rest is quite secondary.

I've seen teams hit a wall of frustration, sort of like this: "We've learned the language quite well. We've bonded with the people. Ours is the best NGO in the country. The team runs like a well-oiled machine. We just don't understand why there isn't any fruit!" Fruitlessness in pioneer situations, of course, is often a matter of hard soil or that it apparently is not yet God's timing. But can it sometimes be due to the fact that we are so busy doing everything in the world other than ministering the Word of God to people?

One of the largest ministries to majority people in the Middle East consists of a "mother church" of 250–300 people which has planted eight daughter churches, all nine churches being in sensitive locations and facing persecution. For over ten years it has been my privilege to receive monthly reports from the team leader and to interact with him on a regular basis. From the earliest days I was struck by how much this young apostle was committed to personal study of the Word. Then, as ministry developed, everything seemed to revolve around how he was teaching this or that passage or how they would take a three-day retreat with the believers to work through the book of Ephesians, or church life in Acts, or whatever. It occurred to me that he was simply planting churches the way Paul did.

Before moving on to some final applications, it is important that we touch on three important "disclaimers":

1. As I am exhorting church planters to really major on studying God's Word and ministering God's Word, I am not talking about mere head knowledge. Obviously feeding on and feeding others with the Word is a lot more than that.

2. I am not saying that studying and ministering the Bible is the *only* important aspect of ministry. Of course there are all the other really vital facets, such as the role of the Holy Spirit, prayer, community and relationships, pastoral care, cross-cultural dynamics, contextualization, etc. But if the Word is the foundation, it is the core of what we convey, what we minister, and our guide for all decisions and strategies.

3. This isn't for all Christians or even for all CP workers. We recall 1 Peter 4:10–11: "As each one has received a special gift, employ it in serving one another as good stewards of the manifold grace of God. Whoever speaks, is to do so as one who is speaking the utterances of God; whoever serves is to do so as one who is serving by the strength which God supplies." There are all the nonspeaking kinds of ministries, which may be the calling of a

few on the team (e.g., facilitators). The applications below apply to teachers, church planters, evangelists, apostles, etc.

APPLICATION #1: HOW YOU SPEND YOUR TIME

Time, for all of us, is limited. It's been said that there are three ways to waste your life: do nothing, do the wrong things, or do so many things that none of them are truly effective. If you are called to be an apostolic church planter, then you want to be like we see the apostles in Acts 6. During that painful crisis between the Hellenistic Jews and the Palestinian Jews they easily could've been pulled into time-absorbing problem-solving and administration. Instead, they clung to their priority: "We will devote ourselves to prayer and to the ministry of the word" (v. 4). What was the result? In verse 7 we read, "The word of God kept on spreading; and the number of the disciples continued to increase greatly in Jerusalem, and a great many of the priests were becoming obedient to the faith." This ain't rocket science. They devoted themselves to the ministry of the Word, and the Word kept spreading, flourishing. That is the apostolic paradigm.

We were pleased to have George Verwer, founder of Operation Mobilisation, speak at our leadership conference in 2000. To this day everyone remembers three words from his talk, even as he yelled them out to the conference hall audience of 1,000 plus: "Cut! Cut! Cut!" He was speaking of the crucial need to prioritize our time and to drop lots of tertiary activities. We must do whatever is necessary in our schedule and workload in order to *major* on the ministry of the Word. Again, the net result of this should be to *lighten* our load, not make it heavier.

Looking back over the years, Martin Luther summed up his world-changing life this way: "I simply taught, preached, wrote God's Word; otherwise I did nothing. And then while I slept, or drank Wittenberg beer with Philip and Amsdorf, the Word so greatly weakened all who opposed me. I did nothing; the Word did it all . . . For it is almighty and takes captive the hearts, and if the hearts are captured, the evil work will fall of itself."[1]

One day a young German pastor came home after work to find his kitten up in a tree. Though it was a young tree, it was tall enough that he couldn't reach the kitten, nor would she come down. He thought to himself: "I have an idea." He grabbed some rope from the trunk of his Volkswagen and tied one end to the rear bumper and the other end to the tree as high as he could reach. Then he eased the car forward slowly, intending to bend the tree down enough to be able to take hold of the kitten. Everything went fine as the car moved several feet forward. But then, "Whoooosh!" You guessed it: one of the knots came loose, the tree flung back, and the kitten disappeared! Gone. Minus one cat.

A few days later, the pastor noticed one of his parishioners in the pet food aisle at the local supermarket. "Frau Schmidt, I didn't know your family had a pet." "Oh Pastor," she replied, "you wouldn't believe what happened. The other afternoon we were all out in the back garden relaxing when my daughter, Ute, came to us almost in tears. 'Mommy, why can't we have a kitten? I really want a kitten! Please, please, please.' I told her we should ask God about it, so right then we prayed together and asked the Lord if He wanted Ute to have a kitten. What happened next was the most incredible answer to prayer I have ever witnessed. God dropped a kitten on us right out of the sky!"

The point is simply this: God is not limited by the sum of our resources, our efforts, our skills. We all long for the kind of ministries where it is clear that God has worked, that God has brought about a harvest well beyond anything that can be attributable to us. It's the Word of God, through the Spirit of God, that is the great, powerful leverage for impact in the life of a people group. We need God-sized results in today's harvest field.

Practically speaking, this means I need to be spending a lot of time in the Scriptures. One approach would be to *read* the Bible every day, reflectively, with a journal. And then also carve out two larger blocks each week in your schedule for in-depth *study*—that is, inductive study of a passage or topic. These study blocks should be free from interruption (door closed, kids knowing it's not a good time to disturb you, etc.).

Billy Graham was asked in an interview, "If you had to live your life over again, what would you do differently?" His answer was this: "One of my great regrets is that I have not studied enough. I wish I had studied more and preached less. People have pressured me into speaking to groups when I should have been studying and preparing. Donald Barnhouse said that if he knew the Lord was coming in three years, he would spend two of them studying and one preaching. I'm trying to make it up."

Some may feel that this doesn't apply as directly in the early days of a church plant, when the team is very busy with language learning, establishing an NGO or tentmaking platform, setting up homes, making acquaintances, learning how to get along as a team, etc. It is true that for a while you may not have believers to disciple or even seekers who are keen to study the Word with you. However, it is all the more important at this stage to build significant habits of Bible study into your schedule, as it will be harder to do so down the road. Beginning this investment now means that you will be ready when the opportunities come.

APPLICATION #2: HOW CHURCHES GET PLANTED

As I mentioned in chapter 2, "What Is a Church?—and How to Plant One," finding a church made up of believers from an unreached people group in a pioneer context is like finding a turtle on a fencepost. Someone has intentionally brought this about; it's not there by accident nor in the natural flow of things. How much more so if the church is healthy! As we have seen, the New Testament teaches various aspects of healthy church life. "They were continually devoting themselves to the apostles' teaching and to fellowship, to the breaking of bread and to prayer" (Acts 2:42). We must not assume, for example, that a fellowship of believers from Hindu background will naturally gravitate toward New Testament patterns of *ekklesia* any more so than churches in the West do. It is the job of the church planting apostles to guide and prepare the new churches for such. I was once asked at a conference what subject I was going to speak on. "The key role of Scripture in planting a new church," I replied. "What a novel idea!" was the somewhat facetious response. Do we use the Bible in our devotions and then in our strategy and problem-solving use everything *except* the Bible?

Think of all the different ministries that must take place in the planting of a new church in a hostile setting. Consider how it is only through the ministry of the Word that the following take place effectively:

- Believers are discipled and encouraged.

- Body life is developed.

- The church gains an understanding and vision for who they are and how they are to live. Believers come to grips with their evangelistic message.

- Essential foundations of sound teaching are laid.

- Every new fellowship struggles with a host of problems, including those arising from character issues, interpersonal relationships, conflicting opinions, disunity, bitterness, and pride. The church planters and local leaders tackle these problems head-on through the Word.

- Transformational ministry occurs. Local believers, as well as expatriate workers, will need to be confronted over sin issues in their lives and gain victory as brothers and sisters around them speak the truth in love. Likewise, as proved to be crucial in the people movement among the Buddhists of Mongolia, future leaders need to be equipped in how to deal with believers' sin.[2]

- Elder candidates are prepared and installed.

- Local teachers and leaders are prepared. I'm always thrilled when I witness an MBB brother or sister who clearly has spiritual gifts of leadership or Bible teaching. The church planters will need to come alongside to cultivate and develop these budding gifts.

So what is the starting point for all this? Is it not the depth of the church planters in their grasp of the Word? It is so crucial in those early months that we are in there equipping the saints. Some say that the church planters should quickly melt into the background and not steer or teach the new fellowship. Now there is a time to strategically withdraw, but the New Testament model is for the apostles to play a vital role of feeding and foundation laying in the early period.

The story goes of a poor man who owned a goat. He fed the goat oats, and the cost of this was getting too much for him. So one day he decided to substitute 10 percent of the oats with sawdust. After a week everything seemed fine, so he made it a 50/50 mixture. After a month he was very pleased, as this was saving him lots of money and the goat seemed to be doing OK. So he went to a 90/10 mixture of sawdust and oats. This went on for a few more weeks and everything seemed fine, until one day the goat just fell over and died. We see lots of HBB, MBB, and BBB fellowships come into existence around the world. Sadly, very many of them just as quickly disintegrate and disappear. We have got to be feeding the new believers. We mustn't shortchange them.

Some might feel that all this only pertains to ministry to believers. What about pioneering ministry that goes on for years without seeing anyone come to faith? What about evangelism in general? Does all this about the ministry of the Word still pertain? The answer, of course, is yes. The evangel is much more than just the basics of *The Four Spiritual Laws*. Among all unreached people groups today, you will find people who are hungry to study the New Testament with you and to learn directly from Scripture about who Jesus really is. I am reminded how in Romans 1:15 Paul equates "the gospel" with all that Paul has to share with the church at Rome, including that incredibly rich epistle.

CONCLUSION

Are you feeling guilty or inadequate in this area? Please don't. What we are talking about is a lifelong process of learning, growing, and developing skills—becoming "a workman [or workwoman] who does not need to be ashamed, accurately handling the word of truth" (2 Timothy 2:15). Could it be that through this chapter the Lord is prompting you to seek out a mentor who can help you develop in this area?

Speaking God's Word, in God's place, with God's authority, and looking for the results that only He can accomplish. This is sobering!

It is also invigorating. It is my earnest hope that this exhortation speaks new hope into your work, and that all this is *releasing* for you, because the power and impact don't have to come from you. The Word of God has been likened to a lion penned up in a cage. Our job is simply to open the cage and release the lion!

Appendix 1
Apostleship in the New Testament

Among New Testament teachings, perhaps none is so important and yet, at the same time, as complex as the notion of apostleship. Obviously the apostles were foundational to the establishment and stability of the first-century church. They were likewise pivotal in the expansion of the church across the known world during the first century and beyond. As good witnesses, they both held ground and gained ground. While there is a good measure of clarity regarding the identity and role of "the Twelve," there are many references to other individuals called apostles. Scholars differ on how the term applies to this latter group. There is therefore a diversity of opinion today as to whether or not the term can appropriately be applied to certain leaders and ministries—and if it can, how? Some denominations will refer to an individual or two in top leadership as apostles, with a view toward hierarchical and organizational authority, while others will insist it applies to pioneer church planters. Let's dive in and explore what apostleship truly meant in the New Testament.

THE WORDS

Two words are of primary concern for us:

1. *apostolos* (αποστολος): noun; "apostle"; literally, "sent one"; *messenger, envoy, representative*; 80 New Testament occurrences. In 2 Corinthians 11:13 we also find the word *pseudapostoloi*, "false apostles."

2. *apostolay* (αποστολη): noun; "apostleship"; 4 New Testament occurrences (Acts 1:25; Romans 1:5; 1 Corinthians 9:2; Galatians 2:8).

Regarding verbs, the classical Greek *pempto* was more common in secular usage for "sending," while *apostello* carried more the sense of "representing, acting on behalf of, being an example or model of the one who sent," and most often referred to a group (e.g., ship or crew). Josephus uses the word once for a particular group of Jews being sent on a mission to Rome. It often carried the notion of an express commission and of being sent abroad. Nonetheless, the verb *apostello* had become extremely common by the first century, so that it normally just meant "sending" and only rarely carried its original sense of "commissioning," though sometimes we do find that (e.g., Acts 22:21; 26:16). Although *apostello* occurs 132 times in the New Testament, because of its broad connotation it is not too helpful in our search for the meaning of *apostle*. We'll focus mostly on the nouns.

THE TWELVE

> It was at this time that He went off to the mountain to pray, and He spent the whole night in prayer to God. And when day came, He called His disciples to Him and chose twelve of them, whom He also named as apostles: Simon, whom He also named Peter, and Andrew his brother; and James and John; and Philip and Bartholomew; and Matthew and Thomas; James the son of Alphaeus, and Simon who was called the Zealot; Judas the son of James, and Judas Iscariot, who became a traitor. Jesus came down with them and stood on a level place; and there was a large crowd of His disciples. (Luke 6:12–17)

We know that Jesus selected these twelve men from a larger group of disciples. Seventy-two men were later sent out for preaching. The gathered believers of Acts 1 were "about one hundred and twenty persons." And, of course, during Jesus' ministry the number of followers ebbed and flowed sometimes in the thousands.

As the primary focus of this appendix is not the Twelve, we won't go into much detail concerning the makeup and commission given to them. But a couple of things are particularly interesting for us. Firstly, it's clear that in replacing Judas in Acts 1 they were keen to get back to exactly twelve. That was the Hebrew number of completeness, corresponding to the number of the tribes of Israel. Eleven was not acceptable and thirteen was not desirable, even though presumably both Joseph and Matthias were qualified.

The twelve apostles played an absolutely essential and unique role that was foundational and sacred. Certain passages refer to the prophets and apostles, meaning the key foundation layers of the Old and New Testament eras respectively (e.g., 2 Peter 3:2; Revelation 18:20). Indeed, the foundation stones of the coming New Jerusalem will have written on them the names of the twelve apostles (Revelation 21:14). No doubt that refers to the Twelve, not to others such as Barnabas or Silas.

Of course, the Twelve didn't just sit around being pillars or foundations. They began with many bold efforts to expand the church among the Jews. Later history also records several examples of these men taking the gospel to nations further afield. Christian tradition has it that Thomas pioneered and established churches in India. Others are believed to have spread the gospel to Turkey, Russia, Ethiopia, and elsewhere.

While the twelve apostles were given broad authority in the church by Christ, the focus of their apostleship was not some form of top-level ecclesiastical governing. For example, at the Jerusalem council of Acts 15, consensus was sought of both "the apostles and the elders" (vv. 4, 6, 23), along with the involvement of "the whole church" (v. 22). Ironically, even this major decision and policy didn't carry overwhelming weight, as the Judaizing controversy persisted well beyond. I personally don't see evidence for believing that apostleship today pertains to a kind of positional, hierarchical governing in church denominations.

PAUL

Paul was the great apostle to the Gentiles (cf. Acts 9:15; Romans 11:13; Galatians 2:8; Ephesians 3:1ff; 1 Timothy 2:7). It is likewise stressed whom he was sent *from*—Jesus Himself (1 Corinthians 9:1; Galatians 1:1; Ephesians 1:1; 1 Timothy 1:1; 2 Timothy 1:1). Of course, this emphasis on *from* and *to* alludes to the pioneer nature of Paul's apostleship. The beginning of his letter to the Romans also makes this extremely clear: "Paul, a bond-servant of Christ Jesus, called as an apostle, set apart for the gospel of God . . . through [Jesus Christ] we have received grace and apostleship to bring about the obedience of faith among all the Gentiles for His name's sake" (Romans 1:1, 5).

Paul's apostleship is particularly curious. He's not one of the Twelve. He would not meet either of the qualifications noted for Judas' replacement in Acts 1:21–22: 1) having been with the original set of disciples from the beginning of Jesus' earthly ministry; and 2) having been a witness of Jesus' resurrection in order to truly *be* a witness (Greek *martus*, which is usually rendered "witness," though sometimes carrying the idea of martyrdom). Paul makes much of Christ's personal appearances to him, but this would still not meet the Acts 1:21–22 requirements. As we will see, neither would James, Barnabas, and others who are later called apostles meet these requirements. Unmistakably, then, another category of apostleship was emerging in the New Testament.

Nonetheless, Paul often refers to his apostolic authority in Christ across the Gentile world. He writes to the Ephesians: "So then you are no longer strangers and aliens, but you are fellow citizens with the saints, and are of God's household, *having been built on the foundation of the apostles and prophets*, Christ Jesus Himself being the corner stone" (Ephesians 2:19–20; emphasis added). Few would argue that Paul wasn't including himself in that "foundation of the apostles."

It would seem, then, that Paul was sort of a bridge between the first apostles—the Twelve—and the later, broader group of apostles. He had broad foundational authority, especially appreciated by the fact that he wrote so much of the New Testament. Nonetheless, most of the references to his apostleship were in the context of his calling to take the gospel to *new, unreached people groups.*

PIONEER GOSPEL WORKERS

While those in this category were not part of the Twelve, their apostolic calling was not of a completely different nature than the first apostles. Let us recall that the original meaning of *apostolos* (noun) and *apostello* (verb) is one being sent from a higher authority to accomplish a particular task, representing that higher authority and speaking for him in the process. Let's look at some passages:

> Acts 1:8
> "You will receive power when the Holy Spirit has come upon you; and you shall be My witnesses both in Jerusalem, and in all Judea and Samaria, and even to the remotest part of the earth."

We're told in verse 2 that this is part of the "orders [given] to the apostles whom He had chosen," part of what He "commanded" (v. 4). This is the core of the commission or mission given to these special *sent ones*: to be witnesses (plural of *martus*), in an ever expanding scope to reach the whole world with the gospel. Bible teachers who see in this verse a threefold outline of the whole of the book of Acts—a) reaching Jerusalem; b) reaching Judea and Samaria; c) reaching the rest of the world—are probably correct. What is crucial for us to see in this foundational verse is that the Twelve were not the only apostles in the book of Acts who would fulfill this core mandate.

> Acts 14
> Verse 4: "But the people of the city were divided; and some sided with the Jews, and some with the apostles [Paul and Barnabas, as seen from the context]."
>
> Verses 13–14: "The priest of Zeus, whose temple was just outside the city, brought oxen and garlands to the

gates, and wanted to offer sacrifice with the crowds.
But when the apostles Barnabas and Paul heard of it,
they tore their robes . . ."

It is unmistakable that in this fascinating account of the "first journey" (Acts 13–14) Luke designates both Paul and Barnabas as apostles.
In fact, Barnabas is mentioned first in verse 14. It must also be observed
that in the beginning of the story, in Acts 13:1–2, Barnabas and Saul are
listed among the "prophets and teachers." *But they are not at that time
called apostles.* Rather it is only as they are engaged in taking the gospel
to the unreached peoples of Cyprus and southern Galatia that they are
labeled *apostles.*

> 1 Corinthians 4:9
> "For, I think, God has exhibited us apostles last of all,
> as men condemned to death; because we have become
> a spectacle to the world, both to angels and to men."

While some might suppose that Paul sometimes used the plural in
sort of a royal "we," he's clearly not doing so here. In this section of
defending his apostleship to the Corinthians, he refers repeatedly (from
3:4) to his work and Apollos' work respectively among them. In 4:6
"myself and Apollos" are the "us," which then carries on as the "us/we"
through verse 9 and beyond. We again note that the context is that of the
initial penetration of Achaia with the gospel. This pioneer effort among
the unreached Achaians resulted in the Corinthian churches, among others. Thus Apollos is clearly called an apostle in this sense.

> 1 Corinthians 9:2
> "If to others I am not an apostle, at least I am to you;
> for you are the seal of my apostleship in the Lord."

The Corinthians had come to faith through Paul's preaching, and
he was the one to first establish this church. That is what he means by
"you are the seal of my apostleship in the Lord." Paul had fulfilled the
apostolic mandate of Acts 1:8 in their case, and it was unmistakably in
the context of pioneer gospel ministry.

1 Thessalonians 2:5–6

"For we never came with flattering speech, as you know, nor with a pretext for greed—God is witness—nor did we seek glory from men, either from you or from others, even though as apostles of Christ we might have asserted our authority."

"Apostles of Christ" here must refer to "Paul and Silvanus [Silas] and Timothy" (1:1). The context is their fruitful "coming" to them (2:1)—that is, bringing the gospel to these unreached Macedonians and planting this pioneer church.

Does this mean that all who joined in pioneer evangelistic and church planting efforts were regarded by the early church as apostles? No. Many in the New Testament were called to be a part of apostolic teams but were never themselves called apostles. Many were called *fellow workers*; only a handful were called *apostles*. While many ministry teams were engaged in "apostolic ministry," the title *apostle* seems to have been applied somewhat sparingly, perhaps only to those men whose fruitfulness, calling, and gifting in pioneer work had become confirmed over time. First Corinthians 9:2 shows that not even Paul's apostleship was universally recognized, as some in Corinth were questioning it. Evidently "apostle" was a special title, not one casually applied. Many started in pioneer ministry as helpers; and only some of these later on were called apostles, no doubt as such a gift was developed and became recognized.

OTHER REFERENCES

1. **James.** After the apostle James, son of Zebedee, is killed in Acts 12:2, James, the brother of Jesus, is spoken of more and more as a major leader in the Jerusalem church. In 1 Corinthians 15:7 and Galatians 1:19 Paul refers to him as somehow among the apostles. He was not one of the Twelve, but clearly had joined their ranks in the endeavor of holding ground and preaching the gospel among the Jews.

2. **False apostles.** See 2 Corinthians 11:13 and Revelation 2:2. That Paul and John could refer to these is clear evidence that "apostles" were a broader collection of gospel workers—some true and some false—rather than a short, closed list.

3. Romans 16:7: "Greet **Andronicus and Junias**, my kinsmen and my fellow prisoners, who are outstanding among the apostles, who also were in Christ before me." As the general context in this passage is various workers taking the gospel, these two were probably fellow workers who, like Paul, had earned prison for their boldness. However, the phrase in the Greek for "among the apostles" could mean that they were considered apostles—and hence not just run-of-the-mill apostles, but "outstanding." Or it could just mean that they were highly regarded *by* the apostles. Scholars differ on whether the name Junias should be taken as masculine or feminine.

4. Philippians 2:25: "But I thought it necessary to send to you **Epaphroditus**, my brother and fellow worker and fellow soldier, who is also your messenger [Greek *apostolos*] and minister to my need." Though Epaphroditus had temporarily joined Paul's apostolic team, he is probably not to be regarded as an apostle in the same sense as Barnabas, Silas, and others. For one thing, he was an *apostolos* of the Philippian church rather than of Christ, as is often designated.

5. Second Corinthians 8:23 refers to the **brethren** who accompanied Paul, taking the large amount of money collected for the needy believers of Judea. As with Epaphroditus, they are called *apostoloi* "of the churches," and hence most translations render them as *messengers* or *representatives*.

Summary of Apostles Other than the Twelve

As H. V. Campenhausen says: "For [Paul] 'the apostles'—and he is deliberately using an existing term—are the foundation-laying preachers of the Gospel, missionaries and church founders possessing the full authority of Christ and belong to a bigger circle in no way confined to the Twelve."[1] The International Standard Bible Encyclopedia takes the position that the primary identity and role of *all apostles*—whether the Twelve or otherwise—was their pioneer calling toward the "propagation of the gospel" (though it does acknowledge some uniqueness and foundational nature of the Twelve).

The primary way in which *apostle* and *apostleship* are used in the New Testament, when not referring to the Twelve, is in regard to the pioneer work of taking the gospel to unreached peoples, resulting in new communities of the body of Christ. Thus "church planting among unreached people groups" would be a fair description of the New Testament concept of apostolic ministry.

Appendix 2
Becoming Someone to Whom Host People Can Talk

by Dr. Lyman Campbell

Lyman Campbell is a language learning consultant with a quarter century of experience helping language learners in many countries. He holds a M.A. and Ph.D. related to language learning theory.

A worker in India once told me, "When a stranger first starts talking to me in Urdu, I often have difficulty understanding him. Once I catch on to the theme, I do a lot better." It interested me that this man had probably been using Urdu for twenty or thirty years, and was effective in relationships and in his work. I encounter similar stories among people who have been working in a language group for five or ten years: "I can understand people who know me, when they are conversing with me, but when they begin conversing with one another, I can easily get lost." That worker in India illustrated that even with many more years, the situation may not change greatly. I believe that this profile—limited, though effective, language ability—often results from what Eddie Arthur calls "speech-led language learning."[1]

Some language learners tell me, "I only learn things that I feel I will have a definite need to say." One such person, attempting to narrate an action cartoon for me in her field language, was unable to express the idea that "a drop of water fell and put out the cigarette." She later commented that she would never want to say that, in any case. This demonstrates a philosophy of language learning that focuses on "things I want to be able to say." The problem is that five minutes from now someone might want to tell me a story in which a drop of water fell and put out a cigarette, or any of trillions of other possible, ordinary life events that might have taken place—events which I might never have thought I would need to know how to communicate about.

Through speech-led learning we may be able to do our work, but not truly be able to share all of life with host people. This condition is sometimes referred to as being a "Terminal 2 Plus"—referring to FSI (Foreign Service Institute) Level 2 Plus. Such people don't grow much because they already can say most of what they think they will ever need to say, plus they don't understand most of what they hear around them—say on TV or in animated conversations that go on between host people. Therefore, on the one hand they may not feel pressure to grow in order to be able to say more, while at the same time the speech going on around them cannot feed further growth because they don't understand it.

In comprehension-led learning, by contrast, we aim for our own speech to be largely based on our growing familiarity with host peoples' speech. Our vision is to move steadily and deliberately toward full comprehension of all we hear and, as a result of that, to keep growing indefinitely.

SOLVING THREE BIG CHALLENGES TO UNDERSTANDING SPEECH

When I ask overseas workers what makes understanding of host speech difficult for them, three that are always mentioned are 1) the speed of speech; 2) unfamiliar words; and 3) not understanding all of the cultural background. I call these, respectively, 1) the processing problem; 2) the vocabulary problem; and 3) the cultural knowledge problem.

Problem 1: The Processing Problem
(Developing a Fast, Efficient "Understanding Machine")

Understanding speech involves a large set of complex processes that convert the vibration of our eardrums into ideas in our heads. These processes take place at an astoundingly high speed. I call the cognitive system that accomplishes this the Understanding Machine. One of the challenges for learners is to develop a large, complex, and rapid-working Understanding Machine. Since the processes involved are influenced by how frequently they are used, it follows that we need to spend a lot of time listening to speech that we *can* understand, in order to speed up those processes.

So how can we make speech understandable to ourselves? First and perhaps foremost, there is a lot of evidence that one of the best ways to make speech understandable for ourselves is to *interact* well with whatever host person might be speaking to us.[2] Early interaction can make use of activities which force learners to interact with their teachers and fellow learners, such as role plays, use of puppets, and interaction around wordless picture stories.

Secondly, our teacher can tailor the speech we hear (often referred to as our "input") to our current level of understanding ability. Healthy chunks of this can be tape recorded and added to our ever-growing listening library. Here are some examples:

A) The easiest level of input is speech about things we can see happening. "Total physical response," a learning activity in which a teacher gives us instructions and we demonstrate our understanding by physically carrying out those instructions, is an example of such input. A bit later, the learner and teacher can cocreate spoken stories based on wordless picture stories, and then the teacher can tape record the story for the learner's listening library.

B) Somewhat more difficult input is speech with highly familiar content, such as stories we knew previously but are hearing for the first time in the host language. We can tape record a story (e.g., Goldilocks) and then we go over it (in the host language) for clarification of parts we didn't understand. This generates valuable interaction, and makes the story more or less fully understandable before we add it to our listening library.

C) More difficult still is speech which is addressed to us newcomers for the very purpose of helping us learn about host life and culture. We recommend hundreds of hours of such interaction in what we call the deep life sharing phase. (See the discussion below of problem 3.) This phase results in a large volume of recordings for the listening library.

D) Finally, more difficult than all of the kinds of speech mentioned above is speech addressed *by* natives *to* natives (native-to-native) with no concessions being made for nonnative listeners. The author of this book gives the example of recording radio phone-in talk shows. Learners might tape these and go over them with a teacher. The tapes are then added to the listening library.

A key at all stages is that we use much of our focused language-growth times to hear input we can understand today, and in the process we eventually grow to the point where what would have been over our heads a few months ago has become understandable to us. The listening library provides a way to increase our experience with understandable input.

Problem 2: The Vocabulary Problem
(and the Iceberg Principle)

We need to be able to understand thousands of words. It is true that a couple thousand high-frequency words account for much of what is said in any language. Unfortunately, speech is also riddled with low-frequency words. Most words that exist are, in fact, low-frequency words! To be able to understand most speech that we will encounter, we need to be able to understand thousands of words that we could not possibly have foreseen needing to know. Here we can exploit what Stevick calls "the comprehension advantage"—that is, the development of our ability to understand can race far ahead of the development of our ability to speak.[3] In fact, when it comes to vocabulary it is normal to understand a large number of words we have not yet spoken. This is even true in our native languages. Yet in learning another language we tend to want to fully master every word the first time that we focus on it, rather than simply beginning to understand it.

We might compare our "mental lexicon" to a growing iceberg. Inside the tip are words that we have used many times already in our own speaking. Nearer the bottom are words with which we have made only some passing acquaintance. Now we might try our best to put every new word that we focus on straight into the tip of our iceberg. This is what Rubin and Thompson seem to suggest: "Whatever technique(s) you are using, always strive for 100% mastery . . . This . . . will probably drop to 70% recall tomorrow and even lower a week later."[4] A month later, the recall may be much lower still! The words are still in the iceberg, and as the learner encounters them again in other contexts those words will rise back to the top. But it was inefficient to try so hard to get them into the tip of the iceberg when many, perhaps most, of them would sink down to the bottom anyway.

But there's a better way. We just start right off by putting all new words into the bottom of the iceberg. In the time it would have taken to put a few words into the peak, we can put dozens into the bottom, which means making sure we have had strong, meaningful encounters with them in which we really focused on their form and meaning in a context of communication. Many of them somehow do rise straight to the top. Others sink further down into the bottom. However, as they are reencountered in more contexts, they keep rising. By listening to a tape from our listening library, we can refresh hundreds of words that have sunk to lower parts of the iceberg. We have found the iceberg principle to be enormously helpful in tackling this second barrier to full understanding, the vocabulary problem.

Problem 3: The Cultural Knowledge Problem

In our growing ability to understand speech, we reach a point where, although we still have great difficulty with native-to-native speech, we can understand explanations of host life and culture that are addressed to us and about which we can interact with the speaker. We have found a great manual for this purpose to be Spradley's book, The Ethnographic Interview.[5] We often begin by asking people to tell us their life stories, or by having representatives of various walks of life tell us about their daily experience. Several hundred hours can be devoted to this deep life sharing. This creates special, close relationships. It also provides opportunity for us to share our own lives deeply.

If a worker is pursuing two years of "full-time language learning" (which I would rather call two years of "highly focused, growing participation in the host society"), then the middle eight months might be devoted to this sort of deep life sharing. We can continue fleshing out our understanding of the host culture during the final eight months of the two-year period, when our primary resource for focused growth times will be native-to-native resources, such as recorded radio phone-in talk shows.

BY NO MEANS THE FULL PICTURE

The focus here has been on learning to understand, recognizing that overseas workers often have a problem in this area. Many seem to assume that as long as they learn to read, write, and speak they will automatically have the ability to understand normal speech. This doesn't appear to be the case. However, developing a powerful Understanding Machine is also far from the full story. Newer understandings of the language learning process are leading to a deeper and richer picture of the whole person as a growing participator in relationships in a host community. This in turn can radically alter our approach to activities with our teacher, since those can now be understood as yet more participation in community, specially enriched to maximize our growth.

Communicative language learning programs tend to mesh better with these richer understandings of the language learning process, and we encourage leaders of programs for overseas workers to consider moving more in this direction, if they have not done so already. While remaining thankful for the widespread fruit of more traditional styles of language programs, I believe the past has just given us a foretaste of what is possible in the future.

Where Do I Go from Here?

Interested in learning more about communicative language learning approaches, and the richer understanding of language learning alluded to above? Here are some possible next steps for you:

1. Check out the wealth of resources at www.equigrp.net/laeg.

2. Come to a field-based workshop. For four or five days learners get together each morning to discuss language learning issues, and then in the afternoons they work with their language teachers, applying some of what was discussed in the mornings. They also evaluate their current learning situation and envision changes and improvements.

3. Get linked up on the field with someone who has received Language Learning Advisor (LLA) training. We recommend that all field teams have this kind of expertise regularly available to them.

Appendix 3
Writing a VSP and MOU

The good team leader wants to clearly articulate where the team is going and how they are going to get there. The target audience for this brief **Vision and Strategy Paper** is potential candidates, organization headquarters, and sending offices, plus anyone else wishing to get a brief understanding of what the team is purposing to do, within security parameters. The "Vision Section" briefly describes the purpose and vision of the team—*what* it intends to accomplish, *where*, and with *what people group(s)*. This should be a page or less.

The "Strategy Section" can be around four pages, and it describes a bit of *how* the team will accomplish its vision. It can include such considerations as entry and residency; language learning; basics concerning evangelism, discipleship, and gathering; what the church(es) will look like; key alliances or partnerships; any unusual obstacles to be overcome; any special subtasks (e.g., translation, vocational training or other projects, microcredit, etc.); basics regarding pre-field preparation of team members, ETA's (estimated time of arrival) of the first group, etc. It should also describe any special team distinctives regarding team functioning, philosophy of ministry, doctrine, or requirements for members. This last part should be brief, since those issues are dealt with more thoroughly in the MOU, which describes how the team will function.

VSPs should not be highly idealized portrayals that include all possible aspirations. Rather, concrete visions and ideas, in the context of reliance on God, are preferred. Team leaders might also want to include a half-page to one-page "bio" with a photo.

The **Memo of Understanding** is a more detailed document that gives the candidate a sharper picture of what everyday life, team life, and ministry will be like on the field. The aim is to minimize surprises and conflicting expectations down the road, as mismatched expectations is perhaps the number one cause of conflict on the field.

The following should be included in an MOU (some of these are optional, depending on your situation):

1. Special doctrinal requirements or emphases.

2. Philosophy of ministry distinctives (e.g., regarding contextualization, church planting movements, charismatic issues, infant baptism).

3. Language learning goals, expectations, and approaches.

4. Whether or not a "bonding experience" is required of new arrivals (living with a local family for a period of time).

5. Tentmaking.

6. Role of the team leader: his responsibility and authority, leadership style, what is expected of team members in this regard, what the oversight of members will look like, and reporting requirements. Some may wish to quote Hebrews 13:17 and explain the implications for the TL-TM relationship.

7. Time stewardship.

8. What decisions must be cleared with team leader beforehand (e.g., housing, jobs, home ministry assignment plans).

9. Decision-making on team matters.

10. Term of commitment.

11. Team life: meetings, social life, expectations regarding "community," etc.

12. Conflict resolution and recourse.

13. Special lifestyle policies (e.g., regarding alcohol, pork or other food issues, dress, housing)

14. Vacations and holidays.

15. Women's roles on the team.

16. Team fund.

17. Children's education.

18. Singles' special lifestyle issues, such as dating.

19. Security (e.g., what can be said in prayer letters and when speaking in churches).

20. Home Ministry Assignments ("HMAs" or "furloughs") and relationship with sending churches.

21. Personal budgets and support-raising.

22. Pre-field preparation.

23. Ongoing training and equipping.

24. Reality check on what life will be like.

25. How future changes can be made to this MOU.

26. Finally, this is also an opportunity for the team leader to address broader issues such as suffering, incarnation, family life, spiritual life on the field, prayer, and personal development.

Appendix 4
Orality, Bible Narratives, and Indigenous Reproducing Churches: The Next Wave of Global Missions?

By Steve Evans

Steve Evans is a communications specialist and field leader serving with the International Mission Board (Southern Baptist Convention) in Africa, the Middle East, and South Asia.

> "Oral Bible development and its use in evangelism, discipleship, and church planting may very well be the missions challenge of the twenty-first century. May we be doing for oral communicators what Gutenberg did for literates!"[1]

A GROWING AWARENESS OF A GLOBAL SITUATION

The gospel is being proclaimed to more people than at any other time in history, yet many of those to whom it is being preached are not really "hearing" it. Unfortunately, most in the evangelical community don't have the slightest idea that there is a problem, and those affected by it are the oral communicators of the world, those who can't, won't, or don't communicate by way of literate means. Ironically, over 90 percent of the world's Christian workers use literate communication styles—either through the printed page or through highly expositional presentations of God's Word—when presenting the gospel, making it difficult, if not impossible, to be heard or understood.

Current estimates indicate that up to two-thirds of the world's population, totaling over four billion people, are oral communicators by necessity or choice. To effectively communicate with them, presentations must match their oral learning styles and preferences. Narrative formats—including stories, songs, proverbs, poetry, drama, and various forms of multimedia—communicate best. In fact, oral communicators find it very difficult to understand literate presentations, especially those containing outlines, lists, steps, and principles.

Add to this the fact that of the more than 6,800 languages spoken in the world, only slightly more than 400 have a complete Bible, with another 1,000 or so having only the New Testament. While another 900 languages, more or less, have at least one book of the Bible, more than 4,450 still do not have even that! It will be decades, at least, before all peoples have God's Word in printed form!

But what if they did? Could they read it with enough understanding to receive the truth, respond to it, and be able to pass it along to others? Could they function in a viable New Testament church? Researchers estimate that at least 70 percent of the world's unreached people groups are oral. How long must they wait to be able to truly receive the good news of God's Word and be able to make a heartfelt response? If the evangelical missions community does not respond to the communication needs of these oral people, up to four billion may never really "hear" the gospel.

What could be one of the greatest obstacles to reaching the unreached peoples of the world and finishing the unfinished task is also one of the greatest challenges the evangelical missions community faces today. Following the unreached peoples movement and church planting movements, evangelicals are facing what could be the next wave of global missions: that of appropriately addressing the oral cultures of this world with narrative presentations of God's Word, leading to viable, sustainable, and reproducing indigenous churches.

Without the presence of God's Word, however, there cannot be such movements. Ultimately they will crash, splinter, fall prey to cults, or face syncretism with existing local beliefs and practices. There must be a commitment to providing God's Word in culturally appropriate ways in order for them to receive, understand, respond to, and reproduce it, providing a foundation to faith, witness, and church. A commitment to this, though, means that one starts oral and remains oral—from evangelism and discipleship to leader training and church planting. Because of the communication and learning styles of oral communicators, as well as their thought and decision-making processes, this must be primarily through narrative presentations of God's Word.

Today, multiple organizations and agencies are working toward a common vision: 1) God's Word for every tribe, tongue, people, and nation; 2) resulting in church planting movements; 3) addressing the issue of orality; and 4) providing resources for Bible storying.

HIGH IMPACT/LOW TECHNOLOGY RESULTS IN TRANSFORMED LIVES

Oral communicators need to hear the rich narratives of God's Word. Without such, how can they know of, meditate upon, and repeat the numerous, wondrous activities of God's interaction with His creation? Gone would be the awe of an awesome God who is present with His people, who is patient with them, provides for them, cares for them, and loves them. Gone would be the stories of wonder and treachery, stupidity and amazement. Without these stories, how can they see that generation by generation God pursued a love relationship with His people, heartbroken for those who were always moving away from Him, turning their backs on Him, yet crying out to Him in times of crisis or trouble? It's the stories of God's Word that transform lives, and without life-transformation they might only have head knowledge and changed outward behavior.

New Testament scholar N. T. Wright said that stories provide a vital framework for experiencing the world. They also provide a means by which views of the world may be changed. "Stories are, actually, peculiarly good at modifying or subverting other stories and their worldviews.

Where head-on attack would certainly fail, the parable hides the wisdom of the serpent behind the innocence of the dove, gaining entrance and favor which can then be used to change assumptions which the hearer would otherwise keep hidden away for safety."[2]

In people groups where oral communicators are predominant, the worldview may differ enough from a biblical worldview that a single presentation of the gospel may not often convince, even when delivered orally. What can be effective in such situations is the oral communication of a set of chronological Bible stories that involve points of similarity between a culture's worldview and a biblical worldview. Over time, confronting worldview barriers with stories of the Bible can lead to accepting a more compelling story than the stories associated with one's own worldview. An oral panoramic presentation of the gospel using stories from Genesis to Revelation has already begun to have an impact on some people groups that, until a few years ago, were still unreached.

In many parts of the unreached world there is open hostility to Christian missionary activity. Crusades, mass evangelism, and public preaching are not taken lightly. Neither is a Bible study nor open witnessing. It is perhaps in these type of situations that chronological Bible storying can be fully appreciated. Storying is not confrontational. It is not preaching. It is not teaching. It is merely conveying the stories of God's Word, leaving the results to God! These stories can go where the printed Bible sometimes cannot go. They can cross borders, enter jail cells, even go into the heart of a Hindu's, Buddhist's, Muslim's, animist's or socialist's home! They can definitely penetrate the heart of the one listening and change that person's life for eternity.

One couple working in a West African village explained how chronological Bible storying helped them go "under the radar," so to speak. "We asked permission of the village chiefs to live among the people in order to learn more about them," the couple said. "They knew we were missionaries. We were asked if we were going to do evangelism. We asked if that meant having a large gathering with singing and drums and show a film. They said that is what they meant. We told them we would not do that. They asked if we were going to build a church. We asked if they meant by that to build a building. When they replied yes, we said we would not build a church building. Permission was given and we were given a house to rent, located among the people . . . When we asked them to tell us what a Christian was they replied, 'I really don't know except they are bad.' 'They pray only once a week when they go into a building.' 'They are drunkards and idolaters.' 'You cannot trust them.' When I asked who Jesus is, one young man said to his friend, 'Isn't he that guy in the movie?'

"Our plans are simple," the couple continued. "We will live among the people and attempt to show them Christ through our lives. We will not discuss the religion of Christianity or talk about 'the Christian way.' We will never discuss Islam, Muhammad, or the Koran or the differences between Christianity and Islam. We are here to teach God's Word under the leadership of the Holy Spirit. We have chosen to use only the storying method, to teach the stories of the Bible chronologically and bring out the truths the people need to know in order to understand the gospel." The next two years saw some amazing results.

Meanwhile, Jeremy was a volunteer in a storying project in a Spanish-speaking country in South America. He was part of a larger team that worked in partnership with members of a translation organization in a language cluster project nearing completion. Working with stories adapted from a neighboring language, Jeremy instilled vision for the storying process in two mother tongue storyers, and coached them through learning the stories and telling them to others. Prior to arriving in the country, Jeremy had not studied Spanish or the indigenous language. Jeremy's two-year involvement has been a significant contributing factor toward a church planting movement that now appears to have resulted in as much as 20 percent of the people group becoming believers. In the few years since Jeremy's departure, storyers continue to go to new unreached villages telling the stories and evangelizing.

In a North African country, seventeen young men (many of whom could barely read and write and some not at all) underwent a two-year leader training program using chronological Bible storying. At the end of two years, the students had mastered approximately 135 biblical stories in their correct chronological order, spanning from Genesis to Revelation. They were able to tell the stories, sing songs that told the stories, and enact dramas about each of the stories. They could tell the stories singly or in clusters, such as the "creation cluster"—dealing with the creation of the spirit world, the heavens and the earth, and man and woman. The students demonstrated the ability to answer questions about both the facts and the theology of the stories, and showed an excellent grasp of the gospel message, the nature of God, and their new life in Christ. They quickly and skillfully referred to the stories to answer a variety of theological questions. Given a theological theme, they could accurately name multiple biblical stories in which that theme occurs. If asked, they could tell each story and elaborate on how it addresses the theme.

A visiting examiner from a theological seminary in the United States concluded, "The training process has successfully achieved its goals of enabling students to tell a large number of biblical stories accurately, to have a good understanding of those stories and the theology that they convey, and to have an eagerness to share the Christian message. The community received the stories and story-songs enthusiastically and have made them part of the culture and church life alike. Various students acknowledged that they entered knowing little of the Old Testament, did not understand the relationship between God and Jesus, did not know the characteristics of God, did not know that God created the angelic beings, had not heard of being born again, and did not know that Christians should not seek help from local deities." He said that upon entering the program these students were unable to communicate the Christian faith to other people. "By the time the training was over they had dramatically improved their understanding of all of these matters and many more," he said.

Bible storying provides a way of engaging a people group that is not highly technological, and it can readily involve oral communicators in efforts to reach their own people group with the gospel. Storying is thus a reproducible evangelistic and church planting approach: new believers can readily share the gospel, plant new churches, and disciple new believers in the same way that they themselves were reached and discipled. While a storying strategy seems to be particularly appropriate with unreached people groups, many involved with people groups where there is an established church found significant benefits to a chronological storying approach in those situations as well. The oral, chronological approach can fill major gaps that literate approaches to evangelism, discipling, church planting, and leadership development have, over the decades, missed.

RESOURCES

Evans, Steve; Green, Ron; Lundberg, Dean; and Payne, David (ed.) (January 10, 2004, revised). "Prospectus: Epic Partners International." Dallas, Orlando, Richmond, and Tyler: SIL/Wycliffe International, Campus Crusade for Christ International, International Mission Board (SBC), and Youth With A Mission, Tyler.

Websites:
www.ChronologicalBibleStorying.com
www.Communication-Strategy.net
www.EpicPartners.org
www.OralBible.com

Appendix 5
Top Ten Team Pitfalls

From my observations, it seems that these strategic issues can make a huge difference in the long run to the team's viability and impact. This is a summary of principles found elsewhere in the book. At the very least, this list of pitfalls can make for a lively team discussion!

10. Not being very clear regarding the people group and location the Lord is calling the team to work amongst.

9. Workers absorbed in high-hours jobs, even when not fully necessary.

8. Male workers trying to do everything out of their home, rather than basing ministry from an office or something. It is very common for team leaders to say they've learned this lesson about 3-year mark.

7. Allowing team misunderstandings or team leader / team member differences to fester and go on too long.

6. The team leader not building the team well. Recruiting anything with a *pulse*, rather than co-workers with a level of proven gifts and maturity.

5. The team leader not responding well to oversight; undervaluing the role of accountability and coaching.

4. Weak commitment to personal and corporate prayer about the work, with expectancy.

3. Not really understanding or being convinced about church planting.

2. Excess time in non-church-planting activities, such as team meetings & team activities, meetings with other workers, correspondence with folks back home, email, etc. [Of course some time spent in these areas is vital. But it can be overdone.] Getting into all forms of field activity other than language learning, evangelism and discipling. Spending too much time in front of computer screens.

1. The team leader being weak, passive, insecure or non-directive in his leadership role—usually due to insecurity and fear of rejection. Not being clear with team members concerning expectations. People begin to operate as a group of "independent contractors" rather than as a team. Team leaders must learn to stay graciously firm about team standards. Likewise there can be insufficient accountability and direction individually of team members' ministries. Weak accountability can lead to permanently weak patterns. Finally, related to this, the team leader can sometimes fail to keep people motivated, eager and expectant about their tasks and goals.

GROUP DISCUSSION:

Hand out this list to everyone on the team. Take 20 minutes for each person to mark each item as to: a) whether or not they agree this is important; and b) rate it 1-to-5 (with 5 being highest) as how much of a problem it currently is to the team. Then discuss as a group.

Bibliography

Adeney, David H. "A Two Stage Approach to Church Planting in a Muslim Context." In *Perspectives on the World Christian Movement*. Edited by Ralph Winter and Steve Hawthorne. 722–728. Pasadena, CA: William Carey Library, 1981.

Allen, Roland. *Missionary Methods: St. Paul's or Ours?* Grand Rapids, MI: Wm. B. Eerdmans Publishing Co., 1962.

———. *Spontaneous Expansion of the Church*. Grand Rapids, MI: Wm. B. Eerdmans Publishing Co., 1962.

Brewster, E. Thomas and Elizabeth Brewster. *Language Acquisition Made Practical*. Colorado Springs, CO: Lingua House, 1976.

Cho, Paul Yonggi. *Successful Home Cell Groups*. With Harold Hostetler. Plainfield, NJ: Logos International, 1981.

Christiansen, Jens. *The Practical Approach to the Muslim*. Upper Darby, PA: North Africa Mission, 1977.

Eims, Leroy. *The Lost Art of Disciple Making*. Grand Rapids, MI: Zondervan Corp., 1978.

Fry, George, and James King. *Islam: A Survey of the Muslim Faith*. Grand Rapids, MI: Baker, 1980.

Garrison, David. *Church Planting Movements*. A booklet. Richmond, VA: International Mission Board of the Southern Baptist Convention, 1999.

———. *Church Planting Movements: How God Is Redeeming a Lost World*. Bangalore, India: WIGTake Resources, 2004.

Gibb, H. A. R. *Mohammedanism: An Historical Survey*. London: Oxford University Press, 1949.

Green, Michael. *Evangelism in the Early Church*. London: Hodder & Stoughton, 1970.

Greeson, Kevin. *Camel Training Manual*. Bangalore, India: WIGTake Resources, 2004.

Hawatmeh, Abdalla. *The Man from Gadara*. With Roland Muller. Philadelphia: Xlibris, 2003.

Hay, Alex Rattray. *The Functioning Church and Church-Planter of the New Testament*. Audubon, NJ: New Testament Missionary Union, 1947.

Hay, Alex Rattray. *The New Testament Order for Church and Missionary*. Audubon, NJ: New Testament Missionary Union, 1978.

Henrichsen, Walter A. *Disciples Are Made, Not Born*. Wheaton, IL: Victor Books, 1974; revised 2002.

Hesselgrave, David J. *Planting Churches Cross-Culturally: North America and Beyond*. 2nd ed. Grand Rapids, MI: Baker Book House, 2000.

Johnstone, Patrick and Jason Mandryk. *Operation World, 21st Century Edition*. Waynesboro, GA: Authentic, 2001.

Latourette, Kenneth Scott. *A History of the Expansion of Christianity*. 7 vols. New York: Harper and Row, 1937–1945.

Leatherwood, Rick. "Mongolia: As a People Movement to Christ Emerges, What Lessons Can We Learn?" *Mission Frontiers* (July/August 1998).

Lin, David and Steve Spaulding, eds. *Sharing Jesus in the Buddhist World*. Pasadena, CA: William Carey Library, 2003.

Livingstone, Greg. *Planting Churches in Muslim Cities: A Team Approach*. Grand Rapids, MI: Baker Books, 1993.

Love, Fran and Jeleta Eckheart, eds. *Ministry to Muslim Women: Longing to Call Them Sisters*. Pasadena, CA: William Carey Library, 2000.

Love, Rick. *Muslims, Magic and the Kingdom of God: Church Planting among Folk Muslims*. Pasadena, CA: William Carey Library, 2000.

———. *Peacemaking*. Pasadena, CA: William Carey Library, 2001.

Marantika, Chris. *Principles & Practice of World Mission—Including a Closer Look in an Islamic Context*. Indonesia: Iman Press, 2002.

McCarthy, Bernice. *The 4MAT System: Teaching to Learning Styles with Right/ Left Mode Techniques*. Arlington Heights, IL: EXCEL, Inc, 1980.

McCurry, Don M., ed. *The Gospel & Islam*. Monrovia, CA: MARC, 1979.

———. *Healing the Broken Family of Abraham: New Life for Muslims*. Colorado Springs, CO: Ministry to Muslims, 2001.

McGavran, Donald A. *Ethnic Realities and the Church: Lessons from India*. Pasadena, CA: William Carey Library, 1979.

————. *Understanding Church Growth*. Grand Rapids, MI: Eerdmans, 1980.

Miley, George. *Loving the Church . . . Blessing the Nations*. Waynesboro, GA: Authentic, 2003.

Neighbour, Ralph W. Jr. *Where Do We Go from Here?: A Guidebook for Cell Group Churches*. With Lorna Jenkins. Rev. ed. Houston, TX: Touch Publications, 2000. Original edition, 1990.

Neill, Stephen. *A History of Christian Missions*. New York: Penguin, 1964.

Nida, Eugene. *Customs and Cultures: Anthropology for Christian Missions*. Pasadena, CA: William Carey Library, 1954.

Parshall, Phil. *Muslim Evangelism: Contemporary Approaches to Contextualization*. Waynesboro, GA: Send the Light, 2003.

————. *The Last Great Frontier*. Quezon City, Philippines: Open Doors, 2000.

Patterson, George and Richard Scoggins. *Church Multiplication Guide: The Miracle of Church Reproduction*. Rev. ed. Pasadena, CA: William Carey Library, 2003.

Register, Ray. *Back to Jerusalem: Church Planting Movements in the Holy Land*. Enumclaw, WA: WinePress Publishing, 2000.

Rowland, Trent and Vivian Rowland. *Pioneer Church Planting: A Rookie Team Leader's Handbook* (98-page handbook). Littleton, CO: Caleb Project, 2001.

Schwartz, Christian A. *Natural Church Development*. Carol Stream, IL: ChurchSmart Resources, 1998.

Scoggins, Dick. *Building Effective Church Planting Teams*. Unpublished manuscript. Available at www.dickscoggins.com.

————. *Church Planting Manual: Planting House Churches in Networks*. Unpublished manuscript. Available at www.dickscoggins.com.

Simpson, Wolfgang. *Houses That Change the World*. Waynesboro, GA: Authentic Media, 2001.

Stedman, Raymond C. *Body Life*. Glendale, CA: Regal Books, 1972.

Steffen, Tom A. *Passing the Baton: Church Planting That Empowers*. La Habra, CA: Center for Organizational & Ministry Development, 1993.

Stott, John. *Christian Mission in the Modern World*. Downers Grove, IL:

InterVarsity, 1975.

Strauch, Alexander. *Biblical Eldership: An Urgent Call to Restore Biblical Church Leadership*. Littleton, CO: Lewis & Roth Publishers, 1988.

Subbamma, B. V. *New Patterns for Discipling Hindus*. Pasadena, CA: William Carey Library, 1970.

Travis, John. "Messianic Muslim Followers of Isa: A Closer Look at C5 Believers and Congregations." *International Journal of Frontier Missions*, 17(1) (2000): 53–59.

———. "Must All Muslims Leave Islam to Follow Jesus?" *Evangelical Missions Quarterly*, 34(4) (1998): 411–415.

———. "The C1–C6 Spectrum." *Evangelical Missions Quarterly*, 34(4) (1998): 407–408.

Tucker, Ruth. *From Jerusalem to Irian Jaya: A Biographical History of Christian Missions*. Grand Rapids, MI: Zondervan, 1983.

VanderWerff, Lyle F. *Christian Mission to Muslims*. Pasadena, CA: William Carey Library, 1977.

Wagner, Peter. *Church Planting for a Greater Harvest*. Ventura, CA: Regal Books, 1990.

Warren, Rick. *The Purpose Driven Church*. Grand Rapids, MI: Zondervan Publishing House, 1995.

Woodberry, J. Dudley. "When Failure Is Our Teacher: Lessons from Mission to Muslims." *International Journal of Frontier Missions*, Vol. 13:3 (July–Sept.1996): 121–123.

Endnotes

Chapter 1

1 While the Great Commission is certainly given to all Christians, Acts 1:8 is in the context of the "orders given to the apostles" (1:2). The threefold worldwide spread of the gospel in the book of Acts takes place through the work of the apostles (the Twelve, Paul, and other apostles) and those teamed with them in apostolic ministry.

2 George Miley, *Loving the Church . . . Blessing the Nations* (Waynesboro, GA: Authentic, 2003), 96.

3 A positive term in the Qur'an referring to Jews and Christians.

4 Sura 19:93. Khatib translation.

5 http://www.wholesomewords.org/children/biostuddcc.html

Chapter 2

1 Trent and Vivian Rowland, *Pioneer Church Planting: A Rookie Team Leader's Handbook* (Littleton, CO: Caleb Project, 2001), 79.

2 B. V. Subbamma, *New Patterns for Discipling Hindus* (Pasadena, CA: William Carey Library, 1970), 79.

3 Made-up name for a real country, for security's sake.

4 Not his real name.

5 Not his real name.

6 David Garrison, *Church Planting Movements: How God Is Redeeming a Lost World* (Bangalore, India: WIGTake Resources, 2004), 39–42.

7 Not the real name of the group.

8 Not his real name.

9 Not his real name.

10 Subbamma, *New Patterns*, 64.

11 David Burnett, "The Challenge of the Globalization of Buddhism," in *Sharing Jesus in the Buddhist World*, ed. David Lin and Steve Spaulding (Pasadena, CA: William Carey Library, 2003), 5–6.

12   International Standard Bible Encyclopedia, General editor, Geoffrey W. Bromiley . . . [et al.] (Grand Rapids : W. B. Eerdmans, c1979).

Chapter 3

1   On the field there are various views concerning the question of women as leaders over mixed-gender teams, and the issue is beyond the scope of this book. As most field church planting teams today are led by men—especially in the Muslim context—masculine pronouns, such as *he*, will mostly be used.

2   The only hint of a solo act was Philip. But in Samaria (modern Nablus) he was quickly joined by Peter and John. And his work with the Ethiopian eunuch was a brief encounter, not an ongoing mode of operation.

3   See Bruce Olson, *Bruchko*, updated ed. (Orlando, FL: Creation House, 1993).

4   Steve Richardson, "Third-Dimension Missionary Teams" (unpublished paper, 1997).

5   Rick Love, "Four Stages of Team Development," *Evangelical Missions Quarterly,* vol. 32, no. 3 (July 1996) <http://bgc.gospelcom.net/emis/1996/fourstages.htm>.

Chapter 4

1   Steve Richardson, "Third-Dimension Missionary Teams" (unpublished paper, 1997).

2   Rick Love, *Peacemaking* (Pasadena, CA: William Carey Library, 2001).

Chapter 5

1   David J. Hesselgrave, *Planting Churches Cross-Culturally: North America and Beyond*, 2nd ed. (Grand Rapids, MI: Baker Book House, 2000), p.42-51.

2   http://www.greatest-quotations.com/

3   http://www.soviet-empire.com/ussr/news/capitalist_watch/us_military.php. Released by the Chief of Naval Operations. Now at www.PoliticsForum.org.

4   David Garrison, *Church Planting Movements: How God Is Redeeming a Lost World* (Bangalore, India: WIGTake Resources, 2004), 230.

5   George Patterson and Richard Scoggins, *Church Multiplication Guide*, rev. ed. (Pasadena, CA: William Carey Library, 2001).

6   Dick Scoggins, "Non-Sequential Phases." Unpublished article.

[7]   Based upon Edition 2.0, February 1998, by Dick Scoggins, James Rockford & Tim Lewis.

[8]   Love, Rick, *Peacemaking*. Pasadena (CA: William Carey Library, 2001).

[9]   Sometimes defined as "Any bold evangelism outside your neighborhood." Usually involves a program, plan or event.

[10]   The Greek New Testament word for *church*.

[11]   While the authors of these Phases see the New Testament teaching a variety of leadership roles for both women and men, they believe that the office of elder is limited to men. That being said, they also recognize and respect that others in the Body of Christ believe otherwise.

[12]   Three or more is better.

Chapter 6

[1]   This "LAMP cycle" methodology is derived from the Larson-Smalley Daily Learning Cycle approach.

[2]   "Timeline of Paul's Life," NIV Study Bible (Grand Rapids, MI: Zondervan, 2002), 1702–1703.

[3]   Greg Thomson, "What? Me Worry about Language Learning?" Unpublished article. Many of Thomson's articles and other valuable resources can be found at http://www.equigrp.net/laeg.

[4]   Foreign Service Institute (USA). Often referred to as "LAMP Levels" in the expatriate worker community.

[5]   Greg Thomson, "The Comprehensible Corpus: A Security Blanket in Challenging Language-learning Situations" (Unpublished article).

[6]   Thomson, "What? Me Worry?"

[7]   Ibid..

[8]   Thomas, Greg, "The Comprehensible Corpus—A Security Blanket in Challenging Language Learning Situations" (in the Proceedings of the First International Congress on Missionary Language and Culture Learning, Herbert Purnell and Lonna Dickerson, eds. 1993).

[9]   Ibid..

[10]   Their most widely used tool was the book *Language Acquisition Made Practical* (Colorado Springs, CO: Lingua House, 1976).

[11] Greg Thomson, "Ad Hoc Language Acquisition Centers: Another Option in Field Language Learning" (Unpublished article; revised March 2002).

[12] http://www.funderstanding.com/right_left_brain.cfm

[13] A language learning method where the learner physically responds to verbal commands in the language.

[14] Greg Thomson, "Alternatives to explicit testing" (presented at the Fifth International Congress on Language Learning, Colorado Springs, October, 2004).

Chapter 7

[1] From Paul's vocation of making tents in the support of his apostolic ministry (Acts 18:3).

Chapter 8

[1] It is particularly regrettable that in this day and age these kinds of draconian restrictions still exist in many countries. Many nations continue to deny their citizens religious freedom even though they have joined the 151 nations that have signed the United Nation's Universal Declaration of Human Rights, which states: "Everyone has the right to freedom of thought, conscience and religion; this right includes freedom to change his religion or belief, and freedom, either alone or in community with others and in public or private, to manifest his religion or belief in teaching, practice, worship and observance" (Article 18) and "Everyone has the right to freedom of opinion and expression; this right includes freedom to hold opinions without interference and to seek, receive and impart information and ideas through any media and regardless of frontiers" (Article 19). See http://www.un.org/Overview/rights.html.

[2] Tan Kang-San, "Elements of a Biblical and Genuine Missionary Encounter with Diaspora Chinese Buddhists in Southeast Asia" (in *Sharing Jesus in the Buddhist World*, ed. David Lin and Steve Spaulding (Pasadena, CA: William Carey Library, 2003), 22.

[3] Not including what occurred in Indonesia in the 1960s.

[4] David Garrison, *Church Planting Movements: How God Is Redeeming a Lost World* (Bangalore, India: WIGTake Resources, 2004), 99.

[5] Ephesians 2:2.

[6] See Acts 5:28–29.

[7]   Greg Livingstone, *Planting Churches in Muslim Cities: A Team Approach* (Grand Rapids, MI: Baker Books, 1993), 152.

[8]   Kang-San, "Elements of a Biblical and Genuine Missionary Encounter," 29.

[9]   Livingstone, "Establishing Significant Relationships" and "Proclaiming the Message," in *Planting Churches in Muslim Cities*.

[10]   John Stott, *Christian Mission in the Modern World* (Downers Grove, IL: InterVarsity, 1975), 127.

[11]   David Garrison, *Church Planting Movements: How God Is Redeeming a Lost World* (Bangalore, India: WIGTake Resources, 2004), 47.

[12]   Ibid., 171.

[13]   Ibid., 177.

[14]   Livingstone, *Planting Churches in Muslim Cities*, 139ff.

Chapter 9

[1]   Jack Welch, *Newsweek International* magazine (April 4, 2005): 45.

[2]   LeRoy Eims, *The Lost Art of Disciple Making* (Grand Rapids, MI: Zondervan Corp., 1978).

[3]   Walter A. Henrichsen, *Disciples Are Made, Not Born* (Wheaton, IL: Victor Books, 1974; revised 2002).

[4]   SEAN International (UK), Park House, 191 Stafford Road, Wallington, Surrey SM6 9BT.

[5]   B. V. Subbamma, *New Patterns for Discipling Hindus* (Pasadena, CA: William Carey Library, 1970), 37, 85, 97.

[6]   A scale from C1 (little or no contextualization to the majority religion) to C5 (highly contextualized).

Chapter 10

[1]   *Encarta Online Dictionary*, http://encarta.msn.com/encnet/features/dictionary/dictionaryhome.aspx.

[2]   Ibid.

[3]   Dallas Willard, *The Divine Conspiracy: Rediscovering Our Hidden Life in God* (San Francisco: HarperSanFrancisco, 1998), 214.

4   Paul McKaughan (President of the Evangelical Fellowship of Mission Agencies), "McKaughan Musing, Memo 1" (unpublished newsletter).

5   The term "Pastoral Epistles" is a misnomer.

6   Bobby Clinton (professor at Fuller Theological Seminary), from a 2004 "Monday Morning Memo" to his mentorees; Article 54: "Problems—The N.T. Church."

Chapter 11

1   Nik Ripken, "Servants in the Crucible: Findings from a Global Study on Persecution and the Implications for Sending Agencies and Sending Churches" (unpublished book, copyrighted, Gupta, 2004).

Chapter 12

1   Mark Dominey, "Anätman as a Metaphor for Japan," in *Sharing Jesus in the Buddhist World*, David Lin and Steve Spaulding, eds. (Pasadena, CA: William Carey Library, 2003), 202–204.

2   David Garrison, *Church Planting Movements: How God Is Redeeming a Lost World* (Bangalore, India: WIGTake Resources, 2004), 21.

3   From a presentation given in 2001.

4   David Garrison, *Church Planting Movements*, a booklet (Richmond, VA: International Mission Board of the Southern Baptist Convention, 1999), 60.

5   B. V. Subbamma, *New Patterns for Discipling Hindus* (Pasadena, CA: William Carey Library, 1970), 23.

6   I do not mean to imply a clergy-lay divide, as if there is a tangible difference in calling. Ephesians 4 teaches the priesthood of all believers. I am using the word *layman* simply to mean one working in the ministry without pay.

Chapter 13

1   Ralph W. Neighbour Jr. with Lorna Jenkins, *Where Do We Go from Here?: A Guidebook for Cell Group Churches*, rev. ed. (Houston, TX: Touch Publications, 2000); original edition published 1990.

2   Paul Yonggi Cho with Harold Hostetler, *Successful Home Cell Groups* (Plainfield, NJ: Logos International, 1981).

3   Unpublished work.

4   George Patterson and Richard Scoggins, *Church Multiplication Guide: The Miracle of Church Reproduction*, rev. ed. (Pasadena, CA: William Carey Library, 2003).

5   B. V. Subbamma, *New Patterns for Discipling Hindus* (Pasadena, CA: William Carey Library, 1970), 84.

Chapter 14

1   See 1 Corinthians 3:6–9.

2   Dr. Tim Keller, Redeemer Presbyterian Church, New York City.

3   B. V. Subbamma, *New Patterns for Discipling Hindus* (Pasadena, CA: William Carey Library, 1970), 92.

4   Available at http://www.desiringGod.org.

Epilogue

1   Calvin, John,. *The Babylonian Captivity*, Selected Works, 399–400.

2   Rick Leatherwood, "Mongolia: As a People Movement to Christ Emerges, What Lessons Can We Learn?" *Mission Frontiers* (July/August 1998).

Appendix 1

1   Brown, Colin editor, *Dictionary of New Testament Theology Vol.1*, "Apostle" (Grand Rapids, MI: Zondervan Publishing House, 1980).

Appendix 2

1   Eddie Arthur, "Speech-led versus Comprehension-led Language Learning"; *Notes on Linguistics* (1993), 60, 22–38.

2   Rod Ellis, ed., *Learning a Second Language Through Interaction* (Amsterdam: J. Benjamins, 1999).

3   Earl Stevick, "Curriculum Development at the Foreign Service Institute," in *Teaching for Proficiency: The Organizing Principle*, ed. Theodore V. Higgs (Lincolnwood, IL: National Textbook Company, 1984).

4   Joan Rubin and Irene Thompson, *How to Be a More Successful Language Learner: Toward Learner Autonomy*, 2nd ed. (Boston: Heinle & Heinle Publishers, 1994), 80.

5   James P. Spradley, *The Ethnographic Interview* (New York: Holt, Rinehart and Winston, 1979).

Appendix 4

[1]   Quote from Rob Hughes of Campus Crusade for Christ International, December 14, 2001.

[2]   Nicholas Thomas Wright, *The New Testament and the People of God* (Minneapolis: Fortress Press, 1992).